WOMEN ON THE
U.S.–MEXICO BORDER

RESPONSES TO CHANGE

THEMATIC STUDIES IN LATIN AMERICA

Series editor: Gilbert W. Merkx, Director, Latin American Institute, University of New Mexico

*in preparation.

WOMEN ON THE U.S.—MEXICO BORDER

RESPONSES TO CHANGE

Edited by

Vicki L. Ruiz

Department of History
University of California, Davis

AND

Susan Tiano

Department of Sociology
University of New Mexico

Boston
Allen & Unwin
London   Sydney   Wellington

Allen & Unwin, Inc.
8 Winchester Place, Winchester, MA 01890, USA.

The U.S. Company of
Unwin Hyman Ltd.

P.O. Box 18, Park Lane, Hemel Hempstead, Herts HP2 4TE, UK
40 Museum Street, London WC1A 1LU, UK
37/39 Queen Elizabeth Street, London SE1 2QB, UK

Allen & Unwin Australia Pty Ltd.
8 Napier Street, North Sydney, NSW 2060, Australia

Allen & Unwin (New Zealand) Ltd, in association with the
Port Nicholson Press Ltd
Private Bag, Wellington, New Zealand

Library of Congress Cataloging-in-Publication Data

Women on the U.S.—Mexico border.

(Thematic studies in Latin America)
Bibliography: p.
Includes index.
1. Mexican American women—Southwest, New.
2. Southwest, New—Social conditions.   I. Ruíz, Vicki.
II. Tiano, Susan.   III. Series.
F790.M5W66   1986   305.4'886872073   86—22305
ISBN 0—04—497038—2
ISBN 0—04—497039—0 (pbk.)

British Library Cataloguing in Publication Data

Women on the U.S.—Mexico border:

responses to change.—(Thematic studies
in Latin America)
1. Women—Mexican—American Border Region
—Social conditions
I. Ruiz, Vicki L.   II. Tiano, Susan
III. Series
305.4'2'097   HQ1462
ISBN 0—04—497038—2
ISBN 0—04—497039—0 (pbk.)

MANUFACTURED IN THE UNITED STATES OF AMERICA

Contents

v

List of Contributors

Raquel Rubio Goldsmith, Department of History, Pima Community College, Tucson, Arizona 87502

Devon Peña, Department of Sociology, Colorado College, Colorado Springs, Colorado 80903

Vicki L. Ruiz, Department of History, University of California, Davis, Davis, California 95616

Rosalía Solórzano-Torres, Chicano Studies Program, University of Colorado, Boulder, Colorado 80309

Kathleen Staudt, Department of Political Science, University of Texas at El Paso, El Paso, Texas 79968

Susan Tiano, Department of Sociology, University of New Mexico, Albuquerque, New Mexico 87131

Norma Williams, Department of Sociology, Texas A & M University, College Station, Texas 77843

Gay Young, Department of Sociology, University of Texas at El Paso, El Paso, Texas 79968

Acknowledgments

We would like to thank Tey Diana Rebolledo, director of Women Studies, and Gilbert Merkx, director of the Latin American Institute at the University of New Mexico, for their unflagging support of this project. Sarah John, Georgina Rivas, and Anita Burdett, former staff members at the Institute of Oral History, University of Texas, El Paso, deserve mention for their invaluable assistance in the preparation of this manuscript. We also appreciate the speedy and accurate word processing skills of Lynnda Borelli Pries, Senior Word Processing Specialist at the University of California, Davis.

We thank Nicolas Kanellos and Arte Publico Press for permission to reprint Pat Mora's poem *Mexican Maid.*

To the women who were interviewed during the course of the research presented here, we thank you for sharing your ideas, experiences, and emotions and it is to you that the anthology is offered.

VICKI L. RUIZ
SUSAN TIANO

Introduction

**Vicki L. Ruiz and
Susan Tiano**

Women have been cast as invisible actors in the social development
drama. Their only accredited roles are those of wife and mother, and
their only acclaimed performances are shrouded within the realm of
domesticity. They tend to be perceived exclusively in terms of their
reproductive activities, as childrearers and domestic workers. Although
many women venture beyond the household into the wage labor force,
their extradomestic roles are typically viewed as temporary aberra-
tions from their true social function. Consequently, the essential productive contributions women regularly make often go unnoticed not
only by society by by women themselves. Their performances are similarly unlikely to bring them adequate monetary compensation. While
women represent one-third of the world's official wage labor force and
perform almost two-thirds of all working hours, they garner only one-
tenth of the global income (United Nations, 1980:7).

This invisibility, nonrecognition, and resultant exclusion from economic opportunities and recompence is especially pronounced for
certain categories of women. Working-class women, women of color,
ethnic women, and women in Third World nations generally hold more
inferior positions than their white middle-class counterparts in indus-
trialized societies. Social class, ethnicity, race, and nationality reinforce
gender inequalities. An illustration of how these factors can combine to
produce a doubly disadvantaged category can be seen in the situation
of Chicanas and Mexicanas in the United States—Mexico border region.
Whether they work as domestic servants in El Paso or as assembly

1

workers in Juarez, whether they are Mexican nationals or U.S. citizens, whether they live north or south of the border, they face common circumstances and share similar problems. Yet as the articles in this volume document, they are not merely the passive victims of discrimination. Today, as in the past, they are active agents directing their own destinies and weaving the economic and cultural fabric of the borderlands. The varied roles of Mexican women in an area undergoing rapid social change form the focus of this book.

The United States–Mexico Border: Continuity within Diversity

From lush valleys to arid deserts, the 2000-mile United States–Mexico border maintains its own special ambiance of ambiguity—*el ambiente fronterizo*, the intermingling of peoples, cultures, and economies. The permeability of the borderlands can be traced to ancient times. Centuries before the birth of Christ, the indigenous peoples of what is now the American Southwest and central Mexico shared common linguistic and cultural patterns and engaged in rudimentary trade. From 300 B.C. onward, the civilizations of interior Mexico directly influenced the development of Native American societies in the Southwest (Chávez, 1984:9–10). The ebb and flow of ideas, institutions, and people did not end with the Spanish victory over the Aztecs. Beginning in 1540 with the Coronado expedition, the settlement of the borderlands by Spanish/ mestizo pioneers added new ingredients to a regional melting pot.

Anglo settlement of Texas during the 1820s generated an uneasy atmosphere of separateness, cultural and political. In 1836 the Republic of Texas established a much-disputed international boundary with Mexico. Ten years later, this territorial conflict provided the justification for the U.S.–Mexican War, as U.S. President James K. Polk forcefully declared, "Mexico . . . had shed American blood upon American soil" (Weber, 1973:2). The Treaty of Guadalupe Hidalgo (1848) and the Gadsden Purchase (1853) carved out the political border separating American soil from Mexican soil. In adjusting to this traumatic turn of events, conflict characterized border life during the remainder of the nineteenth century. Mexicans on the U.S. side of the border became second-class citizens, divested of their property, political power, and social position. Subject to residential segregation, Mexican Americans in the barrios of the Southwest maintained their sense of identity and cultural traditions, traits reinforced by recent arrivals from Mexico (Camarillo, 1979; De León, 1982).

One could argue that during the twentieth century the waves of Mexican immigrants not only revitalized and increased the Hispanic presence in the United States but also led to a Mexicanization of the Southwest. Conversely, the flow of American capital south of the border has led to an Americanization of Mexico. The movements of population and resources back and forth across a political boundary undoubtedly have far-reaching implications for the communities that straddle the border. Some scholars note the "Ellis Island function" of border cities as the gateways to the United States. Prospective immigrants to the United States while living in Mexican border towns receive "anticipatory social-ization" in their contacts with people and things American (Grebler, Moore, and Guzman, 1970:41). Other researchers examine the same areas as havens for (depending on one's perspective) "runaway shops" or "labor-intensive" U.S. industries (Fernández-Kelly, 1983:79−81; Dill-man, 1983:144−152).

Border scholars agree that the region possesses a distinctive culture. A complex set of economic, political, and cultural factors cements the sister cities to each other and renders artificial the international bound-ary. For example, Oscar Martínez's study on Ciudad Juárez and Mario García's monograph on El Paso demonstrate the historical intercon-nectedness of these border cities. As Martínez notes how trends in U.S. history, such as Prohibition, shaped the development of Ciudad Juárez, García carefully gauges the impact of events in Mexico which, in turn, affected El Paso (Martínez, 1973; Garcia, 1981). These studies provide almost complementary halves of a unified history of a metropolitan area.

Despite a shared history marked by fluidity, border life is not without division. Ethnic antagonisms, discrimination, and economic disparities exist in the midst of interdependence. Members of the Border Patrol survey the land before them, making quite real what appears to be an amorphous boundary. The questioning of Hispanic-looking pedestri-ans on El Paso streets by teams of local police and the Border Patrol fosters a sense of separateness not only between Mexico and the United States but also between Mexican and Anglo. The distinctiveness of border life, with all its attendant contradictions and continuities, is reflected in the essays in this book. Indeed, through the study of women, questions concerning the nature of border culture come into sharper focus.

As the first of its kind, this anthology is offered not as the definitive work but rather as a sampling of research on a subject almost totally overlooked by scholars of the United States—Mexico border. Women appear conspicuous by their absence in the mammoth *Borderlands Sourcebook: A Guide to the Literature on Northern Mexico and the American Southwest*. Gender is not included as one of the fifty-nine topics covered in this pioneering reference work (Stoddard, Nostrand, and West, 1983). In general, border scholars either ignore women entirely or rely on well-worn stereotypes. Scholarly and popular images of Mexicanas are distorted by a plethora of misleading and frequently degrading stereotypes. The woman in the cantina, for example, permeates the U.S. mass media from Marty Robbin's famous ballad "El Paso" to Woody Woodpecker cartoons. The standard caricature of the Mexican dance hall girl and/or prostitute has also infiltrated academic scholarship. A one-dimensional perception of women as suppliers of "cheap sex" obscures the experiences of the majority of Mexicanas. Less sensational is the polar opposite of the loose women—the sainted mother. This stereotypical personality enjoys an idyllic, sheltered existence as the revered cornerstone of the Mexican family. Her pervasiveness in popular culture underlies several scholarly myths concerning the roles of Mexican women. Mexicanas tend to be perceived exclusively in terms of their domestic functions, as wives and mothers supported by male breadwinners. It also implies that they are insulated from the vicissitudes of the essentially masculine world of work and politics. A related stereotype holds that Mexicanas are culturally and politically conservative. They presumably preserve and transmit traditional values rather than adopting novel or innovative ways. They do not create culture, but only respond to it. Similarly, they are seen as basically apolitical, uninformed about current events, uninterested in local and national politics, and unable to form or promote organizations which could serve their interests. Those who do engage in politics are presumed to be highly conservative in their orientations, opposing liberal policies and candidates. In sum, according to this view, Mexicanas are obstacles to, rather than agents of, social progress.

Concerning mobility, women are often portrayed as rooted to their native communities. Men try to improve their lives by seeking opportunities on the U.S. side of the border while their wives remain behind to raise the children and maintain the household. Even single women are presumably loath to leave the security of their homeland for parts unknown. Mexicanas' spatial inertia, according to the stereotype, reflects their inherent reluctance to take risks, their devotion to their homes, and their domestic insulation from the lure of economic opportunities.

Since its advent in 1965, the Border Industrialization Program has drawn over 200,000 women into the industrial labor force (*El Nacional*, May 1985). This trend, when viewed through the distorting lens of the aforementioned stereotypes, has led the media and some researchers to place women operatives in a type of "double jeopardy." One view, reflecting the notion of women's hallowed domestic roles, contends that women's industrial employment threatens to destroy the traditional Mexican family. These newly independent women neglect their children and emasculate men, who sometimes resort to alcohol and substance abuse as salve for their "wounded *machismo*." A differing interpretation, rooted in the view of women's inherent conservatism, decries the passivity of Mexicana industrial workers. Twin plant operatives are seen as submissive women who tolerate exploitation. Whether portrayed as irresponsibly independent working women or as tools of manipulative capitalism, twin plant operatives, like other Mexicanas, are the objects of popular and academic criticism.

The stereotypes about women in the United States–Mexico borderlands echo similar notions about women throughout the world. An accumulating body of feminist scholarship challenges the accuracy of these stereotypes while providing insight into their roots and the reasons for their persistence.

Women and Social Change: Two Theoretical Perspectives

Ester Boserup's *Women's Role in Economic Development* (1970) launched a wave of feminist scholarship on women in Latin America and other rapidly changing regions. Her work stimulated a host of case studies supporting her conclusions and embellishing her insights into the theory now known as developmentalism (Elliot, 1977:4–5). Boserup demonstrated empirically that women throughout the world have traditionally made essential productive contributions. Whether engaged in subsistence agriculture, manufacture, or trade, women have produced and distributed goods and services vital to their families and communities. Their productive activities have not only provided the resources crucial to their material well-being, but have offered them at least some degree of personal autonomy and social influence (Etienne and Leacock, 1980). As their societies have modernized according to the Western capitalist model, however, women's position has deteriorated (Youssef, 1976:92). With the transition to a cash-based market economy, men have become the chief wage earners and cash crop producers, while women have been symbolically relegated to the domestic sphere (Blumberg, 1981:41; Saffioti, 1975:83). In part this change reflects the diffusion of European ideologies and economic arrangements that define women exclusively in terms of their productive roles and view commodity production and trade as men's work (Tinker, 1976:22; Boserup, 1970:33). These arrangements have been buttressed by laws circumscribing women's rights to inheritance, property ownership, and political participation (Mernissi, 1976:36). The resulting changes have eroded women's status relative to men, usurping their productive roles and threatening their material well-being.

Paradoxically, as their productive roles have eroded, women's workloads have tended to increase (Black, 1981:267). Men's involvement in market production has often left women with the responsibility for producing food to feed their families (Deere, 1976:12; Blumberg, 1981:41). Further, as men have migrated elsewhere to find employment, women have often remained behind to manage family enterprises (Bossen, 1982:70; Mueller, 1977:155).

Boserup and others in the developmentalist tradition consider the main obstacles to women's welfare to be patriarchal cultural values and sexual discrimination (Jaquette, 1982:272). Developmentalists typically assume that urbanization, industrialization, and other modernization-related changes will eventually improve women's situation, both absolutely and relative to that of men. In the short run, however, concerted policies are necessary to counteract modernization's tendency to marginalize women. They argue that women must be integrated into the modernization process, both as participants and as beneficiaries, so that they will receive their fair share of modernization's many rewards (Tinker, 1976:34). Strategies toward this end include providing health care, family planning technologies, education, and other services that will enhance women's material welfare and prepare them for modern occupations (Papanek, 1977:17; Blumberg, 1976:21).

While many feminists applaud developmentalism for documenting the negative influences of modernization on women in Latin America and elsewhere, others are disenchanted with the developmentalist critique. Integrating women into the capitalist relations of production, they maintain, merely augments women's exploitation. Furthermore, development under capitalist auspices reinforces, rather than eliminates, the patriarchal relations that oppress women. These arguments are the central tenets of socialist feminism.

Socialist feminism synthesizes insights from Marxism and radical feminism into a theory of women's oppression (Sokoloff, 1980). Its aim is to understand two distinct but interrelated structures of women's subordination, capitalism and patriarchy (Eisenstein, 1979:6). Capitalism presumably exploits women both as unpaid household workers and as underpaid wage laborers (Leacock, 1975; Beechey, 1978:196). Patriarchy oppresses women by subjecting them to male domination in the family and in the public sphere (Kuhn, 1978). Socialist feminists argue that although patriarchal relations are universal, capitalism imparts a distinct cast to patriarchy, employing existing relations of gender-based oppression to spur capitalist accumulation (McDonough and Harrison, 1978:13; Beneria and Sen, 1981:280).

Socialist feminist analyses focus on women's roles as reproducers within the private sphere of household and as producers within the public context of wage employment. Their activities in both settings are shaped by the gender-based division of labor and its attendant ideology defining the household as women's primary responsibility (McIntosh, 1978:255). In fulfillment of their duty to hearth and home, women serve capitalism in several ways. They bear and raise new generations of workers; they transmit to their children values and beliefs that make them hard-working, obedient laborers; and they provide their menfolk the food, clothing, sexual services, and nurturance necessary to their continued labor (Fee, 1976:1−8; Beechey, 1978:184). The housewife's only compensation for these services is that share of her husband's wages spent on family upkeep. The husband's employer thereby receives her services in exchange for a "family wage" that is less than their market value, and thus, women's unpaid domestic labor accelerates the rate of capitalist accumulation (Sokoloff, 1980:124−50; Kuhn, 1978:48).

Yet patriarchal relationships, the argument continues, extend beyond the domestic context. When women enter the labor force, the patriarchal image that women belong in the home conditions the terms of their employment (McDonough and Harrison, 1978:30; Rapp, 1982: 172). Viewed as subsidiary wage earners with husbands or fathers to support them, they are typically paid less than men for comparable work and are concentrated in low-paying "female" occupations which are often viewed as extensions of their domestic roles (Beechey, 1978:

191; McIntosh, 1978; 278). Many women hold part-time or temporary jobs exempted from worker protection legislation. Women often accept these conditions without protest because they believe that their primary roles are those of wife and mother, and that wage work is a temporary though necessary deviation from their natural place within the division of labor (Saffioti, 1975:83).

Women on the Border: Myths and Realities

When examined in light of these theoretical considerations, stereotypes about women in the United States—Mexico borderlands come into sharper focus. These one-dimensional images reflect a patriarchal ideology about women's ideal roles which reinforces existing social relationships. The notion that the household is women's primary sphere, and that those who enter wage work do so merely as supplementary wage earners, becomes a justification for paying them low wages and for relegating them to temporary jobs without benefits. Many women so thoroughly believe this ideology that they are ambivalent about their roles as wage laborers and appear willing to accept poor working conditions without protest. In this way the stereotypes serve the economic system, supporting the existing gender-based division of labor and reinforcing women's position as surplus labor. Similarly, the notion that women are apolitical or politically conservative helps preserve the political status quo. On the one hand, the image becomes a self-fulfilling prophecy, leading women to eschew political activities because they believe they are inherently unsuited for politics. On the other hand, the notion becomes an excuse to deny women rights to political participation, as demonstrated in Mexico during the early decades of the twentieth century (Macias, 1982:145).

Several scholars have provided glimpses into the reality of border women's lives, revealing the narrowness of these stereotypes. Although not an exhaustive list, the following works represent some of the more promising lines of research. A pioneering monograph, *For We Are Sold, I and My People*, by María Patricia Fernández-Kelly (1983) is a refreshing, realistic examination of Mexicana industrial labor in Ciudad Juarez. Anthropologist Fernández-Kelly offers a compassionate, rigorously researched portrait of Mexicana operatives employed by multinational corporations. Through participant observation, she examines their day-to-day struggles for dignity and survival. Mexicanas emerge not as faceless statistics or stereotypes but as people whom the reader comes to know and appreciate. Similarly, Laurie Coyle, Gail Hershatter, and Emily Honig in "Women at Farah: An Unfinished Story" (1980) present a stirring account of Mexican American garment workers and their struggle for unionization. Their application of oral history not only yields insight into women's attitudes, life-styles, and political empowerment through labor activism but also reveals the obstacles facing working-class border women. The first article to examine border-region gender issues from a historical perspective is Mario García's "The Chicana in American History: The Mexican Women of El Paso, 1880–1920." García details women's participation in the labor force as well as their roles within the family.

The essays in this book further illuminate the reality of border women's lives. Susan Tiano's work on women's unemployment challenges the conventional notion that women need not work for wages because they are economically supported by men. Her analysis of census data from northern Mexico indicates that a considerable proportion of women work for wages throughout their adult years, that most working women have no male partner to support them, and that women have higher rates of open unemployment than men. Furthermore, Tiano's study of maquiladora and service workers in Mexicali challenges the related notion that the Border Industrialization Program has mobilized a "new" category of women into the workforce who otherwise would remain in the household. To the contrary, most women worked out of economic necessity, making essential financial contributions to their households.

Rosalia Solórzano-Torres offers insight into the lives of undocumented women. Contrary to the commonly held view that women seldom migrate and, when they do, they come as wives and daughters, Solórzano-Torres notes the rise of young immigrant women who arrive in the United States either as solas or as single heads of households. Her interviews with undocumented women in San Diego County illuminate the origins and experiences of a little-known sector of immigrants.

Several works in this volume also belie the notion that women are conservative, apolitical souls who passively submit to exploitation at the workplace. Vicki Ruiz's discussion of domestic workers in El Paso shows that maids began to organize on their own behalf as early as 1933. Since then, they have demonstrated courage in resisting attempts by the Immigration and Naturalization Service to prevent their forays across the border. Moreover, many have retained their personal integrity against the discriminatory treatment and patronizing attitudes they have endured in the course of their employment.

The works by Gloria Young, Devon Peña, and Kathleen Staudt present a consistent portrayal of political and personal empowerment among women workers in Juárez. Young refutes the notion that maquiladora operatives are incapable and unwilling to organize collective protests. A number of women in her sample organized a successful strike, and in the process, expanded their political consciousness as women and as workers. Devon Peña describes informal forms of collective and individual struggle on the factory floor. The majority of workers in his study admitted to restricting their output through a process they call *Tortuguismo* ("working at a turtle's pace"). Moreover, they form cohesive informal networks through which they resist attempts to intensify the labor process through production speed-ups. Kathleen Staudt describes how a program designed to increase women's consciousness successfully provided women with a sense of personal efficacy and, in some cases, of political empowerment.

In a different vein, three essays in this volume document women's contributions to the rich culture flowering in the borderlands. Raquel Rubio Goldsmith's historical study of Mexican nuns in Douglas, Arizona, emphasizes the importance of religion in reinforcing cultural bonds. As newly arrived refugees from the Mexican revolution, these sisters invigorated the Mexicano traditions among their Mexican and Mexican American neighbors. From a sociological perspective, Norma Williams describes Mexican American women's roles in transforming the practices surrounding funeral rites. She argues that these changes were not merely an attempt by Mexican Americans to assimilate Anglo culture but represent instead an innovative adaptation to life in a rapidly modernizing region. Women, as individuals, have also created, preserved, and amplified border arts and customs. A stellar example is Rosa Guerrero, whose internationally respected Ballet Folklorico has enabled audiences throughout the world to appreciate music and dance forms of the borderlands. An oral history edited by Vicki Ruiz chronicles the life of this great women of the arts.

The essays assembled in this collection, concerning women's work and migration, their organization and consciousness, and their contribution to regional culture, are at the cutting edge of scholarship on border women. The interdisciplinary chapters which follow add new perspectives, sharpen existing interpretations, and most importantly, foster a greater understanding of the varying experiences of *las mujeres en la frontera*.

References

Arizpe, Lourdes, 1977. "Women in the Informal Labor Sector: The Case of Mexico City." In Wellesley Editorial Committee (eds), *Women and National Development: The Complexities of Change* University of Chicago Press, pp. 25–37.

Beechey, Veronica, 1978. "Women and Production: A Critical Analysis of Some Sociological Theories of Women's Work." In Annette Kuhn and Ann Marie Wolpe (eds), *Feminism and Materialism*. London: Routledge and Kegan Paul, pp. 155–197.

Beneria, Lourdes, and Gita Sen, 1981. "Accumulation, Reproduction, and Women's Role in Economic Development: Boserup Revisited." *SIGNS*, 7(2):279–298.

Black, Naomi, 1981. "The Future for Women and Development." In Naomi Black and Ann Baker Cottrell (eds), *Women and World Change*. Beverly Hills: Sage Publications, pp. 265–286.

Blumberg, Rae Lesser, 1981. "Rural Women in Development." In Naomi Black and Ann Baker Cottrell (eds), *Women and World Change*. Beverly Hills: Sage Publications, pp. 32–56.

Boserup, Ester, 1970. *Women's Role in Economic Development.* New York: St. Martin's.

Bossen, Laurel, 1982. *The Redivision of Labor.* Albany: SUNY Press.

Bronstein, Audry, *The Triple Struggle.* Boston: South End Press, 1982.

Camarillo, Albert, 1979. *Chicanos in a Changing Society: From Mexican Pueblos to American Barrios in Santa Barbara and Southern California, 1848–1930.* Cambridge: Harvard University Press, 1979.

Chávez, John R., 1984. *The Lost Land: The Chicano Image of the Southwest.* Albuquerque: University of New Mexico Press.

Coyle, Lauri, Gail Hershatter, and Emily Honig, 1980. "Women at Farah: An Unfinished Story." in Magdalena Mora and Adelaida Del Castillo (eds), *Mexican Women in the United States: Struggles Past and Present.* Los Angeles: Chicano Studies Research Publications.

Deere, Carmen Diana, 1976. "Rural Women's Subsistence Production in the Capitalist Periphery." *The Review of Radical Political Economics*, 8(1):9–17.

DeLeón, Arnoldo, 1982. *The Tejano Community, 1836–1900.* Albuquerque: University of New Mexico Press.

Dillman, C. Daniel, 1983. "Border Industrialization." In Ellwyn R. Stoddard, Richard L. Nostrand, and Jonathan P. West (eds), *Borderlands Sourcebook: A Guide to the Literature on Northern Mexico and the American Southwest.* Norman: University of Oklahoma Press, pp. 144–152.

Eisenstein, Zillah, 1979. "Developing a Theory of Capitalist Patriarchy and Socialist Feminism." In Zillah Eisenstein (ed), *Capitalist Patriarchy and the Case for Socialist Feminism.* New York: Monthly Review Press, pp. 5–40.

Elliott, Carolyn, 1977. "Theories of Development: An Assessment." In Wellesley Editorial Committee (eds), *Women and National Development.* Chicago: University of Chicago Press, pp. 1–8.

Etienne, Mona, and Eleanor Leacock, 1980. "Introduction." In Mona Etienne and Eleanor Leacock (eds), *Women and Colonization.* New York: Praeger, pp. 1–24.

Fee, Terry, 1976. "Domestic Labour: An Analysis of Housework and Its Relation to the Production Process." *The Review of Radical Political Economics*, 8(1):1–8.

Fernández, Raul A., 1977. *The United States – Mexican Border: A Politico-Economic Profile.* Notre Dame: University of Notre Dame Press.

Fernández-Kelly, María Patricia, 1983. *For We Are Sold, I and My People: Women and Industry in Mexico's Northern Frontier*. Albany: State University of New York Press.

García, Mario T., 1980. "The Chicana in American History: The Mexican Women of El Paso, 1880–1920: A Case Study." *Pacific Historical Review*, 49:315–337.

García, Mario T., 1981. *Desert Immigrants: The Mexicans of El Paso, 1880–1920*. New Haven: Yale University Press.

Grebler, Leo, Joan W. Moore, and Ralph C. Guzman, 1970. *The Mexican–American People*. New York: The Free Press.

Huston, Perdita, 1979. "Learning, Work, and Aspirations." *Development Digest*, 17(1): 59–68.

International Center for Research on Women (ICRW), 1980. "Keeping Women Out: A Structural Analysis of Women's Employment in Developing Countries." Paper prepared for the Office of Women in Development, U.S. Agency for International Development.

Jaquette, Jane, 1982. "Women and Modernization Theory: A Decade of Feminist Criticism." *World Politics*, 265–284.

Jelin, Elizabeth, 1979. "Domestic Servants in the Latin American Cities," *Development Digest*, 17(1):69–74.

Kuhn, Annette, 1978. "Structures of Patriarchy and Capital in the Family," In Annette Kuhn and Ann Marie Wolpe (eds), *Feminism and Materialism*. London: Routledge and Kegan Paul, pp. 42–27.

Leacock, Eleanor, 1975. "Introduction," to Frederick Engel's *The Origin of the Family, Private Property, and the State*. New York: International Publishers, pp. 7–67.

Lim, Linda, 1983. "Capitalism, Imperialism, and Patriarchy: The Dilemma of Third World Women Workers in Multinational Factories." In June Nash and Maria Patricia Fernández-Kelly (eds), *Women, Men, and the International Division of Labor*. Albany: State University of New York Press, pp. 70–91.

Macias, Anna, 1982. *Against All Odds: The Feminist Movement in Mexico to 1940*. Westport, CT: Greenwood Press, 1982.

McCormack, Thelma, 1981. "Development with Equity for Women." In Naomi Black and Ann Baker Cottrell (eds), *Women and World Change*. Beverly Hills: Sage Publications, pp. 15–30.

McDonough, Roisin, and Rachel Harrison, 1978. "Patriarchy and Relations of Production." In Annette Kuhn and AnnMarie Wolpe (eds), *Feminism and Materialism*. London: Routledge and Kegan Paul, pp. 11–41.

McIntosh, Mary, 1978. "The State and the Oppression of Women." In Annette Kuhn and AnnMarie Wolpe (eds), *Feminism and Materialism*. London: Routledge and Kegan Paul, pp. 254–289.

Martínez, Oscar J., 1975. *Border Boom Town: Ciudad Juárez Since 1848*. Austin: University of Texas Press.

Mernissi, Fatima, 1976. "The Muslim World: Women Excluded from Development." In Irene Tinker and Michele Bo Bramsen (eds), *Women and World Development*. Washington, D.C.: Overseas Development Council, pp. 35–46.

Mueller, Martha, 1977. "Women and Men, Power and Powerlessness in Lesotho." In Wellesley Editorial Committee (eds), *Women and National Development*. University of Chicago Press, pp. 154–166.

Papanek, Hanna, 1977. "Development Planning for Women." In Wellesley Editorial Committee (eds), *Women and National Development*. University of Chicago Press, pp. 14–20.

Rapp, Rayna, 1982. "Family and Class in Contemporary America: Notes toward an Under-
    standing of Ideology." In Barrie Thorne and Marilyn Yalom (eds), *Rethinking
    the Family*. New York: Longman, pp. 168–187.
Rothstein, Frances, 1982. *Three Different Worlds*. Westport, CT: Greenwood Press.
Saffioti, Heleieth, 1975. "Female Labor and Capitalism in the U.S. and Brazil." In Ruby
    Rohrlich-Leavitt (ed), *Women Cross-Culturally: Change and Challenge*. The Hague:
    Mouton, pp. 59–94.
Sokoloff, Natalie, 1980. *Between Love and Money*. New York: Praeger.
Stoddard, Ellwyn R., and Richard L. Nostrand, and Jonathan P. West (eds), 1983. *Border-
    lands Sourcebook: A Guide to the Literature on Northern Mexico and the American
    Southwest*. Norman: University of Oklahoma Press, pp. 144–152.
Tinker, Irene, 1976. "The Adverse Impact of Development on Women." In Irene Tinker and
    Michele Bo Bramsen (eds), *Women and World Development*. Washington, D.C.:
    Overseas Development Council, pp. 22–34.
Weber, David J. (ed), 1973. *Foreigners in Their Native Land: Historical Roots of the Mexican
    Americans*. Albuquerque: University of New Mexico Press.
Youssef, Nadia, 1976. "Women in Development: Urban Life and Labor," in Irene Tinker and
    Michele Bo Bramsen (eds), *Women and World Development*. Washington, D.C.:
    Overseas Development Council, pp. 70–77.

I

LABOR, MIGRATION, AND RELATIONS OF PRODUCTION

1

Women's Work and Unemployment in Northern Mexico

Susan Tiano

A recent pattern in the internationalization of production involves transferring the labor-intensive phases of manufacturing from more- to less-industrialized nations possessing abundant low-waged labor. Proponents of "offshore" manufacturing claim that it provides the Third World worker with employment, a steady income, and useful skills. Critics object, however, that export processing does not alleviate unemployment, for its work force is predominantly female, and unemployment in the Third World is essentially a male problem (Woog, 1980:101; Fernández, 1977:141). Such a claim reflects an inaccurate but common image about women's labor force participation in developing nations. This essay challenges this view with aggregate data on men's and women's employment patterns in northern Mexico. The data indicate that unemployment persists despite considerable investment in export processing industrialization. They provide little evidence, however, that the chief cause of this continuing unemployment is the preferential hiring of women.

Export Processing and Female Employment

Since World War II, the large-scale corporation, spurred by the need to maintain profit margins by minimizing production costs and by ex-

I am grateful to David Maciel, Richard Riger, Barbara Kohl, Karen Bracken, Richard McCleary, and Robert Fiala for their comments on earlier versions of this chapter.

17

panding sales, has evolved into a global enterprise. The constant search
for new markets, inexpensive labor, and reliable sources of raw materials has led North American companies and their European and Japanese competitors to expand into developing nations. This process has
dramatically transformed capitalist investment in the Third World.
Whereas in previous epochs foreign capital financed the extraction of
primary products, today it concentrates in manufacturing. Through
"import substitution industrialization," corporations have avoided pro-
tective tariffs by establishing subsidiaries in the Third World nations
whose markets they have supplied. Because these firms have been
equipped with the same capital-intensive technologies employed in the
home countries, import substitution has tended to displace Third
World workers, thereby limiting the internal markets on which it depends (Barnet and Muller, 1974:123−1147; MacEwan, 1978:481−491).

In the mid-1960s, North American firms developed an alternative
investment strategy. "Export processing industrialization" uses inexpensive Third World labor to produce intermediate products for re-
export to home markets. Items 806.3 and 807 of the U.S. Tariff Schedules
facilitate this process by allowing the export of components, equipment, and raw materials for assembly by foreign subsidiaries or subcon-
tractors. Tariff duties apply only to the value added outside the United
States, largely the relatively low cost of foreign labor (Fernández, 1977:
36; Woog, 1980:16−18). Export processing is suitable not only for labor-
intensive industries such as garments and textiles, but also for high
technology industries with labor-intensive phases, such as electronics.
Third World governments have encourged it as a way to provide jobs,
incomes, and skills to their underemployed populations; to reduce
foreign exchange deficits; and to augment industrialization through
transferring labor-intensive technologies. Incentives to multinational
investment have included establishing free trade zones, offering tax
exemptions, and constructing industrial parks. Some governments
have attempted to increase their nation's "comparative advantage" by
waiving worker-protection legislation which increases labor costs (Safa,
1980:16). Between 1960 and 1968 the number of less-developed nations
which were significant exporters of manufactured goods jumped from
four to thirty (Barnet and Muller, 1974:196). Key sites for offshore sourcing include the Caribbean, Southeast Asia, and the United States−
Mexico border (Hymer, 1978:492−498; Safa, 1980:1−14; Lim, 1981:181−
190; Barnet and Muller, 1974:123−147).

That export processing is leading to a new international division of labor is demonstrated by the increasing geographical dispersion of the electronics industry (Safa, 1980:10). Because this competitive industry is subject to rapid technological innovation, existing production methods soon become obsolete. Firms find it less costly to retrain workers than to continually replace outdated machinery, and thus use labor-intensive techniques for certain production phases. Training is usually minimal, for the labor process has been decomposed through scientific management principles into a series of repetitive, deskilled tasks that are easily transferred to new production sites. By the late 1960s, U.S. electronics firms had removed 90 percent of their labor-intensive assembly operations to the Third World (Lim, 1981:182). Much of this investment has been in Asian nations, which have been integrated into a network of specialized production sites on the basis of labor costs. Headquartered in Hong Kong and Singapore, the industry has concentrated testing operations in Malaysia, and has located the most labor-intensive assembly operations in poorer nations such as Indonesia, the Philippines, and Thailand. By the mid-1970s, semiconductor production had become the fastest growing industry in Southeast Asia, employing over 1 million workers, the vast majority of whom were women (Lim, 1981: 181—190; Grossman, 1979:2—17).

Women, typically aged 16 to 24, constitute 80 to 90 percent of the export processing labor force in Southeast Asia, Mexico, and other export platform nations (Grossman, 1979:3; Woog, 1980:82). This is a radical departure from import substitution, which employs semiskilled and skilled male labor in mechanized firms. It has been argued that export processing is leading to the rapid, large-scale development of a female proletariat in export platform nations (Lim, 1981:186).

Women's Work and the Employment Problem in Developing Countries

A frequent criticism of export procesing is its presumed inability to resolve the employment problems facing many Third World countries. A common explanation for this failure is the "structural imbalance" between the composition of the assembly processing work force and the nature of the employment problems troubling developing nations. According to this argument, Third World unemployment is essentially a male problem (Woog, 1980:51, 101; Fernández, 1977:141), yet women constitute the bulk of the work force involved in export processing. It is also claimed that the large-scale mobilization of young women out of the household and into the labor force may exacerbate unemployment by introducing a new, previously economically inactive category of workers into the labor market (Martinez, 1978:132; Safa, 1980:13; Fernández-Kelly, 1983:45; Fuentes and Ehrenreich, 1983:28). Thus because export processing primarily involves female labor, it does not alleviate, and may even fuel, Third World unemployment.

The view that unemployment is predominantly a male concern pervades much of the literature on Third World labor markets (see Boserup, 1970:194). It is at odds, however, with an accumulating body of literature on women's work in developing nations. As Boserup (1970) and others have effectively demonstrated, unemployment is a considerable problem for Third World women (Chinchilla, 1977:38−56; de Miranda, 1977:261−274; ICRW, 1980). Modernization-related changes frequently displace women from traditional roles in agriculture, handicrafts production, and trade; yet these changes offer them few alternative opportunities in the "modern" sector. Inadequate education and training, socialization into female sex roles, conflicting familial responsibilities, preferential male hiring, and cultural and legal proscriptions excluding women from many occupations combine to limit women's employment options. Yet many women must work to support themselves and their families. A growing proportion (one-third to one-half) of households in Mexico and other developing nations are headed by women, many of whom are their families' sole source of support (ICRW, 1980). Others must work to supplement their husbands' meager wages. The shortage of job opportunities in many Third World cities forces many of these women to eke out a living in the "informal sector" (Arizpe, 1977:25−37). Because informal activities yield neither a secure nor a steady income, and since they contribute little to the city's domestic product, most economists view them as disguised unemployment (Youssef, 1976:70−77). Thus the image that men are the primary breadwinners obscures the suffering that unemployment and underemployment cause women who must work to support themselves and their families. This view is based on a traditional image of women's ideal roles bearing little resemblance to the actual circumstances of working-class women in developing societies.

The claim that unemployment in developing nations is essentially a male problem assumes either that women (1) typically do not work outside the home because (2) they are adequately supported by male breadwinners and thus have no economic need to work, or else (3) are consistently able to secure employment to support themselves. Each of these assumptions will be tested using data from northern Mexico, the site of considerable export processing industrialization. A brief discussion of Mexico's Border Industrialization Program will provide a framework for this analysis. ·

The United States–Mexico Border Industrialization Program

The first region to convert itself to an export platform, northern Mexico has become an important site for export processing. Currently, over half of the imports entering the United States from less-developed nations under the export processing tariff provisions come from this region (Fernández-Kelly, 1983:34). Several factors make this zone attractive to foreign investors. The inability of the economy to absorb the rapidly growing population has created a large labor surplus. The region's proximity to the United States has minimized transportation and communication costs, and has enabled "twin plants" on opposite sides of the border to share managerial expertise and worker training facilities. The Mexican government has encouraged investment in maquiladoras (assembly plants) to foster industrial development and to abate the high unemployment resulting from the termination of the Bracero (guest worker) Program (Bustamante, 1983:242). In 1965 it authorized the Border Industrialization Program (BIP) which offers investment incentives to foreign-owned firms. A firm meeting certain conditions[1] is exempt both from duties and regulations on the importation of raw materials and capital equipment, and from taxes associated with profits, sales, and dividends (Fernández, 1977:135; Peña, 1982:11). After the worldwide 1974–1975 recession, when over a third of the maquiladora work force (23,000) was laid off, 39 North American maquiladoras closed down, and many others threatened to relocate in nations with lower labor costs (Fernández, 1977:148), the Mexican government exempted firms from various worker-protection requirements. Companies are now able (1) to

---

1. Foreign-owned plants must be located within a 12.5-mile strip along the United States–Mexico border; must export 100 percent of the finished product out of Mexico; and must employ predominantly (90 percent) Mexican citizens (Fernández, 1977:135).

dismiss "inefficient" workers without severance pay; (2) to adjust the size of their work force or length of their workday as their needs rquire; and (3) to retain a worker in "temporary" status for ninety days (NACLA, 1979:143). These incentives led to a reproliferation of assembly plants: by 1979 the border region contained 472 firms providing 99,122 workers with salaries and benefits totaling 56 billion pesos (Peña, 1981: 13).

Many analysts agree that the BIP has enabled U.S. multinational companies to reduce production costs and thus to compete more favorably with Japanese and European firms (Woog, 1980:passim; Peña, 1980:2). These savings reflect the investment incentives offered by the BIP, the wage differential between U.S. and Mexican labor, and the higher productivity rate of maquiladora workers[2] (Fernández-Kelly, 1983:28, 32). Motorola, for example, saved $4 million a year by moving from Phoenix to Nogales (NACLA, 1979:133).

✳Yet although the Mexican government developed the BIP in order to alleviate unemployment, augment personal income, increase workers' skills, reduce Mexico's commercial deficit to the United States, and encourage joint ventures between U.S. and Mexican capital, critics claim that it has not accomplished these goals.｜As the events surrounding the 1974 recession illustrate, they argue, the BIP has increased the border region's economic dependence upon the United States (Woog, 1980:104; Fernández-Kelly, 1983:40; NACLA, 1979:135). Critics also deny that the program has stimulated Mexican investment, for the North American firms' drive to maximize profits by continually relocating in areas with lower labor costs has led them to eschew entanglements with Mexican capital (Woog, 1980:98). Nor has the BIP reduced Mexico's balance of payments deficit, for at least half of the Mexican workers' wages are spent across the border (Fernández, 1977:144). They further argue that since many companies supply their Mexican subsidiaries with out-of-date equipment, workers are frequently trained in obsolete production methods (Fernández, 1977:144).

Critics also maintain that the maquiladoras' preference for female labor has prevented the program from alleviating unemployment in northern Mexico. According to this argument, the "traditional" work force in the area is composed of working-age males (Fernández-Kelly,

---

2. Maquiladora workers have been estimated to be 10 to 15 percent more productive than U. S. workers (Fernández-Kelly, 1983:28). One explanation for this high productivity is that the number of supervisors per worker is two to three times larger than is typical in the United States (NACLA, 1979:134).

1983:45), the population sector most troubled by unemployment (Martinez, 1978:132; Fernández, 1977:141; Woog, 1980:51, 101). Indeed, the Border Industrialization Program was originally intended to supply employment for men left jobless by the termination of the Bracero Program in 1965. Yet because over 80 percent of the maquiladora work force is female, critics claim that the program has not provided jobs for those who most need them. They also maintain that many of those employed in assembly plants are young women who ordinarily would not have entered the labor force (Fernández-Kelly, 1983:45). Thus, they argue, the inability of the maquiladora program to resolve the border region's employment problems to a large extent reflects the preferential hiring of women. According to this view, unemployment is not a problem for women in northern Mexico. As has been previously stated, this view assumes either that women typically do not work outside the home because they have husbands to support them, or else that they are consistently able to secure jobs to support themselves.

Patterns of Labor Force Participation in Northern Mexico

One way to explore whether these assumptions accurately describe women's employment situation in the border region is through an examination of aggregate data on men's and women's labor force participation. These data permit only an approximate evaluation, for neither the national nor the occupational censuses presents separate data for the 12.5-mile strip paralleling the United States–Mexico border in which the BIP was implemented. The national census disaggregates data by state, while the occupational census categorizes data by groups of states.[3] These categories include territory external to the border region and thus are not the optimal units on which to base the present

---

3. The border states containing the frontier municipalities include: Baja California Norte, Coahuila, Chihuahua, Nuevo Leon, Sonora, and Tamaulipas. Tables 1.2 and 1.4, which are based on the 1970 national census, present data for these six states. The occupational census employs three regional categories relevant to the present analysis: (1) "Northern," comprising the states of Chihuahua and Durango; (2) "Northwestern," including Tamaulipas, Nuevo Leon, and Coahuila; and (3) "Northwestern," containing Baja California Norte, Baja California Sur, Sonora, Sinaloa, and Nayarit. Tables 1.1 and 1.3 employ this classification.

analysis. More precise data corresponding exactly to the BIP region are not, however, currently available.

It should also be noted that the national and occupational censuses classify data according to nonequivalent age categories,[4] and that neither set of categories corresponds exactly to the age group (16 to 24) from which most maquiladora workers are recruited. This lack of correspondence to some extent limits the precision of the present analysis; nevertheless, it is not so pronounced as to preclude an exploratory consideration of the research questions.

✳ These data reveal patterns inconsistent with the conventional image of women's ideal roles. As the labor force participation rates depicted in Table 1.1 demonstrate, a considerable proportion of women in the border states, as in Mexico as a whole, work outside the home. Throughout Mexico, 21.5 percent of the women aged 12 or older belong to the waged labor force. Women aged 20 to 24 are especially likely to be economically active: about one-third of these women work outside the home. Yet it is not the case, as is commonly believed, that women usually drop out of the labor force to assume full-time roles as wives and mothers as they enter their thirties. On the contrary, in the northern region as in other areas of Mexico, women's labor force participation rates rarely drop below 20 percent until the mid-forties. There is no reason to assume that most women are merely working to pass the time while they wait for a husband to come along. A more plausible explanation is that they work out of financial necessity.

The data in Table 1.2 further challenge the stereotype that Mexican women need not work outside the home because they have husbands to support them. In each of the border states, as in the nation as a whole, between 69 and 81 percent of the economically active female labor force is unmarried.[5] These women's wages are in all probability essential for their own and in many cases their children's support. Should they find

---

4. The national census (Table 1.4) employs the categories 0−9, 10−19, 20−29, and so on; the occupational census (Tables 1.1 and 1.2) use the categories 12−19, 20−24, 25−34, and so on. The occupational census includes 12−15-year-olds in the labor force even though the official minimum working age is 16. They are included because adolescents below this age are permitted to enter the labor force if they have completed six years of primary school. Since children usually start school at age 6, they may be ready to begin working when they are 12. The 12−15-year-old category of workers is considered a special status, and their employers are subject to regulations designed to protect young workers. The government created this special status in part to protect women from the lower classes who enter domestic service at young ages.
5. These figures exclude women in "free unions" whose marital status is ambiguous.

TABLE 1.1
Labor Force Participation by Age and Sex, for Republic of Mexico and Northern, Northwestern, and Northeastern Regions, 1979

	Total	12–19	20–24	25–34	35–44	44–54	55–64	65+
National								
No.	19,839,222	3,390,612	3,120,226	4,772,140	3,704,271	2,529,468	1,440,234	861,310
Rate	45.5	25.3	56.8	59.5	59.0	55.3	49.4	29.7
Men								
No.	14,976,232	2,358,533	2,162,013	3,612,320	2,900,574	2,019,930	1,192,144	716,408
Rate	71.3	35.4	82.5	95.9	96.7	93.4	85.1	53.2
Women								
No.	4,862,990	1,032,079	958,213	1,159,820	803,697	509,538	248,090	144,902
Rate	21.5	15.4	33.4	27.3	24.5	21.1	16.3	9.3
Northern								
No.	918,007	141,473	161,727	215,339	192,922	115,590	61,943	28,307
Rate	41.24	19.55	56.48	57.76	56.30	51.01	44.58	21.52
Men								
No.	670,775	91,421	102,813	152,771	152,243	91,409	54,638	24,774
Rate	64.25	25.53	78.05	93.34	94.27	87.28	83.92	43.14
Women								
No.	247,232	50,052	58,914	62,568	40,679	24,181	7,305	3,533
Rate	20.92	13.70	38.10	29.92	22.46	19.84	9.89	4.77
Northeastern								
No.	1,721,544	283,527	272,028	408,561	336,611	214,661	125,032	79,201
Rate	43.66	24.05	56.40	58.05	57.63	50.31	46.58	26.90
Men								
No.	1,333,033	166,142	190,306	321,881	273,771	180,452	106,729	72,176
Rate	70.09	32.04	78.93	96.85	97.52	94.17	78.71	52.57

(continued on next page)

25

TABLE 1.1 (Continued)

	Total	12–19	20–24	25–34	35–44	44–54	55–64	65+
Women								
No.	388,511	97,385	81,722	86,680	62,840	34,209	18,303	7,025
Rate	19.03	16.29	33.88	23.34	20.72	14.55	13.78	4.47
Northwestern								
No.	1,566,264	237,658	252,136	384,044	309,253	200,136	117,545	63,119
Rate	41.74	20.11	57.30	55.44	56.33	51.61	46.46	26.81
Men								
No.	1,258,994	160,915	175,338	306,242	269,887	179,252	107,321	58,083
Rate	68.40	26.94	84.34	95.17	97.09	93.78	83.91	52.16
Women								
No.	307,270	76,743	76,798	77,802	39,366	20,884	10,224	5,036
Rate	16.07	13.13	33.08	20.97	14.53	10.62	8.17	4.06

SOURCE: Encuestra Continua Sobre Ocupacion, Secretaria de Programacion y Presupuesto (SPP), Coordinacion General del Sistema Nacional de Informacion, Serie 1, Vol. 7, Trimestre 1, 1979, Mexico, February 1980.

TABLE 1.2
Marital Status of Economically Active Women in Frontier States and Republic of Mexico, 1970

Place	Total Econ. Active	Married	Free Union	Widowed, Divorced, Separated	Single
Mexico (Estados Unidos Mexicanos)	2,466,257 100%	587,092 23.80%	151,544 6.14%	392,530 15.92%	1,335,091 54.13%
Baja California	48,693 100	11,826 24.29	3,266 6.71	7,015 14.41	26,586 54.60
Coahuila	47,081 100	9,705 20.61	1,681 3.57	6,675 14.18	29,020 61.64
Chihuahua	73,708 100	16,664 22.61	4,323 5.87	11,550 15.67	41,171 55.86
Nuevo Leon	107,195 100	17,785 16.59	2,605 2.43	11,462 10.69	75,343 70.29
Sonora	50,549 100	9,536 18.86	3,278 6.48	6,632 13.12	31,103 61.65
Tamaulipas	69,349 100	14,006 20.20	4,267 6.15	10,452 15.07	40,624 58.58

SOURCE: IX Censo de poblacion.

27

themselves unemployed, they would be under considerable financial pressure to secure a new source of income. Clearly for this sector—actually a substantial majority—of the female labor force, unemployment could be a formidable problem.

The alternative justification for the claim that unemployment is not typically a problem for Mexican women is that those women who desire and/or need a job are able to find one. The information in Table 1.3 challenges this assumption. These data measure open unemployment, which underestimates joblessness by neglecting the "discouraged worker"[6] who has abandoned his or her job search. Even these underestimates show unemployment to be a problem for women in northern Mexico and in the nation as a whole. The highest unemployment rates correspond to the 12−19- and 20−24-year old categories, which encompass the age range most heavily represented in the ma-quiladora work force. To anticipate the subsequent discussion, it apears as though these women provide an available labor pool for the assembly plants.

In sum, the argument that unemployment in northern Mexico is essentially a male phenomenon is not only unreasonable but empirically inaccurate. A more plausible version of the argument might be that because maquiladoras hire predominantly women, they cannot alleviate more than half the unemployment in the region, namely that affecting women. This argument assumes that (1) by providing jobs for women, maquiladoras lessen or resolve female unemployment, and (2) because maquiladoras hire few men, they do not reduce male unemployment. Further, maquiladoras may exacerbate male joblessness by attracting migrants from the interior who compete with border residents for jobs (Bustamante, 1983:244; Fernández, 1977:141).[7] In this case, male unemployment in the northern region should be as high or higher than female joblessness, or at least the ratio of female to male unemployment rates should be lower in the north than in Mexico generally.[8]

---

6. Evidence from the United States demonstrates that the "discouraged worker" effect is more pronounced among women than men.

7. Migration could contribute to male unemployment even though the majority of migrants are not men. If men and women are equally represented in the migration stream, but maquiladoras hire mostly women, migration could augment male joblessness.

8. The cross-sectional data presented here do not permit a precise determination of the impact of the maquiladora program on men's and women's labor force participation. Such an assessment would require comparable longitudinal data collected prior to the

A comparison of the employment and unemployment rates in northern Mexico with those for the nation as a whole challenges these assumptions. There is no evidence that the maquiladora program has led to a disproportionately high level of female labor force participation in northern Mexico. The data in Table 1.1 show women's average rates of economic activity to be no higher in the northern region than in the nation generally. On the contrary, they are somewhat lower, ranging from 16 percent to 20.9 percent as compared to the national average of 21.5 percent. Even for the 12−19- and 20−24-year age categories, from which the majority of maquiladora work force is recruited, employment rates are not consistently higher than the national averages for comparable age categories. This casts doubt on the notion that the maquiladora program has brought into the work force a new category of workers, young women, who otherwise would not participate in the paid labor force.

One might postulate, perhaps, that northern Mexican women are less likely than their counterparts elsewhere in Mexico to enter the labor force because for whatever reason they are more apt to have husbands to support them financially. Yet the data in Table 1.2 do not justify this presumption. In all but one of the border states, the percentage of married women in the economically active population is lower than the national average. Similarly, the female labor force in the northern states contains a larger proportion of unmarried women than the Mexican average. This suggests that northern Mexican women may be even more likely than their counterparts in other regions to work out of financial necessity.

Table 1.3 provides further evidence that women's employment problems remain despite the Border Industrialization Program. Female unemployment rates in the border region are not noticeably lower than the national average. Even within the younger age categories, unemployment rates are consistently below the national average in only one of the three border regions. And just as throughout Mexico, unemployment is most pronounced among women aged 12 to 24, so too in the north, younger women have the highest rate of joblessness. Unemploy-

---

initiation of the Border Industrialization Program and at appropriate intervals subsequent to its onset. These data can, however, be used to indirectly evaluate claims about the program's impact, by comparing male and female labor force participation rates in the north with those for the nation generally.

TABLE 1.3
Levels and Rates of Open Unemployment by Age and Sex, for Republic of Mexico and Northern, Northwestern, and Northeastern Regions, 1979

	Total	12–19	20–24	25–34	35–44	44–54	55–64	65+
National								
No.	662,635	266,516	162,360	117,589	57,745	33,766	17,382	6,297
Rate	3.34	7.86	5.49	2.53	1.58	1.33	1.22	.74
Men								
No.	418,136	153,606	100,853	78,052	40,018	24,491	14,815	5,321
Rate	2.79	6.51	4.67	2.16	1.38	1.21	1.24	.74
Women								
No.	224,499	112,910	61,507	39,537	17,727	9,275	2,567	976
Rate	5.03	10.94	6.42	3.41	2.21	1.82	1.04	.67
Northern								
No.	34,819	13,592	8,396	4,952	3,342	2,887	1,267	383
Rate	3.79	9.61	5.19	2.30	1.73	2.50	2.05	1.35
Men								
No.	23,475	7,556	5,836	3,958	2,028	2,445	1,267	383
Rate	3.50	8.27	5.68	2.59	1.33	2.67	2.32	1.55
Women								
No.	11,344	6,036	2,558	994	1,314	442	—	—
Rate	4.59	12.06	4.34	1.59	3.23	1.83	—	—

Northeastern								
No.	66,724	28,598	13,491	11,564	7,116	3,449	1,723	783
Rate	3.88	10.09	4.96	2.83	2.11	1.61	1.38	.99
Men								
No.	41,541	17,047	6,288	7,654	4,597	3,449	1,723	783
Rate	3.12	9.16	3.30	2.38	1.68	1.91	1.61	1.08
Women								
No.	25,187	11,551	7,203	3,910	2,519	—	—	—
Rate	6.48	11.86	8.81	4.51	4.01	—	—	—
Northwestern								
No.	39,636	14,801	7,402	8,186	4,189	2,443	1,662	953
Rate	2.53	6.23	2.94	2.13	1.35	1.22	1.41	1.51
Men								
No.	30,883	11,918	6,211	5,734	3,211	1,683	1,173	953
Rate	2.45	7.41	3.54	1.87	1.19	.94	1.09	1.64
Women								
No.	8,753	2,883	1,191	2,452	978	760	489	—
Rate	2.85	3.76	1.55	3.15	2.48	3.64	4.78	—

Source: Encuestra Continua Sobre Ocupacion, Secretaria de Programacion y Presupuestra (SPP), Cordinacion General del Sistema Nacional de Informacion, Serie 1, Vol. 7, Trimestre 1, 1979. Mexico, February 1980.

ment continues to be a problem for that sector of the female labor force from which maquiladoras draw the majority of their workers.

One might question why, when such a large proportion of maquiladora workers consists of women aged 16 to 24, unemployment rates are so high among young border state women. The data presented in Table 1.4 suggest a partial explanation. Women aged 10 to 29 make the largest contribution to the migration stream to the border states. Because these data tell us nothing about these women's reasons for moving, they provide no information about the role of maquiladoras in drawing young women to the north. These data do demonstrate, however, that the largest proportion of female migrants belongs to the age categories from which the maquiladoras recruit their labor force. Whether the assembly plants induce these women to migrate, or merely utilize the labor of movers coming for diverse reasons, it appears that the steady northward flow of young women helps maintain unemployment levels in the face of job shortages and replenishes the supply of potential maquiladora workers.

These data provide no evidence that maquiladoras exacerbate male unemployment in northern cities. If such a claim were correct, one might expect men in the northern region to have higher unemployment rates than the national averages. However, Table 1.3 indicates that with the exception of the 12−19-year category, unemployment rates for northern Mexican men are about equal to or somewhat lower than those for men in other regions.

A comparison of the male and female unemployment rates in Table 1.3 similarly provides no evidence that the BIP has given women an advantage over men in the labor market. Women in each of the three northern regions are more likely to be unemployed than comparably aged men. These differences parallel the pattern for Mexico as a whole.

The empirical evidence fails to support even the more plausible version of the argument advanced by Woog and others. Despite the presence of the Border Industrialization Program, joblessness remains a problem for women of all ages. It is particularly high among those aged 12 to 24, the sector which provides the bulk of the assembly plant labor force. Further, women have not acquired a privileged position relative to men in the labor market: women of most ages are twice as likely as men to be unemployed. The same conditions that weaken women's employment status in other parts of Mexico operate in the north, despite whatever job opportunities maquiladoras might offer.

TABLE 1.4
Population Who Have Changed Their Place of Residence, by Age and Sex, for Republic of Mexico and Frontier States, 1970

Place	Total	Less Than 9	10–19	20–29	30–39	40–49	50–59	60+
Mexico	7,406,390	949,160	1,439,440	1,585,174	1,258,222	921,485	585,400	667,509
Men	3,572,268	477,787	675,083	749,684	618,456	458,609	285,049	307,600
Percent of total no. of male migrants		13.37	18.90	20.99	17.31	12.84	7.98	8.61
Women	3,834,122	471,373	764,357	835,490	639,766	462,876	300,351	359,909
Percent of total no. of female migrants		12.29	19.94	21.79	16.69	12.07	7.83	9.39
Baja Calif.	361,847	41,405	71,575	77,389	65,813	49,679	29,285	26,758
Men	179,092	20,605	34,390	35,912	32,963	26,651	15,291	13,280
Percent of total no. of male migrants		11.51	19.20	20.05	18.41	14.88	8.54	7.42
Women	182,755	20,800	37,185	41,477	32,850	23,028	13,937	13,478
Percent of total no. of female migrants		11.38	20.35	22.70	17.97	12.60	7.63	7.37
Coahuila	148,588	17,475	24,713	25,953	24,107	19,372	14,923	22,045
Men	71,933	8,798	11,990	11,929	11,512	9,461	7,262	10,981
Percent of total no. of male migrants		12.23	16.67	16.58	16.00	13.15	10.10	15.27
Women	76,655	8,677	12,723	14,024	12,595	9,911	7,661	11,604
Percent of total no. of female migrants		11.32	16.60	18.29	16.43	12.93	9.99	14.43

(continued on next page)

TABLE 1.4 (Continued)

Place	Total	Less Than 9	10–19	20–29	30–39	40–49	50–59	60+
Chihuahua	188,344	21,346	35,298	36,514	31,129	25,053	17,546	21,458
Men	92,792	10,762	17,342	17,157	15,203	12,798	8,890	10,640
Percent of total no. of male migrants		11.60	18.69	18.49	16.38	13.79	9.58	11.47
Women	95,552	10,584	17,956	19,357	15,926	12,255	8,656	10,818
Percent of total no. of female migrants		11.08	18.79	20.26	16.67	12.83	9.06	11.32
Nuevo Leon	424,083	46,897	86,894	98,218	73,014	51,848	31,805	35,407
Men	206,867	23,791	41,437	47,694	36,598	25,597	15,126	16,624
Percent of total no. of male migrants		11.50	20.03	23.06	17.69	12.37	7.31	8.36
Women	217,216	23,106	45,457	50,524	36,416	26,251	16,679	18,783
Percent of total no. of female migrants		10.64	20.93	23.26	16.76	12.09	7.68	8.65
Sonora	171,798	17,897	32,095	36,436	31,691	23,927	14,819	14,933
Men	89,168	9,127	15,729	17,693	17,073	13,460	8,197	7,889
Percent of total no. of male migrants		10.24	17.64	19.84	19.15	15.10	9.19	8.85
Women	82,630	8,770	16,366	18,743	14,618	10,467	6,622	7,044
Percent of total no. of female migrants		10.61	19.81	22.68	17.69	12.67	8.01	8.52
Tamaulipas	343,859	34,318	56,576	68,851	64,112	48,075	32,558	39,369
Men	168,749	17,349	26,917	31,500	31,420	24,504	16,774	20,285
Percent of total no. of male migrants		10.28	15.95	18.67	18.62	14.52	9.94	12.02
Women	175,110	16,969	29,659	37,351	32,692	23,571	15,784	19,084
Percent of total no. of female migrants		9.69	16.94	21.33	18.67	13.46	9.01	10.90

SOURCE: IX Censo de Poblacion.

Discussion

The evidence presented here challenges the claim that unemployment in northern Mexico is basically a male rather than a female problem. The assumption that women have no need to work for wages outside the home because they are adequately supported by male breadwinners runs counter to the fact that a considerable proportion of women are in the work force. Similarly, the tendency to define all women as full-time wives and mothers has little basis in reality: between 70 and 80 percent of economically active women are unmarried. Such an image appears to reflect cultural definitions of women's ideal roles rather than portraying their real-world situations. Most unpartnered women must, in all probability, earn an income to support themselves and perhaps other family members. While these aggregate statistics provide no way of estimating how many of the remaining, stably partnered women work out of economic need, it is likely that many are an essential income source for the family wage economy (Fernández-Kelly, 1983:11). Nor do these data support the alternative claim that all women who need to work are able to find employment. For the woman whose wages are essential to her own, and in many cases other family members', economic support, unemployment would be a considerable problem.

This study has found no evidence that the maquiladora program has enhanced northern Mexican women's position in the labor market, relative to men in the region or to women in Mexico generally. Nor do they support the related claim that the program contributes to male unemployment through the large-scale mobilization of young women out of the household and into the labor force. Women in the north do not have higher labor force participation rates or lower unemployment rates than the average for the nation as a whole. The highest unemployment is found among women from the younger age categories, the sector from which the bulk of the maquiladora labor force is recruited. Similarly, northern Mexican men are no more likely to be unemployed than their counterparts in other parts of Mexico. Finally, unemployment rates for northern Mexican women, like those for women in the rest of the country, are generally twice as high as comparable rates for men.

The claim that the Border Industrialization Program has failed to solve the border region's employment problems thus appears to be correct, but for the wrong reasons. The maquiladora program has not placed men at a disadvantage relative to women in the labor market. On the contrary, the program has not attenuated unemployment among members of either sex. Although unemployment is more pronounced for women, it continues to be a problem for both sexes.

How then might one account for this persistent unemployment, particularly among young women, despite considerable maquiladora investment? It is well understood, by both opponents and supporters of the Border Industrialization Program, that the key incentive to maquiladora investment is the abundance of inexpensive labor (Fernández-Kelly, 1983:40). High rates of natural population increase and internal migration to the region in recent decades have led to considerable population growth in northern Mexico. The border economy's inability to provide enough jobs for the rapidly expanding population has produced a large pool of surplus labor (Fernández, 1977:166, 140; Bustamante, 1983:231). Women are especially likely to constitute this labor reserve: as the aggregate data have demonstrated, their unemployment rates are generally twice those of men. Most apt to be among the surplus labor reserve in northern cities are women aged 24 or younger. Not only do they have higher unemployment rates than women of other age categories, but they are disproportionately represented in the migration stream which continually replenishes the surplus labor pool.

Over 70 percent of the economically active women in the north are unmarried; most of these women work out of financial necessity. For the woman who must support herself and perhaps other family members, maquiladora employment is preferable to domestic service, prostitution, or petty sales, which may be her only other options (Fernández-Kelly, ND:23; Lim, 1981:1978). Because gender-typed definitions of "appropriate" roles for women tend to exclude them from many occupations, and because few women have the necessary training for better female jobs such as nursing or teaching, many women have few alternatives to maquiladora employment. It has been estimated that for every worker hired, some twenty applicants are turned away (NACLA, 1979: 134). Such intense competition for assembly plant jobs helps explain why wages rarely rise much above the federally mandated minimum (Fernández-Kelly, 1983:114). In sum, the notion that women—particularly young, unmarried women—constitute a ready supply of available low-waged labor from which maquiladoras can recruit their labor force is consistent with these data. This labor pool is a key factor drawing export processing investment to the Mexican north.

To put the matter differently, by ensuring a steady labor supply and by creating a competitive situation holding wages to a minimum, female unemployment encourages the establishment of maquiladoras. It is probable that a rough equilibrium is maintained between levels of unemployment and maquiladora investment. If the BIP and its labor force were to grow so rapidly as to substantially reduce the pool of surplus female labor, this would eliminate the major incentive attracting maquiladoras to the border zone. Multinational companies would look to other regions with larger labor surpluses as sites for new offshore plants, building few new maquiladoras in northern Mexico. Some established maquiladoras would transfer their operations to other locations, pursuing more abundant low-waged labor. The resulting decline in maquiladora investment would limit the creation of new jobs while eliminating some existing ones. Yet at the same time that the maquiladora work force was failing to expand or contracting, female migration to the border region would continue to augment the female labor reserve. Female unemployment would thus rise up to or above its original level. While the growth of the BIP might, therefore, temporarily decrease female joblessness, such reductions would not be long-lasting. By eliminating the key incentive for further maquiladora investment, substantial long-term reductions of the female labor reserve would ultimately bring the program's demise. Ironically, a requirement for the maintenance of the maquiladora program is the very condition which the program was implemented to eliminate.

To summarize, the program's critics miss the boat when they view the region's continued unemployment as mainly a reflection of the maquiladoras' preference for women workers. A more accurate analysis would attribute causal priority to the large numbers of young women who must work to support themselves, yet may be unable to secure employment. To put the matter simply, it is not so much that the maquiladoras have contributed to unemployment in the region, but rather that the existence of a pool of surplus female labor has led to proliferation of maquiladoras. Without a fundamental change in the economic and demographic factors contributing to rapid population growth in northern Mexico, unemployment is likely to persist despite the existence of the maquiladora program.

Although caution should be employed in generalizing these findings from northern Mexico to other export platform nations, there is no reason to assume that this case is atypical. These results are consistent with a growing body of research on women in a variety of developing nations. Throughout the Third World, economic necessity forces women to earn an income to support themselves and their families, yet their position in the labor market is generally weaker than that of their male counterparts. Women's wages are consistently lower than men's, their employment options are restricted to a range of jobs deemed appropriate for women, and they are less likely than men to be organized into unions which might enhance their bargaining power and working conditions (ICRW, 1980). Women are an optimal work force from the standpoint of transnational corporations, who engage in offshore sourcing primarily to reduce labor costs. It is no accident that women form the bulk of the export processing work force not only in northern Mexico, but in the Caribbean, Central America, and southeast Asia. Women will, in all probability, continue to function in this capacity as export processing industrialization expands into new Third World contexts. As the findings of this study indicate, women's relatively vulnerable position in Third World labor markets is at the root of their common role as assembly workers within the global division of labor. Future studies of women's role in export processing should attempt to elucidate the social structural, demographic, and economic factors underlying women's employment situation in developing countries.

References

Arizpe, Lourdes, 1977. "Women in the Informal Labor Sector: The Case of Mexico City." In Wellesley Editorial Committee (eds), *Women and National Development: The Complexities of Change*. University of Chicago Press, pp. 25−37.

Barnet, Richard, and Ronald Muller, 1974. *Global Reach: The Power of Multinational Corporations*. New York: Simon and Schuster.

Boserup, Ester, 1970. *Women's Role in Economic Development*. New York: St Martin's Press.

Bustamante, Jorge, 1983. "Maquiladoras: A New Face of International Capitalism on Mexico's Northern Frontier." In June Nash and Maria Patricia Fernández-Kelly (eds), *Women, Men, and the International Division of Labor*. Albany: SUNY Press, pp. 224−256.

Chinchilla, Norma, 1977. "Industrialization, Monopoly Capitalism, and Women's Work in Guatemala." In Wellesley Editorial Committee, pp. 244−260.

De Miranda, Glaura Vasques, 1977. "Women's Labor Force Participation in a Developing Society: The Case of Brazil." In Wellesley Editorial Committee, pp. 261−274.

Ehrenreich, Barbara, and Annette Fuentes, 1981. "Life on the Global Assembly Line." *Ms.* (January), pp. 53−59.

Fernández, Raul, 1977. *The United States−Mexican Border: A Politico-Economic Profile*. University of Notre Dame Press.

Fernández-Kelly, María Patricia, 1983. *For We Are Sold: I and My People*. Albany: SUNY Press.

————, ND. "Maquiladoras and Women in Ciudad Juarez: The Paradoxes of Industrialization under Global Capitalism." Stanford: Calif.: Center for Latin American Studies.

Fuentes, Annette, and Barbara Ehrenreich, 1983. *Women in the Global Factory.* New York: South End Press, 1983.

Grossman, Rachael, 1979. "Women's Place in the Integrated Circuit." *Southeast Asia Chronicle,* no. 66 (January–February), pp. 2–17.

Hymer, Stephen, 1978. "The Multinational Corporate Capitalist Economy." In Richard Edwards et al. (eds), *The Capitalist System.* Englewood Cliffs, N.J.: Prentice-Hall, pp. 492–498.

International Center for Research on Women (ICRW), 1980. "Keeping Women Out: A Structural Analysis of Women's Employment in Developing Countries." Prepared for the Office of Women in Development, U.S. Agency for International Development, April.

Lim, Linda, 1981. "Women's Work in Multinational Electronics Factories." In Roslyn Dauber and Melinda Cain (eds), *Women and Technological Change in Developing Countries.* Boulder, Colo.: Westview Press, pp. 181–190.

MacEwan, Arthur, 1978. "Capitalist Expansion and the Sources of Imperialism." In Richard Edwards et al., pp. 494–498.

McCormack, Thelma, 1981. "Development with Equity for Women." In Naomi Black and Ann Baker Cottrell (eds), *Women and World Change.* Beverly Hills, Calif.: Sage, pp. 15–30.

Martinez, Oscar, 1978. *Border Boom Town: Ciudad Juarez Since 1948.* Austin: University of Texas Press.

North American Congress on Latin America (NACLA), 1979. *Beyond the Border: Mexico and the United States Today.* New York.

Peña, Devon, 1980. "Las Maquiladoras: Mexican Women and Class Struggles in the Border Industries." *Aztlan: International Journal of Chicano Studies Research XI:2 (Fall).*

————, 1981. *Maquiladoras: A Select Annotated Bibliography and Critical Commentary on the United States–Mexico Border Industry Program.* Center for the Study of Human Resources, University of Texas, Publication No. 7–81.

————, 1982. "Emerging Organizational Strategies of Maquila Workers on the Mexico–U.S. Border." Tenth Annual Meeting of the National Association for Chicano Studies (NACS), Arizona State University, Tempe, March.

Safa, Helen, 1980. "Export Processing and Female Employment: The Search for Cheap Labor." Paper prepared for Burg Wautenstein Symposium, No. 85, August.

Woog, Mario, 1980. *El Programa Mexicano de maquiladoras.* Instituto de Estudios Sociales, Universidad de Guadalajara.

Youssef, Nadia, 1976. "Women in Development: Urban Life and Labor." In Irene Tinker and Michele Bo Bramsen (eds), *Women and World Development.* Overseas Development Council, pp. 70–77.

2

Female Mexican Immigrants in San Diego County

Rosalía Solórzano-Torres

Even though the presence of Mexican immigrants and its impact on the sites of destination in the United States has been the focus of decades of intense social scientific and policy-oriented research, very little about this phenomenon is known as it affects the lives of women.

Most of the studies that have been conducted are primarily male-centered, especially when the focus of concern becomes the undocumented immigrant (Gamio, 1930; Bustamante, 1975, 1978, 1979; Cornelius, 1976, 1978, 1980, 1982; North and Houston, 1976; and Villalpando, 1977). However, I contend that the process of migration incorporates women as well as men, that is, households, at both national and international scenarios.

There exists a historical trend showing the process of migration to be gender-selective, and the Mexican male immigrants have been shown to be the protagonists (Goodman and Rivera, 1982), yet very little is known about how the process affects the lives of women. The female component has been often neglected because the migration of women is seen as an "associational" affair. Women are seen as members of whole family units which migrate together, or as dependents of males who already have established permanent residence in the United States (Cornelius, 1978).

Let us at this point consider a general assumption espoused in the undocumented migration literature: If undocumented migration tends to reflect mostly recent arrivals of unattached males who migrate for short periods of time and who are engaged particularly in the agricultural economic sector (Cornelius, 1981; and Dinerman, 1982), then this pattern does not reflect the characteristics of a more stable household, headed by women or men, with or without children. Nor do we know the characteristics of more temporary female Mexican immigrants, whether they occupy urban- versus rural-based jobs, their places of origin in Mexico, in summary, their socioeconomic and demographic characteristics. At a purely speculative theoretical level, the male and female characteristics merit further research.

This chapter is divided into two sections: The first section emphasizes the relative "invisibility" of women immigrants from Mexico into the United States. Research data on women will be utilized and compared with male immigrants in order to present a gender-differentiated demographic analysis. The second section provides a preliminary profile of the socioeconomic and demographic characteristics of the female Mexican immigrants. Because as mentioned before, studies have been male-centered, and because a random sample of the undocumented Mexican immigrants is not possible, samples of this population have often been interviewed at Immigration and Naturalization Service detention centers. I find that these studies tend to underrepresent women. Henceforth, the findings reported in this chapter will shed light on the distinctive and similar characteristics of male and female Mexican immigration.

The Data

The data were randomly selected from two samples of female interviews conducted by myself and anthropologist Ana García, of the U.S.-Mexican Studies Center at the University of California, San Diego. The sample was extracted from a major health study on the population of Mexican origin in the San Diego County, conducted from March 1981 to September 1982 under the direction of Dr. Wayne Cornelius.

In the San Diego County study, 2300 persons of Mexican origin were interviewed in their San Diego residences, which were scattered throughout the county. Approximately 50 percent of the total sample are women. To this date, the San Diego County study represents the most detailed data bank anywhere in the nation on mostly undocumented persons of Mexican origin. It is also the most detailed and in-depth interview schedule especially as it focuses on the female Mexican immigrant. The findings to be reported in the second section of this chapter are preliminary. It is important to mention that the results presented here do not claim to be representative of the female Mexican immigrant universe in the United States.

The data were gathered at both urban- and rural-based communities throughout the San Diego County. The selected sample to be presented represents women who were interviewed in San Diego (especially its southeast region), Chula Vista, National City, and San Ysidro. There were a total of 107 female Mexican immigrants selected from urban based communities. Seventy-seven other women were interviewed mostly in the rural areas of Ramona, Vista, Valley Center, Rincon, San Luis Rey, Fallbrook, San Marcos, Carlsbad, Bonsall, and Leucadia, and the cities of Escondido and San Deigo. Both samples combined give a total of 184 female Mexican immigrants interviewed by myself and Ana García. These women were residing in the San Diego County at the time of the interviews, from March 1981 to February 1982.

The methodology utilized was the "snowball sample" technique. This method proved to be an excellent way to explore the life experiences of both male and female undocumented immigrants in the United States. Because the San Diego County study focused on health issues, it was feasible to relate to the informant's experiences by overtly ignoring any reference to the women's legal status. As a result, about 98 percent of the informants revealed their status before the interviewer probed into this issue.

One of the drawbacks that emerged from utilizing this technique is a bias favoring representation of permanent settlers (Melville, 1978). However, the biases can be eased somewhat by interviewing the sample of the population selected in both rural- and urban-based communities, where there is some probability that newcomers and seasonal workers will be included. As a matter of fact, this method allowed the author new information on single, temporary female Mexican immigrants and their socioeconomic characteristics, a sample of the undocumented population generally ignored in the current literature.

Representation from both regions was ensured by broadening the sources of initial contact, by comparing with other population samples, and by tapping into kin and friendship networks of the informants. These techniques gave some indication of the male-female ratio of the Mexican immigrant population under study. Other methodologies utilized in this section of the study were participant observation, in-depth open interviews, structured interviews containing closed and open questions, direct observation, and in some situations, utilization of a tape recorder and a camera (with the informant's consent). Interviewing female Mexican immigrants was possible without major inconveniences to either the informant or the interviewer once entrance had been made into a particular network. It is also important to emphasize at this point that all interviews were conducted by a bilingual Spanish/English staff in Spanish, and at the informants' homes. In addition, because I am a Mexicana, women found it easy to talk about their life experiences in an open and free style.

The combination of techniques allowed me to provide a more complete sketch or profile of the lives of female Mexican immigrants in San Diego County. It becomes important to supplement personal interviews with "qualitative," enthnographic data gathered through less structured methodologies.

The Migration Literature: Where Are the Women?

Previous studies of undocumented migrants, aside from indicating a gender-selectivity, suggest that the bulk of them are young and unattached, have less than 5 years of education, and held their first job in Mexico (Cornelius, 1979; Bustamante and Martínez, 1980). What are the findings concerning Mexican women immigrants? There have been a few studies that reported data on women; however, because the representativeness of the samples is indeterminable, these data must be interpreted with care.

The CENIET Survey conducted from October through November 1977 at the ports of entry to Mexico released information on female Mexican undocumented immigrants. The findings show that 12 percent of the total surveyed sample were women who had been detained at the INS centers. For every female caught, 7.2 males were apprehended.

Another study conducted by North and Houston (1976) reported that there were ten males apprehended for every female. Other policy-oriented reports have completely omitted the female immigrant (Villalpando, 1977; Comisión Intersecretarial, 1972). In contrast, Margarite Melville, Lourdes Arguelles, Esther Bach-y-Rita, and scholars associated with the Orange County Task Force and the San Diego County study are among the few who have incorporated women respondents to a significant degree (Melville, 1978; Arguelles, 1981; Orange County Task Force, 1978; San Diego study, 1982).

NACLA (1979) conducted a study on fifty undocumented immigrants (mostly women), by tapping into the informants' kin and friendship networks. As contended by Portes (1981), these networks form the microstructures of migration. Bach-y-Rita (1981), by utilizing the same technique, interviewed fifteen undocumented female Mexican immigrants in Northern California and found that more than half were productive members of the economic labor force of that region. Cárdenas and Flores (1980) noted that 63.8 percent of the informants who were parents of children attending schools for the undocumented were female immigrants. Likewise, Van Ardol et al. (1979) indicated the 38 percent of the applicants for immigration status adjustment were female. These studies suggest that migrant women are anchored in well-defined social as well as economic structures, and that immigration is far from being overwhelmingly male. This pattern either suggests an actual increase in the relative numbers of women migrants or else reflects the different manner in which the information was gathered in the past; perhaps both factors are operating concurrently.

The Findings

The following findings represent the characteristics of female Mexican immigrants residing in the San Diego County from March 1981 to February 1982. Contrary to what is otherwise believed, female Mexican immigrants have a predominantly urban-based origin. Almost two-thirds of the respondents declared their place of origin to be a city, 15.7 percent from small pueblos, 13.8 percent from ranchos or haciendas, and a mere 5.9 percent from ejidos (see Table 2.1). Unlike the findings that have been reported for male undocumented immigrants, women seem to originate from mostly urban-based communities. In contrast, slightly over half of the male sample of the 1977 Ceniet survey came from rural communities. These findings illuminate the heterogeneity of the immigrants.

The place of origin cited by the informants and by federal studies tends to confirm the six traditional areas of the Mexican Republic that represent the majority of Mexican undocumented immigrants. Hence, almost three-fourths of the total sample of females interviewed came from the states of Baja California Norte, Chihuahua, Zacatecas, Jalisco, and Guerrero. Of these women, slightly less than half declared one of the Mexican northern border states of Baja California Norte, Chihua-

TABLE 2.1
Type of Place of Origin of a Sample of Female Mexican Immigrants in San Diego County before Entering the United States

Type of Place of Origin	Number	Percentage
Rancho o hacienda	25	13.8
Ejido	11	5.9
Pueblo	29	15.7
Ciudad	119	64.6
TOTAL	184	100.0

SOURCE: A total sample of 184 women was extracted from the major San Diego County Health study conducted from March 1981 to September 1982 and presently in progress: 107 women were selected at random from a 215 sample conducted by the author while she was part of the fieldwork personnel of the U.S.-Mexican Studies Center of the University of California at San Diego; 77 women were selected from the total sample of women interviewed by anthropologist Ana Garcia, staff member at this center. The first sample was interviewed at an urban-based environment and the second one in mostly rural-based communities. For analysis of data and presentation of the findings these two samples were combined.

hua, Sonora or Coahuila as their place of origin (see Table 2.2). Because they live in close proximity to the United States, it is probable that crossing the border into the United States does not represent the same economic, social, and psychological opportunity expense as for those who reside in farther regions.

It is also interesting that when place of birth of these women is considered, the findings show that about 83 percent of them had previous migration histories. Migration into the northern Mexican cities that border with the United States constituted for many women an intermediate stage, before their migration to the United States. About 62 percent of the women interviewed at rural sites were women who had left their rural place of origin in Mexico, had migrated to the cities in Mexico in search of an improvement of their living standards, and then retired al norte. In addition, through their networks of friendship and kin, they served as information agents to others who followed their steps at later dates. There were also cases of undocumented women residing in San Diego County who provided shelter, food and in some cases, income to the newly arrived paisana, or relative. In repeated situations encountered during the interview, it was found that many of the already established females serve as contacts for employment for the neophytes, who often report to work in less than one week after immigrating to San Diego County.

Table 2.3 categorizes the female Mexican immigrants by place of birth. Jalisco represented the place of birth of 22.8 percent of the total

TABLE 2.2

Place of Origin of a Sample of Female Mexican Immigrants in the San Diego Couty by Federal Entity

State	Number	Percentage
Baja California Norte	70	38.0
Chihuahua	12	6.5
Colima	5	2.7
Coahuila	1	0.5
Distrito Federal	5	2.7
Durango	2	1.1
Guanajuato	6	3.2
Guerrero	9	4.8
Jalisco	19	16.6
Mexico	1	0.5
Michoacan	13	7.0
Nayarit	4	2.2
Oaxaca	2	1.1
Queretaro	1	0.5
San Luis Potosi	2	1.1
Sonora	4	2.2
Sinaloa	4	2.2
Tlaxcala	1	0.5
Zacatecas	10	5.4
TOTAL	183	100.0

SOURCE: A total sample of 184 women was extracted from the major San Diego County study conducted from March 1981 to September 1982 and presently in progress. U.S.–Mexican Studies Center, The University of California at San Diego.

population sample followed by Michoacan, Baja California Norte, and Zacatecas with 11.6 percent, 7.6 percent and 8.7 percent, respectively. The state of Guerrero followed with 5.9 percent, Chihuahua with 5.5 percent, Durango with 5.5 percent, and Sonora with 4.9 percent. The migration process seems to be incorporating both male and female immigrants from states that have had a long tradition of sending migrants into the United States (CENIET, 1977). These flows are far from diminishing in the near future. Contrary to what might otherwise seem to be the case, the migration flows tend to increase and become more selective through time; such is the case of the incorporation of the female Mexican immigrant into the United States.

Current migration patterns extending through Latin American countries show that at a national level, more women are migrating to the cities than their male counterparts (Arizpe, 1978; Benería, 1979; Safa,

TABLE 2.3
Place of Origin of a Sample of Female Mexican Immigrants in San Diego County by Federal Entity

State	Number	Percentage
Baja California Norte	14	7.6
Baja California Sur	2	1.1
Chihuahua	10	5.5
Coahuila	1	0.5
Colima	6	3.2
Curango	10	5.5
Distrito Federal	7	3.8
Guanajuato	8	4.4
Guerrero	11	5.9
Hidalgo	1	0.5
Jalisco	42	22.8
Mexico	1	0.5
Michoacan	21	11.6
Nayarit	5	2.7
Nuevo Leon	1	0.5
Puebla	1	0.5
Oaxaca	4	2.1
San Luis Potosi	4	2.1
Sonora	9	4.9
Sinaloa	8	4.4
Veracruz	2	1.1
Zacatecs	16	8.7
TOTAL	184	100.0

SOURCE: A total sample of 184 women was extracted from the major San Diego County study conducted from March 1981 to September 1982 and presently in progress. U.S.–Mexican Studies Center, The University of California at San Diego.

1981). A pattern reflected since the 1960s indicates that more younger women are migrating out of their rural places of origin into urban communities (Cardona and Simmons, 1975). Downing (1975) has argued that for the last three decades, the male and female immigrant ratio from Mexico has been narrowed. A report prepared for the Office of Women in Development, conducted by the U.S. Department of Commerce, shows that in 1979 the median age of rural Mexican women migrants found in the cities was about 17 years old. For other Latin American countries, similar patterns were observed (U.S. Bureau of the Census Report issued in June 1980).

The age ranges reflected in my findings coincide with the recent literature. Slightly less than 50 percent of the total sample fell within the age range under 30 and not younger than 17 years old. The mean age for the total sample was 29.8 years, and about one-third of the sample fell in the 30 to 41 age range with about 30 percent of the women indicating they were more than 42 years old (see Table 2.4). This last group represented a component of the population who were permanent settlers, having resided in the United States for at least 25 years.

When age is analyzed according to the place where the women were interviewed (be it an urban or rural based community), findings show that women from the oldest and youngest age categories were more likely to live in urban communities, while women aged 30–52 were more likely to live in rural areas. For the older women in the 42 to 47 range, it was found that these women cross into the United States to visit friends and relatives and perhaps help them with domestic work, but without remuneration. Of the women in the older age brackets, those who work for wages are concentrated in domestic related services outside of the formal sector of the economy.

Legal Status

Out of the 184 women interviewed, almost 60 percent reported to be undocumented residents of San Diego County. Of the women who

TABLE 2.4

Age of a Sample of Female Mexican Immigrants in San Diego County by Place of Interview

Age	Urban	Rural	Urban & Rural	Percentage
17–23	40	13	53	28.8
24–29	22	14	36	19.5
30–35	12	19	31	16.8
36–41	11	17	28	15.2
42–47	1	8	9	4.8
48–52	2	5	7	3.8
53 +	19	1	20	21.1
TOTAL	107	77	184	100.0

SOURCE: A total sample of 184 women was extracted from the major San Diego County study conducted from March 1981 to September 1982 and presently in progress. U.S.–Mexican Studies Center, University of California at San Diego.

reported having papers, 40 percent had obtained them after they joined their husbands in the United States, or had migrated as a family unit. Two women openly admitted having a birth certificate that was bought from someone else; one woman came to the United States with a student visa that had elapsed before the time of the interview (see Tables 2.5 and 2.6). More than 45 percent of the women who reported crossing into the United States with documents were "local" card holders. Of 85 percent of the sample who held jobs, 35 percent stayed overnight at their working sites. These women, usually domestic workers, commuted to Mexico once a week; 15 percent of the wage earners returned home to Mexico every two weeks and 28 percent returned once a month. Only 22 percent remained in their working sites for more than two months, typically for a maximum of one year, after which they returned to their homes in Mexico.

Most of the female Mexican immigrants interviewed were well informed and felt secure because they relied on their kin and friendship networks. People enmeshed within these nets may very well have families with previous migration histories. This was found to be the case with the women who reported their place of origin within the interior of Mexico: Michoacan, Jalisco, and Zacatecas.

Education

The mean number of years of schooling for the women in this study is 6.8 years. This can be explained by the fact that most of the women immigrated from urban areas in Mexico (see Table 2.7). Only 8.1 percent

TABLE 2.5
Residence in the United States of a Sample of Female Mexican Immigrants in the San Diego County by Legal Status

Legal Status	Number	Percentage
Without documents	109	59.4
With documents	70	38.0
Missing cases	5	2.6
TOTAL	184	100.0

Source: A total sample of 84 women was extracted from the major San Diego County study conducted from March 1981 to September 1982 and presently in progress. U.S.–Mexican Studies Center, the University of California at San Diego.

TABLE 2.6
Legal Documents Lacking in a Sample of Female Mexican Immigrants in the San Diego County by Type of Document

Missing Document	Number	Percentage
Residence	42	60.0
False documents	2	2.5
Visa student	1	1.5
Local card	25	36.0
TOTAL	70	100.0

SOURCE: A total sample of 184 women was extracted from the San Diego County study conducted from March 1981 to September 1982 and presently in progress. U.S.–Mexican Studies Center, the University of California at San Diego.

TABLE 2.7
Years of Schooling of a Sample of Female Mexican Immigrants in the San Diego County

Years of Schooling	Number	Percentage
Illiterate (0 years of school)	15	8.1
1 to 5 years	75	40.5
6 years (completed *primaria*)	45	25.5
Secondary school (*secundaria comercio*)	28	15.2
Preparatory school (*Preparatoria*)	10	5.4
University	6	3.3
Professional degree completed	5	2.0
TOTAL	184	100.0

SOURCE: A total sample of 184 women was extracted from the major San Diego County study conducted from March 1981 to September 1982 and presently in progress. U.S.–Mexican Studies Center, the University of California at San Diego.

of the women were illiterate and had 0 years of education. Many (40.5 percent) had from 1 to 5 years of schooling. An astounding 51.4 percent had completed at least 6 years of formal education, or *escuela primaria*. This is a significant finding since the mean education level typically reported for male immigrants is less than 5 years (Bustamante, 1979). Both male and female undocumented immigrants have educational levels clearly above the national average of 3.4 years. The findings in this report correspond with the ENEFNEU results, which showed that the educational levels of the emigrants were significantly higher than that of Mexico as a whole. For most of the *indocumentados*, the findings suggest that Mexico is exporting its better educated and perhaps more productive workers. Taking into consideration the ages of these individuals, they constitute a human resource and capital loss to the Mexican Republic. Of the sample, 15.2 percent of the women had more than 7 years of education, and 8.7 percent had 7.1 to 15 years of education. Almost 2 percent of the women had completed university-level training for professional careers. These young immigrants are spending most of their productive years in the United States (Newman, 1982:18).

Marital Status

The findings allowed us to evaluate the hypothesis that there exists an inverse relationship between the marital status of the female Mexican immigrant and the type of receiving community she selects. If the woman is married, she is more likely to be found in a rural community in the San Diego County. However, if the woman migrant is single, she appears more likely to be found in the urban communities. Out of a total of 107 women interviewed at urban communities in San Diego County, 72 percent reported to be single and never married; in contrast, only 6.5 percent of rural dwellers were single. An inverse relationship is also seen when we consider that for a total of 77 women interviewed at rural communities, 85 percent were married; in contrast, only 8.4 percent in the urban communities were married. Women who were widowed, divorced, or separated were almost evenly distributed between rural and urban communities.

One last point to consider is that 10 out of the 12 women who reported to be living in consensual unions were women who were left *abandonadas* by their mates. However, the category, *abandonadas*, was omitted since only 2 women reported to be single at the time of the interview (see Table 2.8). For the total sample, 44.5 percent were single and never married. This category is particularly significant because about half of these women were single mothers. Slightly more than one third of the never-married women who did not have children remitted one-half of their total income to their families in Mexico. These findings correspond to those of María Patricia Fernández-Kelly (1980), who

TABLE 2.8
Civil Status of a Sample of Female Mexican Immigrants in the San Diego County by Urban and Rural Places of Interview

Civil Status	Urban	Percentage	Rural	Percentage	Total	Percentage
Single	77	71.9	5	6.5	82	44.5
Married	9	8.4	65	84.4	74	40.2
Widowed	6	5.6	—	—	6	3.3
Divorced	3	2.8	3	3.9	6	3.3
Separated	2	1.8	2	2.6	4	2.2
Consensual union	10	9.5	2	2.6	12	6.8
TOTAL	107	100.0	77	100.0	184	100.0

Source: A total sample of 184 women was extracted from the major San Diego County study conducted from March 1981 to September 1982 and presently in progress. U.S.–Mexican Studies Center, the University of California at San Diego.

found that female maquila workers are key wage-earners for Mexican households.

Women in the Labor Force

The process of industrialization in Mexico has not improved the endemic unemployment and subemployment that many of her citizens suffer. The industrialization of a few urban centers which have become poles of attraction for domestic migrants has not alleviated the unemployment and subemployment, that presently exist. For example, the maquiladoras' absorption of women into their labor force has been a highly selective process. Often by the time the woman reaches her late twenties she is no longer employable by this sector. Most maquiladora workers have few skills which could help them find alternative employment in Mexican cities after they leave the maquilas. This is crucial to our understanding of the relation between internal and international migration of women to the United States. The maquilas have failed to provide employment opportunities to those who are most likely to migrate, men (Fernández-Kelly, 1980; DeBuen Rickarday and Fernández, 1981). While these enterprises constitute powerful poles of attraction, especially for women migrants from other regions of the Mexican Republic, these export processing plants have not led to a reduction of male unemployment. It has been argued and even publicized by the mass media that the maquilas have created a new type of "macho": one who lives off the labor of his mate (*El Fronterizo*, October 14, 1981).

The findings on the partial sample from the San Diego County Study indicate that there may be a relationship between the maquila program and undocumented immigration of women to the United States. As the data displayed in Table 2.9 reveal, almost 60 percent of the women surveyed had worked in Mexico prior to moving to the United States. Out of the 92 women who had held formal sector jobs, 65 percent worked in industry, 4.3 percent in commerce-related activities, 16.3 percent in the services sector, 7.1 percent in agricultural related activities, and 7.1 percent held professional positions (see Table 2.10). Thus almost two-thirds of women with employment histories prior to migrating had been in the industrial or maquila sector. Most of them were single household heads raising one or more children, whose salaries were their only source of income. Expulsion from the maquila

TABLE 2.9
A Sample of Female Mexican Immigrants in San Diego County by Previous Work in Mexico before Entering the United States

Worked in Mexico before entering the United States	Number	Percentage
Yes	108	58.7
No	74	40.2
No response	2	1.1
TOTAL	184	100.0

SOURCE: A total sample of 184 women was extracted from the major San Diego County study conducted from March 1981 to September 1982 and presently in progress. U.S.–Mexican Studies Center, the University of California at San Diego.

work force may have been a primary factor inducing these women to immigrate to the United States.

According to my findings, the first job women tend to hold once in the United States tends to be in domestic services. Often, women enter jobs that have very little mobility and are located at the bottom rung of the occupational ladder. There is clearly a loss of status when one compares their previous employment in Mexico with their first job in the United States. Yet, because even low wages in the United States are attractive in comparison to those in Mexico, undocumented women, especially those working in factories, can be counted on to accept harsh conditions and perform difficult menial, often tedious, and eye-straining tasks for low pay. The median yearly income for the total sample of women was $6055. For the women who declared themselves to be heads of household, median income was even lower: $5430. Clearly, these figures place these women significantly below the federal poverty line. The types of employment engaged in by the women in my sample are as follows: 12.7 percent in agriculture, 24.0 percent in the light industries, 9.8 percent in commerce, 49.2 percent in the services sector, and 4.3 percent in construction (see Table 2.11).

Forty-five women reported working as domestic servants in private homes. Domestic service is often not considered a stable job because there is no contract between employer and employee. Women can be fired, or can enter or leave their jobs at various times during their lives. In San Diego County, domestic work has been institutionalized as an occupation performed almost entirely by undocumented females. This

TABLE 2.10
A Sample of Female Mexican Immigrants in San Diego County by Economic Sector of Employment in Mexico, before Entering the United States

Sector of Employment	Number	Percentage
Industry	60	65.2
Commerce	4	4.3
Services	15	16.3
Agriculture	5	7.1
Other not declared	5	7.1
TOTAL	92	100.0

SOURCE: A total sample of 184 women was extracted from the major San Diego County study conducted from March 1981 to September 1982 and presently in progress. U.S.–Mexican Studies Center, the University of California at San Diego.

TABLE 2.11
A Sample of Female Mexican Immigrants in San Diego County by Sector of Employment in the United States

Sector of Employment	Number	Percentage
Agriculture	9	12.7
Industry	17	24.0
Commerce	7	9.8
Services	35	49.2
Construction	3	4.3
TOTAL	91	100.0

SOURCE: A total sample of 184 women was extracted from the major San Diego County study conducted from March 1981 to September 1982 and presently in progress. U.S.–Mexican Studies Center, the University of California at San Diego.

pattern can also be found in other U.S. border cities, such as El Paso, Texas (see Ruiz's chapter in this volume). Indeed, undocumented women form a significant proportion of domestic workers in other southwestern cities and even as far away as New York and Washington (Lewis, 1979).

Out of the 27 percent of the Mexicanas who reported not working at the time of the interview, most did have an employment history in San Diego County. It is quite probable that many of them worked in seasonal agricultural occupations, especially those interviewed in rural settings.

Of those who reported not working either in the United States or in Mexico, some probably engaged in home-based informal tasks. For example, many of these women sold Avon products to their acquaintances and relatives. In addition, some women assembled computer chips in their homes, receiving $8 per completed box of chips. An intermediary would come to their homes to pick up and deliver these products in much the same way as do home work contractors in the garment industry. In sum, female immigrants from Mexico appear to be contributing in varied ways to the economy of San Diego County.

My study represents a small segment of the female undocumented population, a group so often neglected in the migration literature. Further research is needed to comprehend more fully the experiences of this significant sector of Mexican migrants. Furthermore, a theoretical frame of reference must be developed in order to analyze gender as well as class and race within the global process of migration.

References

Arizpe, Lourdes, 1978. *Migración, etnicismo y cambio económico*. México, D.F.: Centro de Estudios Sociológicos, El Colegio De México. México.

Arguelles, Lourdes, 1981. "Undocumented Female Labor in the United States Southwest: An Essay on Consciousness, Oppression and Struggle." To be published in *Mexicana/Chicana History*. UCLA: Chicano Studies Research Center.

Bach-y-Rita, Esther W., 1981. "A Study of Fifteen Undocumented Mexican Women: Immigrants in a Northern California Community." Unpublished paper, Wright Institute, Berkeley, Calif.

Benería, Lourdes, 1979. "Reproduccion, produccion y division sexual del trabajo." *Cuadernos Agrarios*, no. 9, pp. 3–32. Mexico.

Bustamante, Jorge, 1975. "Espaladas mojadas: materia prim a para la expansión del capital Norteamericano." Cuadernos del Centreo de Estudios Sociológicos del Colegio de México. México, D.F.

———, 1977. "Undocumented Immigration from Mexico: Research Report." *International Migration Review* 11(2): 149–177.

———, 1979. "Emigración indocumentada a los Estados Unidos." *Indocumentados: Mitos y Realidades*. México, D.F.: Centro de Estudios Internacionales,. El Colegio de México.

———, and Gerónimo Martínez, 1980 "Emigración a la frontera norte del pais y los Estados Unidos," in *Migraciones Internacionales en Las Americas*. Venezuela: CEPAM.

Cárdenas, Gilbert, and Estevan T. Flores, 1980. "Social and Economic, Demographic Characteristics of Undocumented Mexicans in the Houston Labor Market: A Preliminary Report." Houston, Tex.

Cardona, Rene, and Simmons, F., 1980. "Toward a Model of Migration in Latin America." In Brian M. Du Toit (ed), *Migration and Urbanization*. Chicago: Morton Publishers.

Comisión intersecretarial para el estudio del problema de la emigración subrepeticia de trabajadores Mexicanos a los Estados Unidos de América, 1972. Unpublished research report, Secretaria de Relaciones Exteriores, México, D.F.

CENIET, 1977. "Analisis de algunos resultados de la primera encuesta a trabajadores Mexicanos no documentados de los Estados Unidos." Encuesta Nacional de emigracion a la frontera Norte del Pais y a los Estados Unidos. México, D.F., October 23−November 13.

Cornelius, Wayne, 1976. "Mexican Migration to the U.S.: The View from Rural Sending Communities." Monograph #c76-12, Migration and Development Center, Cambridge, Mass.

————, 1978. *Mexican Migration to the United States: Causes and Consequences, and U.S. Responses*. Cambridge, Mass.

————, 1979. "Migration to the U.S.: The View from Mexican Communities." *Development Digest* 17: 90−101.

————, 1980. "Legalizing the flow of Temporary Migrant Workers from Mexico: A Proposal." Working Papers in the U.S.-Mexican Studies, No. 7. Program in the U.S.− Mexican Studies, University of California, San Diego; La Jolla.

Cornelius, Wayne, Leo Chávez, and Jorge Castro, 1982. "Mexican Immigrants and Southern California: A Summary of Current Knowledge." Working Papers in the U.S.− Mexican Studies, No. 36. Program in the U.S.-Mexican Studies, University of California, San Diego; La Jolla.

Dinerman, Ina, 1982. "Migrants and Stay-at-Homes: A Comparative Study of Rural Migration from Michoacan, Mexico. Monograph Series, No. 5. U.S.-Mexican Studies, University of California, San Diego; La Jolla.

Fernández-Kelly María Patricia, 1980. *Chavalas de Maquiladora: A Study of the Composition of the Female Labor Force in Ciudad Juarez Offshore Production Plants*, Ph.D. dissertation, Rutgers University.

Gamio, Manuel, 1930. *Mexican Immigration to the United States*. University of Chicago Press.

Goodman, P., and Rivera, Julius, 1982. "Clandestine Labor Circulation: A Case of the U.S.−Mexican Border." *Migration Today* X(1): 21−26.

Johnson, Kenneth F., and Nina M. Ogle, 1978. *Illegal Mexican Aliens in the U.S.: A Teaching Manual*. Washington: University Press of America.

Lewis, Sasha G., 1979. *Slave Trade Today: An Exploitation of Illegal Aliens*. Boston: Beacon Press.

Melville, Margarita B., 1978. "Mexican Women Adapt to Migration." *International Migration Review* 12(2).

Newman, Allen, 1982. "The Impacts of Emigration on the Mexican Economy." *Migration Today* X(2): 17−21.

North, David, and Marion Houston, 1976. "The Characteristics and Role of Illegal Aliens in the U.S. Labor Market: An Exploratory Study." Report prepaed for the Employment and Training Administration, U.S. Department of Labor.

Orange County Task Force, 1978. "Economic Impact of Undocumented Immigrants and Public Health Services in Orange County, Ca." Report presented to the Orange County Board of Supervisors. Santa Ana, Calif., March.

Rickarday, De Buen Bertha Elena, and Fernández, J. L., 1981. "Los Limites del programa de industralizacion fronteriza para el abatimiento de las tasas de desocupacion y calificacion de la fuerza de trabajo." Presentado en El Primer Encuentro sobre . Impactos Regionales de Relaciones Mexico y Estados Unidos, Guanajuato, July 7—11.

Safa, H. I., 1981. "Runaway Shops and Female Employment: The Search for Cheap Labor." *Signs, Journal of Women in Culture and Society*, Winter Special Issue.

Van Ardol, et al., 1979. Non-Apprehended and Apprehended Undocumented Residents in Los Angeles Labor Market: An Exploratory Study." Los Angeles: University of Southern California, Population Research Laboratory. 1979.

Villapando, Vic, et al., 1977. Study of the Socio-economic Impact of Illegal Aliens in the County of San Diego. Human Resources Agency, County of San Diego, January.

3

By the Day or the Week: Mexicana Domestic Workers in El Paso

Vicki L. Ruiz

In a controversial series, journalists for the *El Paso Herald Post* offered the following description of Mexicana domestics. "Even though they risk being overworked, swindled, and even sexually abused, they come to El Paso by the thousands, taking off their shoes, rolling up their pants and wading the Rio Grande in the early morning hours" (Quintanilla and Copeland, 1983:83). Segmented by class, gender, and ethnicity, Mexican women workers have historically occupied the bottom rung of the economic ladder (Segura, 1084:57−91; Barrera, 1979: 131, 151; Ruiz, 1984:1−4). As marginalized members of the work force, they have also been marginalized in academic scholarship. Their day-to-day struggles for survival and dignity have gone largely unrecorded in the annals of Chicano history, labor theory, women's history, and border studies. While some scholars decry the paucity of research materials in documenting the lives of Mexican women, an important resource is as accessible as the nearest tape recorder. Oral history not only increases the visibility of minority women but fosters understanding and appreciation as well. Oral interviews, housed at the Institute of Oral History, University of Texas at El Paso, form the core of this study.[1]

I would like to acknowledge my research assistants for this project: Sylvia Hernández, Julieta Solis, and Anna Montalvo. ¡Gracias por todo!

1. The Institute of Oral History at the University of Texas at El Paso has the largest collection of taped-recorded interviews (over 700) dealing with the United States−Mexico border. A significant portion of these holdings focus on the lives of Mexicana and Mexican American women workers, many of whom were interviewed as part of the

Economic Background

El Paso is one of the most improverished cities in the United States. In terms of per capita income, only 5 other urban areas (out of a total of 303) rank lower than this border community. More importantly, El Paso has the dubious distinction of having the lowest per capita income level of any population center exceeding 100,000 inhabitants. The city also has the reputation of being a "minimum wage town," yet 15 percent of El Paso County households earn less than the minimum wage of $6968 per year (Rebchook, 1983a: 74; 1983b:66). Unemployment, furthermore, exceeds both the national and the state averages. While unemployment figures hovered around 7.1 to 7.8 percent for the state of Texas and for the nation as a whole during the winter of 1985, El Paso experienced a jobless rate approaching 12 percent (Texas Employment Commission, 1985).[2]

An ethnic dimension complicates the earnings and employment patterns as 63 percent of the city's population has been classified as of "Spanish Origin." For instance, a representative Anglo head of household earns $20,400 annually in contrast to a Hispanic counterpart whose yearly income averages $12,600. In addition, 85 percent of El Paso residents whose income dips below the poverty level are Mexican. Conversely, Anglos compose 81 percent of persons earning $50,000 or more per year. Comparing types of employment, 40 percent of Hispanic workers hold blue-collar jobs while 47 percent of Anglo employees fill high-level professional positions (Copeland, 1983a:12; 1983b:21).

The economic situation in Ciudad Juárez appears even more dismal. Despite an absence of reliable employment figures for El Paso's sister city, a safe estimate would place joblessness at between 10 and 15 percent of the area work force. Salaries for blue-collar operatives are extremely low when compared to those in the United States. In the twin plants (maquiladoras), the take-home pay for line personnel averaged 523 pesos per day or $3.48, a wage set by the Mexican government (Summer, 1983). With such a low pay scale, it is not surprising that thousands of Juarenses (both men and women) cross the Rio Grande in search of employment. In fact, a typical domestic worker can earn almost five times the wage garnered by her peers in the maquiladoras.

Institute's Border Labor History Project. From August 1983 to May 1985, I served as the director of the Institute of Oral History.

2. The El Paso figure is 11.9 percent, which translates as 24,175 unemployed persons actively seeking work.

Twin plant employers, however, hold out the promise of business and government-sponsored social service benefits, the lure of which prove more attractive to workers than the actual pay (Brannon, 1985; Skodack, 1983:68−69; *El Paso Herald Post*, 1985b).[3] As a 20-year-old Mexicana employed by AMF remarked, "If I didn't work here, I don't know if I would have a job. Maybe I would be a maid" (Skodack, 1983:69). The choice for many Juárez women seems clear: employment as trabajadoras in the twin plants or as maids in either Ciudad Juárez or El Paso.[4]

How many women work as dometics in El Paso? There are no reliable estimates. According to the 1980 census, 1063 El Paso women identified themselves as maids in private homes. This figure is very low, for it does not include Juárez commuters with work permits or undocumented women who compose the bulk of the city's domestic labor force. Nestor Valencia, director of the City Planning, Research, and Development Department, stated, "if only 10 percent of El Paso's households had maids that would be more than 13,400 maids and a significant employment sector" (Quintanilla and Copeland, 1983:86). Although impossible to measure accurately, probably more than 10 percent of El Paso homemakers hire domestic help. Perhaps as many as 15,000 to 20,000 women are private household workers.

The salaries of Mexican domestics are sadly deficient when compared with those earned in other parts of the nation for similar work. In El Paso a daily maid (a woman who comes in to clean once a week) earns an average of $15 per day, while a live-in household worker receives from $30 to $60 per week. Some employers, however, offer no more than $80 per month for live-in services. The ready availability of domestic help at bargain basement prices have led to the common expression: "The best thing about El Paso is the cheap maids" (Quintanilla and Copeland, 1983:86; *El Paso Shopping Guide*, 1983; *El Paso Herald Post*, 1985a; *El Paso Times*, 1985).[5]

Domestic workers are so welded into the city's life-style, particularly for middle- and upper-income families, that many homes contain areas identified as "maid's quarters." These accommodations vary from large, light airy rooms with a separate bath and entrance to a small bed

3. The extent to which these promises of benefits are realized is currently the subject of considerable controversy.
4. Employment in the El Paso apparel trades is considered a step up from domestic work, both in terms of pay and prestige. Most maids would view sewing slacks at Farah as a "good" job.
5. Source includes personal observations by the author.

nestled against the washer and dryer. It is very fashionable to have domestic help. As one person observed, "Once you get a microwave, the next status item is a maid." Not only Anglos employ household workers, but also Mexican Americans and Mexican nationals residing in El Paso. In fact, many working-class homes benefit from live-in labor. Mexican American factory operatives frequently hire domestic help (Quintanilla and Copeland, 1983:83, 86; Mr. M., 1983).[6] The presence of Mexicana maids does not stem originally from the recent economic crises in Mexico. Rather, Mexican domestic workers have played important roles in El Paso's economy at least since the turn of the century.

Historical Background

According to a sample of 393 families taken from the 1900 census, only 23 El Paso homes had live-in maids. Of the 23, only one family had a Spanish surname and was, in fact, the family of the Mexican Consul. Many Anglos, however, hired Mexicanas as day servants (García, 1981: 254n). El Paso native Elizabeth Rae Tyson explained:

> Every Anglo American family had at least one, sometimes two or three servants: a maid and laundress, and perhaps a nursemaid ... .The maid came in after breakfast and cleaned up the breakfast dishes, and ... last night's supper dishes, ... did the routine cleaning, washing, and ironing, after the family dinner ... washed dishes again, and then went home to perform similar service in her own home (Barton, 1950:15).

These Mexicanas worked from 7 A.M. to 5 P.M. for $3 to $6 per week (García, 1981:77).

Domestic labor provided the most common form of employment for Mexican women during the first half of the twentieth century. In 1919, the U.S. Employment Bureau opened an office in El Paso. According to historian Mario García, bureau personnel expended large amounts of time and energy in placing Mexican domestics in area residences. For example, in November, 1919, 1740 Mexicanas applied to the agency for employment assistance and 1326 found work. During the 1930s and 1940s, the Rose Gregory Houchen Settlement House, operated by the Methodist Church, also found jobs for Mexican women as domestics.

6. Source includes personal observations by the author. Note that real estate brokers frequently mention "maid's quarters" in advertising their listings.

Staff members operated an informal bureau endeavoring to find Christian homes for Christian women. The settlement also provided child care and medical services to the people of El Segundo, a poor, predominately Hispanic, neighborhood (García, 1981:60; Ruiz, 1983:37–38).

In 1933, in the midst of the Great Depression, many El Paso housewives were horrified to learn that over 500 domestics had organized themselves into the Domestic Workers' Association. In other words, they formed a maids' union. These women, led by political and labor activist Charles Porras, had banded together because they simply could not support their families on the average wage of $1.75 per week (*El Paso Herald Post*, 1933; Porras, 1975).[7] Porras recalled:

> I organized the Domestic Workers' Association—all women, local from *here*. Mind you, $3 a week! I wouldn't let them take a nickel less; and they had to get car fare ... . You'd be surprised to see the number of women, I mean the upper class women *here* that went to the Immigration outfit and tried to get me deported ... or arrested because I was getting these women to stay away from them (Porras, 1975).[8]

Although these Mexicanas received financial and organizational support from a few area locals affiliated with the American Federation of Labor, the maids' association appears to have been short-lived (*El Paso Herald Post*, 1933). Community hostility to the union, as well as rampant unemployment on both sides of the border, ensured a ready supply of domestic servants for El Paso middle- and upper-income housewives at whatever wage these homemakers deemed suitable.

Anglo housewives formed an organization of their own in 1953— the Association for Legalized Domestics. This was in response to the McCarran–Walters Immigration Act, which placed controls on the flow of Mexican nationals coming into the United States. The Association for Legalized Domestics sought the assistance of the Immigration and Naturalization Service (INS) in contracting (legally) the labor of Juárez women. Members of this organization desired the importation of domestic help along the lines utilized by Southwest agribusiness in re-

7. Gracias a Mario García for providing the news clipping.
8. During this period in other sections of the United States, domestic workers generally earned $3 per week (Lois Rita Helmbold, "Class Conflict and Class Cooperation among Women during the Depression," paper presented at the Fifth Berkshire Conference on the History of Women, June 1982, p. 5)

cruiting Mexicanos to work as farm labor under the Bracero Program. Maids, classified as "nonimmigrants," would be contracted to specific employers with specific conditions (*El Paso Times*, 1953; *El Paso Herald Post*, 1953a; Acuña, 1981:144–150).[9] The provisions of the proposed "Bracero Maid" contract follow:

1. The non-immigrant must be asked for by name and must be between the ages of 18 and 35.
2. The non-immigrant must supply the prospective employer with an acceptable health certificate . . . .
3. Non-immigrant must supply the prospective employer with a certificate from Mexican authorities stating that they are free of any civil or criminal record . . . .
4. Non-immigrant must have character references . . . .
5. The contractor must pay a minimum salary of $15 a week.
6. The contractor must provide acceptable living quarters and food . . . .
7. The non-immigrant . . . must have at least one and one-half days of rest per week, at which time the non-immigrant is free to leave the premises and return to Mexico.
8. The non-immigrant may visit Mexico within a limited area designated by the Immigration and Naturalization Service . . . .
9. A $10 fee must be paid by the prospective employer to the INS . . . .
10. Non-immigrant domestic working visas will cost the prospective employer $41.50. This sum will be paid to the U.S. Consular Service.
11. The contract may be terminated by either employer or employee and employee returned to Mexico at any time . . . .
12. The contract and working period . . . is for a period of one year and may be renewed at that time for a fee of $10 providing the U.S. Labor Department states that no qualified domestics are available in the United States . . . (*El Paso Herald Post*, 1953a).

Mexican American household workers protested vehemently the proposal generated by the Association for Legalized Domestics. In a letter to a local advice columnist, one El Paso maid stated that an ample of supply of domestic help existed on the Texas side of the border; however, local housewives preferred women from Juárez since these Mexicanas will work for lower wages. "We charge $3 a day and most ladies want to pay just $12 or $14 a week." The columnist responded by chiding the woman for not accepting the pay scale offered by El Paso homemakers. However, she also realized the enormity of

9. One of the most comprehensive accounts of the Bracero Program is Ernesto Galarza's *Merchants of Labor: The Mexican Bracero Story*, Charlotte, N.C.: McNally and Loftin Publishers, 1964.

household tasks assigned to many domestics. "I think that the amount of work . . . and the hours have a lot to do with the wages," Mrs. Carroll wrote, "that $14 and $12 a week can be too little when a maid is expected to do everything but breathe for her employer" (El Paso Herald Post, 1953b). Reflecting conventional attitudes of the 1950s, Carroll rebuked housewives for their reliance on household workers:

> I think American women could do more housework than they are doing these days . . . . I believe that a good healthy tiredness from housecleaning and cooking a mighty good meal for their family or digging in the garden would stave off more nervous breakdowns than all this hub-bub and how-dya-do over civic . . . duties. I have heard doctors say so (El Paso Herald Post, 1953c).

The Department of Justice ended the controversy generated by the Association of Legalized Domestics by refusing to consider a bracero-type program for Mexican maids (El Paso Herald Post, 1953d, 1953e).

Life-Styles and Employer Attitudes

El Paso homemakers have always had household help, and the experiences of the Mexicanas performing these services have ranged from rewarding, fulfilling employment to sexual abuse. While one woman proudly displays pictures of the Anglo children she helped rear, another recounts how she was sexually harassed and even assaulted by her employers' husbands (Quintanilla, 1983b; Rocío, 1979). Subtle day-to-day humiliation, however, often leaves the deepest scars. As domestic worker Enriqueta Morales recounted:

> There are those that treat me very well. I feel even as if I were one of the family. And with others, it was very different. They humiliated me. With some, they give something to eat . . . they sit you down at the table and everything. As we sit together, we eat, we talk—it's all the same. And others, well, its different. They only give you a sandwich and a glass of water. And that's all they put on our plate. They say "Look, this is your lunch." In time, you may be given a glass of tea, even a soda. Or sometimes, they didn't give me any lunch. That hurts" (Morales, 1979).

Many domestics provide a variety of services for little pay. One employer while entertaining friends instructed his Mexican maid to wash all of the guests' automobiles. The book, Your Maid from Mexico: A

Home Training Course for Maids, encourages Mexicanas to "always . . .
find new ways to help and please your employers." These little extras
range from hair styling to sewing to shining shoes. The duties of
most household workers include cleaning, babysitting, cooking, even
gardening, for a mere $30 to $60 per week. Little wonder, then, that
many El Paso women emphatically declare, "I couldn't live without
my maid" (Quintanilla and Copeland, 1983:84; Hawkins, Soper, and
Henry, 1959:6, 8).[10]

Many señoras have little understanding of the everyday realities
facing the women they employ. Although written over generation ago,
the following excerpt from *Your Maid from Mexico* reflects the apparent
ignorance and patronizing attitudes characteristic of many contemporary El Paso homemakers:

> You girls who work in homes can soon become more valuable to your
> employers than girls who work in offices, stores, or factories because our
> homes . . . are closest to our hearts . . . . Remember, as you learn new skills
> day by day, you are not only learning how to become a better wife and
> mother . . . but you are learning to support yourself and your family in a
> worthwhile career in case you must be the breadwinner (Hawkins, Soper,
> and Henry, 1959:2).

In fact, some women believe that they are doing Mexicanas a favor by
hiring them. As one poorly phrased classified advertisement stated:
"Permanent live-in child carer [sic] of 3 in exchange for private room
and food" (*El Paso Herald Post*, 1985). This potential employer obviously
did not feel compelled to offer any sort of monetary remuneration.

Mexicanas become domestics out of economic necessity. Many live-
in maids have their own families in Ciudad Juárez, their own children
generally cared for by relatives. Typically, they visit their families
on weekends. Younger women, some recruited from the interior of
Mexico, often stay with a family for months at a time. A youthful Mexicana
may work as a household worker in order to earn money for her family or
to save for her own marriage. "I go home about once every month,"
one 18-year-old domestic stated. "Sometimes I stay a week . . . . Most of
the time I go home for the weekend. I miss my family . . . . Sometimes I
miss them too much" (Quintanilla and Copeland, 1983:84; Quintanilla,
1983a:87).[11]

---

10. Source includes personal observations by the author.
11. Source includes personal observations by the author.

Commuter maids, of all ages, form the majority of the live-in domestic labor force in El Paso. These women wade across the river early Monday morning, catch a Sun City Area Transit (SCAT) bus, work all week, and then return to Ciudad Juárez for the weekend. While their pay remains low, it is enough to provide food, clothing, and shelter for their families in Ciudad Juárez. In fact, their earnings are comparable to those garnered by white-collar Juarenses (Quintanilla and Copeland, 1983: 84−86; Brannon, 1985).

Prize-winning poet Pat Mora has clearly captured the divergent worlds of the Mexican maid and her Anglo employer in the poem "Mexican Maid."

> Would the moon help?
> The sun did,
> changed the señora's white skin
> to red, then copper.
> "I'm going to take a sun
> bath, Marta, sun bath, sí?
> Marta would smile, nod,
> look at her own dark skin
> and wish
> that she could lie
> outside at night
> bathed by moonlight,
> lie with her eyes closed
> like the señora wake to a new skin
> that would glisten white
> when she stepped off the dusty bus
> at the entrance to her village (Mora, 1984:36).

Middle-and upper-income residents, in particular, often have definite opinions concerning domestic workers. Echoing common sentiments, Mike Trominski, a deputy director of the Immigration and Naturalization Service (INS), succinctly stated, "People think that it is a God-given right in El Paso to have a wet maid that they can pay a few dollars and will do anything they want." These employers, whether Anglo or Mexican American, are generally unappreciative of the household services they enjoy. At social functions, some women swap maid stories that begin, "My maid is so stupid that—" (Copeland, 1983b).[12]

12. Source includes personal observations by the author.

This denigration of intelligence has not been lost on the domestic worker, even though she often cannot speak the language of her employer. Describing her communication skills in relating to her Anglo *patrona*, one Mexicana poignantly revealed:

> She didn't know any Spanish and I no English. But she has learned much from me. I believe I have learned very little from her because, well, Mexicans, we aren't, well, I'm not so intelligent (Morales, 1979).

The low self-esteem of this woman is undoubtedly the product of years of prejudice and humiliation. INS official James Smith sums it up: "It's human nature—the abuse and the exploitation" (Quintanilla and Copeland, 1983:84).

Life may not be any easier for maids employed by Mexican Americans. Some women assert that Hispanics treat them worse than Anglos. *Mexicanos: es lo peor*, one woman simply stated. Many prefer working for Anglos newly arrived in El Paso. Perhaps these newcomers (often first-time *patronas*) feel a bit guilty about hiring Mexicanas for such bargain rates. As a result, they may be more considerate and appreciative of their household workers (Carlos, 1979; Mrs. C., 1983).[13]

It is important to remember that not all domestics internalize the negative attitudes imposed upon them. Even if they experience psychological and physical abuse, many retain their sense of humor, their pride, their integrity. When María Christina Carlos left her job in a private home to work in a tortilla factory, her employer refused to pay her for her final two weeks' work. Adding insult to injury, the *patrona* then spread the rumor that her maid had robbed her. With rising indignation, Señora Carlos recalled, "But just who had robbed who?" (Carlos, 1979). Another woman recounted how her employer's husband had offered her twenty dollars if she would take off her clothes and dance on the dining room table. Although trembling inside, she managed to reply, "I'm not looking for that kind of work. There are many places where you can see women dance and for less money" (Rocío, 1979).

The "superior" attitudes assumed by many *patronas* can reach preposterous proportions. Some women, perhaps unwittingly or perhaps deliberately, forget to pay their housekeepers at the end of the day or week. Then when the maids ask for their wages, these employers act offended as if to convey the message: "Just who do you think you are?"

---

13. Source includes personal observations by the author.

In addition, *patronas* sometimes believe that they are entitled to regulate the private lives of their domestic workers. When one Mexicana who cleans several homes in the Coronado area (a middle- to upper-middle-class, largely Anglo neighborhood) informed her clients that she was pregnant with her second child, she received mixed responses. While two of her employers have offered Señora Chavarría maternity leaves with pay, another callously issued an ultimatum, "Get an abortion or lose your job." In Señora Chavarría's words, "I tell her, I get other work" (Hernández, 1983; Chavarría, 1983).

Blatant discrimination can even be detected through perusing the classified ads in El Paso's newspapers and shopping guides. Advertisements appearing under the "Domestic Help" sections frequently contain such phrases as "must be clean," "neat appearance," and the ubiquitous "some English necessary." A few area women desire domestic labor but refuse to hire Mexicanas. One recent advertisement noted, "Wanted, European housekeeper" (*El Paso Times*, 1984; *El Paso Herald Post*, 1984; *El Paso Shopping Guide*, 1983, 1984).

One Anglo businessman offered the following reasons why he and his wife are delaying parenthood:

> The major dilemma would be what to do with the child. We don't really like the idea of leaving the baby at home with a maid ... for the simple reason if the maid is Mexican, the child may assume that the Mexican is its mother. Nothing wrong with Mexicans, they'd just assume that this other person is its mother. There have been all sorts of cases where the infants learned Spanish before they learned English. There've been incidences of the Mexican maid stealing the child and taking it over to Mexico and selling it. (Lyons, 1984).

This winding statement reveals the (at best) ambivalent attitudes many Anglo El Pasoans harbor toward Mexicans and their culture.

Of course, strong, harmonious relationships can develop between a Mexican domestic worker and her El Paso employer. For instance, when one Mexicana's infant became ill with severe diarrhea, she called her *patrona*, Mrs. C. who escorted the mother and baby to Thomason General Hospital. During the early morning hours, both Mr. and Mrs. C. waited with the mother in the hospital until the child was examined, and then they drove the woman and her infant home. This display of genuine concern may be uncommon, but it does indicate that the relationship between a private household worker and her *patrona* need not result in humiliation, callousness, or exploitation (Mrs. C., 1983).

Related Concerns

Homemakers are not the only El Pasoans who claim that they "couldn't live without their maids." Domestic workers make significant contributions to the city's economy. Nestor Valencia, director of the city planning office, remarked, "It's an industry that is part of the fiber of the community." In fact, the Sun City Area Transit (SCAT) depends on domestic workers for at least half of its riders. One SCAT official even claimed, "If they ever cracked down on domestic help, especially illegals, we would lose our ridership." By midafternoon in this West Texas community, the suburban bus stops are thronged with Mexicanas, some wearing old sweaters in the winter or holding umbrellas in the summer, some sitting on benches, others on hard pavement. The city bus system is so clearly identified with its Mexican clientele that the Border Patrol routinely boards SCAT vehicles to check the citizenship documents of the passengers (Quintanilla and Copeland, 1983:84).[14]

The apprehension of undocumented maids is not a high priority for the Immigration and Naturalization Service. While the Border Patrol will take women into custody at the river or from city buses, these officials will not search private residences. The rationale for this policy centers on the fact that domestic work is not a lucrative position coveted by U.S. citizens. INS Deputy Director Trominski bluntly pointed out, "it doesn't make sense looking for one illegal maid in Eastwood when we could be removing an alien from a good paying job . . . ." Still, commuter maids are routinely picked up near the river and driven back to Juárez. Border Patrol agents apprehend some women so frequently that they call them by name. "Norma, again?" they asked, after detaining one woman for the third time in a single day (Quintanilla and Copeland, 1983:83, 85; Copeland, 1983; Quintanilla, 1983a).

Mexicana domestics have developed elaborate strategies for crossing the United States—Mexico border. Some time their routes precisely so that they will arrive at a border bus stop at the same time as the scheduled bus. Rocío remembered that once when she and several other women were crossing the river near a Border Highway bus stop, the driver purposely held his vehicle for them; and after they had boarded, he offered each of them a tissue so that they could wipe their mud-streaked legs (Avila, 1979; Rocío, 1979).

Others prefer to cross before daybreak and then depend on rides to

14. Source includes personal observations by the author.

the downtown plaza, where they can make their SCAT connections all over the city. However, women dread accepting rides from strangers (often *coyotes* who demand a small *mordida* for their services) and indeed, they could be and have been sexually assaulted. *"Tu cuerpo es tu morida."* 'Your body is your bribe' may not be an uncommon phrase among coyotes. Because of their dubious status in the United States, these rape victims do not report the incidents. Women also fear crossing the four-laned Border Highway and the six lanes of Interstate 10. The gangs of Mexican and Mexican American youth that congregate on both sides of the river pose another threat. When considering all the factors involved, many Mexicanas cross in groups and often with family or friends (Avila, 1979; Quintanilla, 1983a:87; Chavarría, 1983).

Some household workers take a more direct approach. With some knowledge of English and El Paso, they cross at one of the three bridges and declare their citizenship as "American." One woman who has used this tactic remarked that she preferred Anglo to Mexican American immigration officials because the former tend to ask fewer questions (Rocío, 1979).

Another government service agency concerned about the role of domestic workers in the El Paso economy is the local branch of the Social Security Administration. By law, if any person hires another and pays that person more than $50 over a three-month period, both parties must pay 6.7 percent of the weekly wages in social security taxes. Even if the employee is undocumented, the employer must still pay the tax. The reasoning behind this regulation is simple: After 40 to 50 years of service, a domestic worker who has received wages on a cash-only basis throughout her life is often left with nothing in her declining years. However, even if her *patrona* has paid into the social security system, she still cannot collect benefits unless or until she has legal resident status in the United States. This law is flagrantly violated. Employers appear reluctant to deduct these taxes and to keep the appropriate records. Domestic workers, too, seem unwilling to give up any of their meager, hard-earned wages. "I want my money now," one Mexicana succinctly stated (Copeland, 1983c; Quintanilla and Copeland, 1983:84; Quintanilla, 1983a:87).

Another piece of legislation ignored by most patronas is the minimum wage law. Few Mexican domestics receive $3.35 per hour, a wage to which they are entitled regardless of their citizenship or residence. The average daily wage of $15 for a woman who cleans once a week for approximately 6 to 8 hours translates into $2.50 to $1.88 per hour. The hourly wage of a live-in maid earning from $30 to $60 per week is considerably less. Interestingly, Social Security did not extend to private household workers until 1952 and these women had also been excluded from minimum wage legislation until 1974 (Copeland, 1983c; *El Paso Herald Post*, 1985; *El Paso Times*, 1985; Kessler-Harris, 1981: 84).

As long as there remains high unemployment and a surplus labor pool on both sides of the border, El Paso homemakers will continue to employ Mexican household workers at bargain wages. Economic segmentation and sexual exploitation are likely to continue as Mexicana household workers face a quadruple whammy—class, gender, ethnicity, and citizenship. Their dubious status in the United States compounds the barriers confronted by working-class women of color. Further research by historians and social scientists is needed in order to comprehend fully the economic contributions and experiences of Mexicana domestics on the United States–Mexico border. Though frequently victimized, Mexicana domestics are not victims, but women who meet each day with integrity and endurance. As one woman states, "I go where I have to go. I do what I have to do."[15]

References

Acuña, Rodolfo, 1981. *Occupied America: A History of Chicanos*, 2d ed. New York: Harper & Row.

Avila, Esperanza, May 10, 1979. Interview conducted by Mario Galdos and Sarah John. On file at Institute of Oral History, University of Texas at El Paso.

Barrera, Mario, 1979. *Race and Class in the Southwest: A Theory of Racial Inequality.* University of Notre Dame Press.

Barton, Mary Wilson, 1950. "Methodism at Work among the Spanish-Speaking People of El Paso, Texas," M.A. thesis, Texas Western College.

Brannon, Jeffrey T., March 27, 1985. Interview, conducted by the author.

Mrs. C., June 1, 1983. Interview, conducted by the author.

Carlos, María Christina, June 20, 1979. Interview, conducted by Oscar Martínez. On file at Institute of Oral History, University of Texas at El Paso.

Chavarría, Monica Santos de, December 13, 1983. Interview, conducted by the author.

Copeland, Peter, 1983a. "Border Ambiente.", *Special Report: The Border. El Paso Herald Post,* Summer.

———, 1983b. "INS Checks Maids' U.S. Entry." *Special Report: The Border. El Paso Herald Post,* Summer.

———, 1983c. "Social Security Head Went on Warpath." *Special Report: The border. El Paso Herald Post.*

15. Personal observations by the author.

———, 1983d. "The Two Cities of El Paso." *Special Report: The Border. El Paso Herald Post,* Summer.

García, Mario T., 1981. *Desert Immigrants: The Mexicans of El Paso, 1880–1920.* New Haven: Yale University Press.

González, Irene, October 12, 1979. Interview, conducted by Mario Galdos and Virgilio Sanchez. On file at Institute of Oral History, University of Texas at El Paso.

Hawkins, Gladys, Jean Soper, and Jane Pike Henry, 1959. *Your Maid from Mexico: A Home Training Course for Maids in English and Spanish.* San Antonio: Naylor.

Hernández, Martina, November 29, 1983. Interview, conducted by Sylvia Hernández. On file at the Institute of Oral History, University of Texas at El Paso.

Kessler-Harris, Alice, 1981. *Women Have Always Worked: A Historical Overview.* Old Westbury, N.Y.: Feminist Press.

Lyons, Robert, July 23, 1984. Interview, conducted by Mary Ann White. On file at Institute of Oral History, University of Texas at El Paso.

Mr. M., June 8, 1983. Interview, conducted by the author.

Mora, Pat, 1984. "Mexican Maid," in *Chants.* Houston: Arte Publico Press.

Morales, Enriqueta, June 14, 1979. Interview, conducted by Oscar Martínez, Mario Gáldos, and Sarah John. On file at the Institute of Oral History, University of Texas at El Paso.

El Paso Herald Post, September 23, 1933.

———, October 12, 1953a.

———, October 15, 1953b.

———, October 30, 1953c.

———, November 9, 1953d.

———, November 18, 1953e.

———, February 17, 1984.

———, March 26, 1985a.

———, April 8, 1985b.

El Paso Shopping Guide, December 21, 1983.

———, February 14, 1984.

El Paso Times, September 25, 1953.

———, February 20, 1984.

———, April 9, 1985.

Porras, Charles, November 18, 1975. Interview, conducted by Oscar Martínez. On file at the Institute of Oral History, University of Texas at El Paso.

Quintanilla, Michael, 1983a. "Illegal Maid: She Plays Cat and Mouse with La Migra." *Special Report: The Border. El Paso Herald Post,* Summer.

———, 1983b. "Legal Maid: She Devotes Her Life to Others." *Special Report: The Border. El Paso Herald Post,* Summer.

———, and Peter Copeland, 1983. "Mexican Maids: El Paso's Worst-Kept Secret." *Special Report: The Border. El Paso Herald Post,* Summer.

Rebchook, John, 1983a. "El Paso is a Minimum Wage Town." *Special Report: The Border. El Paso Herald Post,* Summer.

———, 1983b. "The Poor in El Paso." *Special Report: The Border. El Paso Herald Post,* Summer.

Rocío, May 29, 1979. Interview, conducted by Oscar Martínez and Mario Gáldos. On file at the Institute of Oral History, University of Texas at El Paso.

Ruiz, Vicki L., 1983. "A History of Friendship Square: Social Service in South El Paso." Unpublished manuscript.

————, 1984. "Working for Wages: Mexican Women in the American Southwest, 1930–1980." Working Paper No. 19, Southwest Institute for Research on Women, University of Arizona.

Segura, Denise, 1984. "Labor Market Stratification: The Chicana Experience." *Berkeley Journal of Sociology* 29.

Skodack, Debra, 1983. "Border Business: Twin Plants Give Boost." *Special Report: The Border. El Paso Herald Post,* Summer.

Texas Employment Commission, 1985. "Labor Force Estimates for Texas Counties—Feb. '85." Prepared by the Economic Research and Analysis Department.

4
Maquiladoras in Mexicali: Integration or Exploitation?

Susan Tiano

Export processing industrialization reflects an ongoing process of international capitalist expansion. It involves transferring the labor-intensive phases of production to Third World nations which possess abundant low-waged, typically female labor. A heated debate has ensued concerning the effects of participation in assembly processing on women workers and their families. Some view it as a way of integrating women into modern industry with its attendant economic and nonmaterial benefits. Others see it as but another form of capitalist exploitation and patriarchal oppression. Social scientists have only begun to supply the data necessary for evaluating these arguments. This chapter reports some preliminary findings of a study of export processing workers in Mexicali, Mexico. Its focus is on the characteristics of assembly workers and the economic consequences of employment in export processing firms.

"Integration" or "Exploitation"?

The increasing involvement of Third World women in export processing factories has sparked a debate in the women-in-development litera-

Prepared for the annual meetings of the American Sociological Association, New York, August 1986. The data for this study were collected in collaboration with Karen Bracken.

ture. Some consider export processing a valuable means for integrating women into national development by incorporating them into modern industry (see Safa, 1980:17). This view shares many assumptions of modernization theory and its feminist variant, developmentalism (El- liott, 1977:4−5). According to this perspective, Third World women tend to be marginal to their societies' development efforts (Boserup, 1970: passim, McCormack, 1981:24). Confinement to traditional roles in the household or the informal economy presumably prevents them from influencing the direction or sharing the benefits of modernization. Their marginality is detrimental not only to themselves and their fami- lies, but to the larger society, for it wastes human resources. Advocates of export processing consider it a way to more fully utilize women's productive potential while increasing their economic and personal wellbeing. Assembly plants are seen as a stable employment source yielding incomes and supplemental benefits which provide economic security for women and their families. Assembly work also presumably transmits productive skills that increase a woman's competitiveness in the labor market and promote upward mobility within and among industrial firms. The availability of assembly jobs supposedly expands women's employment options and offers them an economic alternative to early marriage and childrearing (Grossman, 1979:11). Access to stable waged employment presumably enhances a woman's self-image and increases her personal autonomy (Lim, 1981:187; 1983:83). Work in modern factories also presumably exposes Third World women to value systems and social organizational forms that inculcate a "modern" worldview emphasizing equality between the sexes and nontraditional gender roles (see Inkeles and Smith, 1974). In sum, employees of multi- national factories are generally better off than workers in locally owned enterprises (Lim, 1983:82,85).

An alternative perspective stresses the negative consequences of export processing. This view, which shares many socialist-feminist assumptions (see Sokoloff, 1980), holds that multinational corporations take advantage of and reinforce women's structural vulnerability within the labor market and the family (see Lim, 1983; Nash, 1983; Fernández-Kelly, 1983b:219). On the one hand, assembly processing presumably immerses women within capitalist relations of production that exploit workers. On the other hand, multinational companies deepen preexist-ing patriarchal relations that oppress women (Enloe, 1983; Lim, 1983). According to this argument, widespread norms defining women's pro-per roles as wives and mothers disadvantage them economically. Ac-

cess to better-paid, skilled occupations is limited by their lack of qualifications and by discriminatory hiring practices that reserve the best jobs
for men. The common image that women work only to supplement
their partner's earnings becomes a justification for paying them less
than men. Thus, working-class women presumably form a vulnerable,
low-waged labor force with little choice but to work under terms dic-
tated by multinational companies (Lim, 1983; Enloe, 1983). According to
this view, assembly workers do repetitive, monotonous tasks for minimal wages; they have little job security or advancement opportunity
(Enloe, 1983:415; Fernández-Kelly, 1983b:220). Although many assembly
tasks impair their physical and mental health, workers are often denied
insurance and disability benefits (Fuentes and Ehrenreich, 1981;
Abraham–Van Der Mark, 1983:381). Many companies, often with the aid
of the Third World government, either tacitly or explicitly prohibit
employees from organizing or joining unions through which they could
collectively press for change (Enloe, 1983:420; Abraham–Van Der Mark,
1983:381).

Women's entrance into assembly processing jobs, and their submis-
sion to unsatisfying working conditions presumably reflect their subordination to patriarchal relations in the family and on the factory floor
(Lim, 1983; Enloe, 1983). Women are assumed to participate in export
processing not so much as independent individuals but as members of
patriarchal families whose survival often depends upon the woman's
wage (Fernández-Kelly, 1983b:217). Elder daughters may be forced to
quit school, taking assembly jobs to support parents or to subsidize the
educational expenses of their brothers (Salaff, 1981). They often have
little control over their wages, handing them over to fathers or mothers
who determine their disposition. Parents may discourage young women from marrying, living on their own, or quitting their jobs to further
their studies, because they cannot afford to live without their daughter's
income. A strong sense of filial duty compels many young women to
comply with familial demands; those taking a more independent route
often suffer guilt for putting their own wishes above their family's
welfare. These dynamics, assumed to reflect patriarchal relations deep-
ly imbedded within the family, presumably explain why women enter
and remain in assembly firms despite alienating working conditions
(Enloe, 1983:412).

Yet patriarchal relations, the argument continues, have ramifications
beyond the family context from which they originate (Lim, 1983:77).
Multinational corporations supposedly use them to ensure their female

employees' conformity to company rules and standards. Beauty pageants, makeup demonstrations, cooking classes, and sex education seminars all reinforce workers' traditional notions of femininty. Supervisors, both male and female, act as parent surrogates for their "girls," closely monitoring not only their output but frequently their personal lives. Loyalty to the company is expected, and strengthened through gifts, favors, and other paternalistic techniques (Ehrenreich and Fuentes, 1981). Thus, rather than encouraging autonomy, independence, and self-reliance, work in assembly plants is assumed to deepen obeisance to authority and acquiescence to traditional sex roles (Fernández-Kelly, 1983a,b; Safa, 1980; Grossman, 1979).

This chapter explores the assumptions underlying these two positions using data from Mexicali, Baja California, the site of considerable export processing industrialization. A brief description of Mexico's Border Industrialization Program sets the stage for this analysis.

The U.S.–Mexico Border Industrialization Program

Since 1965, when the Mexican government authorized the Border Industrialization Program to stimulate foreign investment, northern Mexico has become a key export processing site. This region is responsible for more than half of the imports entering the United States from Third World nations under the export-processing tariff provisions (Fernández-Kelly, 1983a:34). The region's proximity to the United States and its large labor surplus account for its attractiveness to multinational investors. It has been estimated that by the end of 1985, 260,000 people were employed by maquiladoras (assembly plants) along the U.S.–Mexico border (El Nacional, May, 1985).

Despite the large number of jobs created by the BIP, its critics claim that it has not alleviated unemployment in northern Mexico. According to this view, the "traditional" work force in the area is composed of working-age males (Fernández-Kelly, 1983a:45), and thus unemployment is essentially a male problem (Martinez, 1978:132; Fernández, 1977:141; Woog, 1980:51,101). However, because women constitute over 80 percent of the maquiladora work force, critics claim that the program has not provided jobs for those who most need them. A related argument is that the BIP has drawn into the work force a new category of workers, young women, who would not otherwise be economically active (Fernández-Kelly, 183a:45; 1983b:219; Martinez, 1978:132). Some have argued that multinational companies have consciously targeted and incorporated young women, "a new source of cheap factory labor" into the maquiladora work force (Fuentes and Ehrenreich, 1983:28). This thesis holds that without the BIP, most women currently in the maquiladora work force would have been instead full-time homemakers or students, supported by husbands or fathers.

The short- and long-term consequences of the BIP for women workers and their families have only begun to be explored. Escamilla and Vigorito's (1977) analysis of garment workers in Mexicali was the first to use extensive participant observation and survey research to study maquiladora workers. Research on worker−management conflicts (De la Rosa Hickerson, 1979; Hernandez, 1980; Carrillo, 1980) and workers' organizational forms (Peña, 1980) has illuminated the political dimensions of maquiladora employment.

One of the most comprehensive studies of maquiladora workers to date is that of Fernández-Kelly (1983a), who documented the employment histories, family situations, and working conditions of electronics and apparel assemblers in Ciudad Juárez, Chihuahua. She argues that the contrasting organizational structure of the electronics and apparel industries underlie differences in the composition and working conditions of their labor forces. Although both industries are susceptible to market fluctuations and both are highly labor intensive, the apparel industry is decentralized and technologically backward, while electronics production is dominated by a few large firms and is subject to rapid technological innovation (Fernández-Kelly, 1983a:102−103). Most electronics maquiladoras are direct subsidiaries of transnational parent firms, while garment assembly firms are typically Mexican-owned enterprises operating as subcontracted shops. The latter are usually smaller, more unstable, and less able to offer worker benefits than are subsidiaries of transnational firms.

The organizational advantage of the electronics industry enables these firms to recruit workers considered more "desirable" according to management standards (Fernández-Kelly, 1983a:106). Electronics workers tend to be younger and better educated, and are more often single and childless, than women in the apparel industry. They are frequently new entrants into the labor market who are essential providers for parents and siblings. Garment workers are more likely than electronics workers to be single household heads or to be living with un- or underemployed male partners (Fernández-Kelly, 1983a:50−54). While both groups of women work out of economic necessity, they have different employment opportunities and career trajectories. Fernández-Kelly concludes that multinational firms take advantage of these differences, establishing subdivisions in the labor market that stratify the female labor force (1983a:106).

Fernández-Kelly presents numerous findings relevant to the "integration" and "exploitation" theses. In general, they suggest that the effects of the BIP are neither consistently beneficial nor uniformly detrimental to women and their families. The consequences of maquiladora employment not only vary according to firm type and economic cycles, but must be evaluated relative to women's alternative employment options.

The present study examines some of these questions using data from a sample of workers in Mexicali, the capital of Baja California. In 1982 I conducted a study of women workers in three sectors of the Mexicali labor market. I drew comparable subsamples of workers in the electronics and garment industries and from various jobs in the service sector. This sampling frame facilitates comparisons between the two types of maquila workers and between them and women employed as domestics, waitresses, clerks, and other lower-level service workers. The sample contains 66 women from electronics firms, 58 from apparel maquiladoras, and 70 from the service sector. Respondents selected through quota sampling procedures were administered an interview of typically an hour's duration consisting of both closed- and open-ended questions. Because the representativeness of the sample is indeterminable, caution must be employed in generalizing from these findings to the population of women workers in northern Mexico. There is no reason to assume, however, that the sample composition is skewed in a way that would introduce systematic bias into the analysis. In order to better interpret the resulting information, I also interviewed personnel directors and other managers of electronics and garment maquiladoras.

The following discussion reports some preliminary findings relevant to the "integration" and "exploitation" theses. First I consider demographic characteristics affecting the labor market status of the three categories of women workers. I next explore economic and nonmaterial consequences of working in the different economic sectors. If the integration thesis is correct, workers in the more "modern" electronics factories should be better off than their counterparts in apparel firms, and both should have more rewarding jobs than service workers. The exploitation thesis, by contrast, suggests that maquiladora workers should enjoy few advantages over service workers.

Findings

If it is true that electronics maquiladoras are able to recruit the more "privileged" members of the female labor force, then electronics workers in the sample should be younger and less likely to be married or have children, than the other women in the sample. The data in Tables 4.1 through 4.3 suggest that this is the case. Electronics workers were on the average younger (22.6 years) than their counterparts in garment maquiladoras (27.9) or service occupations (27.2). They were also less likely than other women in the sample to have children. The relative youth and childlessness of electronics workers are linked to a third difference between them and other workers: They were more apt to be single. Over two-thirds (65 percent) of the electronics workers, as compared to half (52 percent) and less than half (45 percent) of the garment and service workers, have never been married.

TABLE 4.1
Age by Type of Work

	Mean	Std Dev	Cases
Total	25.8093	8.5884	194
Electronics maquila	22.5606	7.0430	66
Clothing maquila	27.8793	9.4388	58
Service sector	27.1571	8.3936	70

Total cases = 194

TABLE 4.2
Number of Children by Type of Work

	Mean	Std Dev	Cases
Total	1.2216	1.7653	194
Electronics maquila	.7424	1.4709	66
Clothing maquila	1.6552	1.9245	58
Service sector	1.3143	1.7981	70

Total cases = 194

TABLE 4.3
Marital Status by Type of Work

	Electronics Maquila	Clothing Maquila	Service Sector	Row Total
Single				
Number	43	30	32	105
Subset percentage	65.2%	51.7%	45.7%	54.1%
Divorced, separated				
Number	8	8	16	32
Subset percentage	12.1%	13.8%	22.9%	16.5%
Married, free union				
Number	15	20	22	57
Subset percentage	22.7%	34.5%	31.4%	29.4%
Column Total				
Number	66	58	70	194
Subset percentage	34.0%	29.9%	36.1%	100.0%

Number of missing observations = 0

When questioned about their hiring standards, several managers told me that it is not so much their youth, but rather their recent entrance into the labor market, which makes young women preferred employees. They claimed that younger, inexperienced workers are easier to train because they have not developed previous work habits. Also, they are usually untainted by past encounters with labor unions, and thus less likely than more mature workers to be "troublemakers." In other words, they form a more tractable labor force. They also maintained that single, childless women make better employees than married mothers. Domestic and childrearing responsibilities, employers believe, often interfere with optimal on-the-job performance. Lack of concentration, absenteeism, and frequent resignations, they told me, are common among wives and mothers, who put their family's welfare above their job-related responsibilities. These notions, expressing traditional images of women's ideal roles, underlie the selective recruitment practices of electronics firms (see Fernández-Kelly, 1983b:220).

One might question why these employment criteria do not seem to apply to garment assemblers in the sample, whose ages and domestic statuses are more similar to those of service workers than electronics assemblers. On the one hand, the selective hiring practices may be confined to multinational companies, which institute them to homogenize, and thereby more efficiently manage, their geographically dispersed labor force. Research on electronics workers in Asia (Lim, 1981, 1983; Fuentes and Ehrenreich, 1983; Grossman, 1979), as well as other parts of Mexico (Fernández-Kelly, 1983a,b), suggest that these policies are fairly universal among export processing subsidiaries. On the other hand, employers in locally owned apparel firms might also prefer young, single workers but not be in a position to recruit them. The Mexican owner of a small garment assembly firm operating under subcontract with various U.S. and Mexican companies complained bitterly to us about his inability to recruit hardworking, skilled seamstresses. He told us he would prefer younger, unmarried workers, but was forced to hire almost any woman who could operate a sewing machine and would report to work punctually. Other garment firm managers we interviewed shared his lament. The preference for young, single workers appears to be fairly widespread, although electronics multinationals are better able than many locally owned establishments to recruit more desirable members of the female labor force.

Education is another factor held to increase a woman's competitiveness in the labor market. Managers and workers in electronics firms, as well as women employed elsewhere, repeatedly told us that electronics workers were required to have completed secondary school. Previous studies in Mexico (Fernández-Kelly, 1983a) and Southeast Asia (Lim, 1981; Grossman, 1979) report higher educational attainment among women in electronics firms than in many other urban jobs. The data in Table 4.4 only partially reflect this expectation. These numbers may be difficult to interpret because they represent educational categories rather than years of schooling. The education measure is a categorical variable ranging from 1 (no schooling) to 12 (finished three years of preparatory school plus some additional commercial training). A score of 4 indicates completing 6 years of primary school; 5 denotes primary

TABLE 4.4
Education by Type of Work

	Mean	SD	Cases
Total	6.8705	2.8721	193
Electronics maquila	7.5152	2.7301	66
Clothing maquila	5.2456	2.3167	57
Service sector	7.5857	2.9117	70

Total cases = 194; missing cases = 1, or 0.5%

plus some commercial or technical training; 6 indicates some secondary school; 7 reflects some secondary plus commercial or technical training; 8 denotes completing the three years of secondary school, and so forth.

These data show a substantial difference between the education levels of workers in apparel firms, whose mean score is 5.2, and those in electronics firms and service jobs, whose averages are 7.5 and 7.6. Electronics workers were generally better educated than seamstresses but not service workers. Service sector establishments appear as able as electronics firms to attract relatively well-educated workers. Furthermore, a secondary-level education does not appear to be a hard-and-fast requirement for all MNC employees. Electronics workers in the sample reported average schooling levels somewhat below the minimum employment criterion. Electronics firms apparently relax their hiring standards on some occasions.

If electronics firms actually favor inexperienced workers, then electronics assemblers should have had more limited employment histories than other women in the sample. Previous research (Fernández-Kelly, 1983a; Lim, 1981; Fuentes and Ehrenreich, 1983) supports this expectation, as do the data in Table 4.5. In electronics firms, 44 percent of the workers, as compared to 25 percent of those in apparel firms and 31 percent of those in the service sector, were holding their first job at the time of the study. Only 3, or 5 percent, of the electronics workers had held more than two previous jobs; 30 percent of the apparel workers and 37 percent of the service workers had equally lengthy employment histories. Garment workers, who averaged 1.26 prior jobs, were more similar to service workers (1.43) than electronics workers (.75). Newness to the labor market and the resulting inexperience with labor unions appear to be other factors leading multinational corporation managers to favor young women.

A common theme in the critical literature is that women are attractive as maquiladora workers because they constitute an available supply of surplus labor. If this argument is true, then many women in this sample could be expected to have experienced a time in which they were excluded from the formal labor force. The data in Table 4.6 shed light on this issue. Respondents were asked about the longest time they had been without a job despite their active search for employment. About half of the sample reported never having been in such a predicament. Only a small proportion (14%) claimed to have been unemployed for longer than six months. Electronics workers reported the greatest

TABLE 4.5
Number of Previous Jobs by Type of Present Job

	Electronics Maquila	Clothing Maquila	Service Sector	Row Total
0				
Number	29	14	22	65
Subset percentage	43.9%	25.0%	31.4%	33.9%
1				
Number	21	15	10	46
Subset percentage	31.8%	26.8%	14.3%	24.0%
2				
Number	13	10	12	35
Subset percentage	19.7%	17.9%	17.1%	18.2%
3				
Number	0	5	12	17
Subset percentage	.0%	8.9%	17.1%	8.9%
4				
Number	0	2	4	6
Subset percentage	.0%	3.6%	5.7%	3.1%
5				
Number	3	10	10	23
Subset percentage	4.5%	17.9%	14.3%	12.0%
Column Total				
Number	66	56	70	192
Subset percentage	34.4%	29.2%	36.5%	100.0%

Number of missing observations = 2

incidence of unemployment: 37 percent as compared to 22 percent of the textile workers and 29 percent of service workers had been unemployed for longer than a month. One might question why electronics assemblers, many of whom were younger and better educated than women in apparel firms, were more likely to have been unable to find employment. Perhaps these workers were more selective in their job choices, holding out for certain types of service jobs or a position in the more desirable electronics industry. Their household status may have facilitated this selectivity, for they were less likely to be single heads of households who were the sole support of dependent children. Also, since many had only recently entered the labor force, they may have been less aware than more experienced workers of the procedures for seeking employment.

To summarize, multinational companies do not appear to recruit from the most vulnerable sector of the female labor force, as the exploi-

TABLE 4.6
Longest Time Unemployed by Type of Job

	Electronics Maquila	Clothing Maquila	Service Sector	Row Total
No Time				
Number	31	30	34	95
Subset percentage	47.0%	54.5%	50.0%	50.3%
Few days—4 weeks				
Number	10	13	14	37
Subset percentage	15.2%	23.6%	20.6%	19.6%
1—6 months				
Number	21	9	13	43
Subset percentage	31.8%	16.4%	19.1%	22.8%
Longer than 6 months				
Number	4	3	7	14
Subset percentage	6.1%	5.5%	10.3%	7.4%
Column Total				
Number	66	55	68	189
Subset percentage	34.9%	29.1%	36.0%	100.0%

Number of missing observations = 5

tation thesis maintains. Rather, they are able to hire workers whose domestic status and educational attainment give them an advantage in the labor market. Locally owned establishments, particularly in the apparel industry, typically hire workers whose labor market status is somewhat weaker. Do multinational companies enjoy this recruitment advantage because they offer better economic incentives, as the integration thesis suggests? Or do they merely take advantage of patriarchal relations that force young women to enter and remain in the labor force, as the exploitation thesis maintains? Data from the Mexicali sample illuminate these questions.

In order to explore the importance of workers' wages for their family's economic well-being, we questioned respondents about the size and composition of their households. Tables 4.7 and 4.8 summarize their answers. Electronics workers' households averaged 6.3 members, while those of garment assemblers and service workers averaged 5.6 and 5.1. Almost two-thirds of electronics assemblers, compared with less than half of the garment and service workers, lived with one or both parents and siblings. The percentage of garment assemblers who were single heads of households is fairly small (8.6), departing from Fernández-Kelly's (1983a:55) sample in which 31 percent of the seam-

TABLE 4.7
Number of Persons in Household by Type of Work

	Mean	SD	Cases
Total	5.6406	2.8360	192
Electronics maquila	6.2769	3.0286	65
Clothing maquila	5.5614	2.5844	57
Service sector	5.1143	2.7691	70

Total cases = 194; missing cases = 2, or 1.0%

TABLE 4.8
Household Composition by Type of Job

	Electronics Maquila	Clothing Maquila	Service Sector	Row Total
Husband, partner				
Number	16	21	19	56
Subset percentage	24.2%	36.2%	27.1%	28.9%
Household head				
Number	4	5	14	23
Subset percentage	6.1%	8.6%	20.0%	11.9%
Parents, siblings				
Number	42	28	33	103
Subset percentage	63.6%	48.3%	47.1%	53.1%
Other				
Number	4	4	4	12
Subset percentage	6.1%	6.9%	5.7%	6.2%
Column Total				
Number	66	58	70	194
Subset percentage	34.0%	29.9%	36.1%	100.0%

Number of missing observations = 0

stresses had this type of household. Service workers, rather than apparel assemblers, were most likely to head their own households.

Relatively few of the women in the sample were the sole supporters of their household. Not shown in these tables is the fact that only 33, or 17 percent were exclusively responsible for their family's financial support. The average number of wage earners per household was somewhat larger among electronics assemblers (2.7) than garment workers (2.3) or service workers (2.4). The economic burden shouldered by wage earners in respondents' households can be evaluated by comparing household size to the number of regular contributors to household income. The averages among the three subgroups are almost identical, ranging from 2.3 for service workers through 2.5 for electronics workers to 2.6 for apparel workers. Although electronics assemblers typically shared financial responsibility with more income earners than did garment or service workers, the larger average size of their households overrides this potential advantage. In sum, these data provide no indication that most electronics workers single-handedly supported parents and siblings. For them, like other women in the sample, it was common for two or more members to pool their wages to cover household expenses. On the other hand, neither they nor other workers in the sample were peripheral to the family wage economy. Their financial contributions were in most cases essential to their household's support.

To further explore the importance of women's wages, we posed the question: "If for some reason you were unable to work here, would you need, for economic reasons, to find another job?" The overwhelming majority of the sample, 85 percent, answered that they would (Table 4.9). Electronics assemblers were somewhat more likely to answer affirmatively (88 percent) than seamstresses (83 percent) or service workers (83 percent). When interpreted vis-à-vis the household composition data, these responses suggest that most women had to earn a wage to support not only themselves but other family members. The maquiladora program does not appear to have mobilized into the labor force a "new" category of workers who otherwise would not enter paid employ-

TABLE 4.9
Perception of Economic Need by Type of Job

	Electronics Maquila	Clothing Maquila	Service Sector	Row Total
No				
Number	7	8	11	26
Subset percentage	11.9%	17.4%	17.5%	15.5%
Yes				
Number	52	38	52	142
Subset percentage	88.1%	82.6%	82.5%	84.5%
Column Total				
Number	59	46	63	168
Subset percentage	35.1%	27.4%	37.5%	100.0%

Number of missing observations = 26

ment because they are adequately supported by husbands and fathers. This pattern is consistent with both the integration and the exploitation theses, each of which stresses the economic imperative underlying women's employment.

One way to evaluate these competing explanations is to examine women's attitudes toward their work. The exploitation hypothesis that women are often reluctant and temporary breadwinners for patriarchically organized families would predict that most women would quit their jobs if they could. The integration hypothesis that work provides intangible benefits reinforcing job commitment suggests that economic need is but one cause of women's labor force participation. We explored this issue by asking respondents whether they would continue working even if they did not need the money. Their answers are summarized in Table 4.10. Over two-thirds of the electronics and service workers, and over half of the seamstresses, claimed they would keep working. This finding is more consistent with the integration than the exploitation thesis. Most women do not apear to have been victims of oppressive arrangements that forced them to work against their will. Rather, a considerable proportion of women preferred waged work to

TABLE 4.10

Percentage of Respondents Who Would Keep Working Even If They Did Not Need the Money

	Electronics Maquila	Clothing Maquila	Service Sector	Row Total
Strongly disagree				
Number	10	21	21	52
Subset percentage	15.2%	36.2%	30.0%	26.8%
Disagree				
Number	11	4	2	17
Subset percentage	16.7%	6.9%	2.9%	8.8%
Agree				
Number	18	10	11	86
Subset percentage	27.3%	17.2%	15.7%	20.1%
Strongly agree				
Number	27	23	36	86
Subset percentage	40.9%	39.7%	51.4%	44.3%
Column Total				
Number	66	58	70	194
Subset percentage	34.0%	29.9%	36.1%	100.0%

Number of missing observations = 0

full-time domestic responsibilities. Employees of multinational firms were no different in this regard from other women in the sample.

To summarize, it appears that economic necessity propels most women workers into the labor force, although many work for other reasons as well. Younger, single women have an advantage over more mature, partnered women in the competition for positions in electronics firms. It remains to be seen whether electronics workers parlay their competitive advantage into concrete economic gains. The integration thesis has it that work in transnational firms provides job stability, adequate wages, and other benefits. The exploitation thesis maintains that maquiladora employment is temporary, subject to layoffs and production stops, and poorly remunerated. The data in the following tables provide a way of evaluating these hypotheses.

According to the exploitation hypothesis, the preference for younger, single workers combines with dissatisfying working conditions to cause rapid turnover among the maquiladora labor force. The data in Table 4.11 provide qualified support for the notion that maquiladoras typically offer short-term employment. Half of the workers in garment firms, and 39 percent of those in electronics plants, had been at their

TABLE 4.11
Length of Time at Present Job by Type of Job

	Electronics Maquila	Clothing Maquila	Service Sector	Row Total
0−6 months				
Number	26	29	19	74
Subset percentage	39.4%	50.0%	27.1%	38.1%
6 + months−4 years				
Number	9	6	16	31
Subset percentage	13.6%	10.3%	22.9%	16.0%
18 + months−8 years				
Number	20	11	18	49
Subset percentage	30.3%	19.0%	25.7%	25.3%
4 + years−8 years				
Number	4	7	9	20
Subset percentage	6.1%	12.1%	12.9%	10.3%
8 or more years				
Number	7	5	8	20
Subset percentage	10.6%	8.6%	11.4%	10.3%
Column Total				
Number	66	58	70	194
Subset percentage	34.0%	29.9%	36.1%	100.0%

Number of missing observations = 0

present jobs for six months or less. These proportions are considerably higher than that for service workers, 27 percent of whom had recently assumed their present positions. Electronics firms may provide slightly more stable employment than apparel firms, and service sector establishments typically retain their workers somewhat longer than assembly firms. It should be stressed that none of the three subgroups had experienced considerable longevity at their present jobs. While service workers were somewhat more likely than maquiladora employees to have held their jobs for four or more years, the proportion (24 percent) is not large, and does not contrast substantially with those for garment (21 percent) and electronics workers (17 percent). These data suggest that not merely maquila workers, but urban women generally, rarely acquire significant seniority at their workplace. On the other hand, the fact that about a fifth of the maquiladora workers had held their jobs for over eight years demonstrates that such employment need not always be temporary.

A second indication of the instability or security of maquiladora employment is the frequency of layoffs and work stoppages. We asked respondents whether there were times other than holidays when their workplace closed down completely or continued operating with a reduced labor force. Their responses, summarized in Table 4.12, demonstrate considerable variation among the sample subgroups. Almost 80

TABLE 4.12
Production Stops and Layoffs by Type of Job

	Electonics Maquila	Clothing Maquila	Service Sector	Row Total
Never				
Number	2	9	63	74
Subset percentage	4.1%	33.3%	91.3%	51.0%
Stops production, no layoffs				
Number	8	13	5	26
Subset percentage	16.3%	48.1%	7.2%	17.9%
Layoffs, no production stops				
Number	39	5	1	45
Subset percentage	79.6%	18.5%	1.4%	31.0%
Column Total				
Number	49	27	69	145
Subset percentage	33.8%	18.6%	47.6%	100.0%

Number of missing observations = 49

percent of the electronics workers reported that their firms regularly laid off part of their work force during autumn months when shipments of components declined, but did not completely cease production. Some workers returned to their jobs once work picked up again around the first of the year, but others were compelled to seek other employment. Apparel assemblers portrayed a somewhat different picture: A third of the subsample stated that their firm never stopped production or suspended workers, and only 19 percent reported layoffs of part of the work force. The most common pattern among apparel firms, described by 48 percent of the garment workers, was for the plant to cease production entirely when materials were unavailable, temporarily laying off all workers. It is debatable which pattern entails the most job instability. For the individuals involved, the answer hinges on seniority, since electronics firms typically suspend those most recently hired while continuing to employ long-term workers. Seniority, however, will not help those in apparel firms that close completely for short periods, for they suspend all workers. Few service workers report layoffs or closures of their workplaces. These findings must be interpreted with some care owing to the fairly large number of respondents, all but one of whom were maquiladora workers, for whom we have no information on this item. Most simply did not know whether layoffs or closures occurred; in other cases, the interviewers skipped this item because it was politically volatile and might have jeopardized their ability to interview in the factory. Nevertheless, these data do not portray an image of job security, particularly among electronics workers.

Tables 4.13 and 4.14 provide data on the wages earned by the three categories of workers. Most maquiladora workers (88 percent and 90 percent) earned the federally mandated minimum of 3661 pesos per week. Electronics operators were paid no better than seamstresses. This suggests that maquiladoras rarely pay their workers more than the legal minimum despite their length of time on the job. Although 47 percent of the electronics operators had held their present job for over eighteen months, only 10.6 percent earned even slightly more than a minimum wage. The same could be said of garment assemblers: 20 percent had been at their jobs for four or more years, yet only 7 percent earned slightly above the legal minimum. On the other hand, maquiladora workers rarely received less than a minimum wage. Firms do not appear to flagrantly violate minimum wage standards, as some critics of export processing have suggested (NACLA, 1979). If one were to generalize from these patterns, one might conclude that the federal minimum is both a

TABLE 4.13
Minimum Wage by Type of Job

	Electronics Maquila	Clothing Maquila	Service Sector	Row Total
Under minimum				
Number	1	2	12	15
Subset percentage	1.5%	3.4%	17.1%	7.7%
Minimum				
Number	58	52	15	125
Subset percentage	87.9%	89.7%	21.4%	64.4%
Somewhat over minimum				
Number	5	4	24	33
Subset percentage	7.6%	6.9%	34.3%	17.0%
Substantially over				
Number	2	0	19	21
Subset percentage	3.0%	.0%	27.1%	10.8%
Column Total				
Number	66	58	70	194
Subset percentage	34.0%	29.9%	36.1%	100.0%

Number of missing observations = 0

TABLE 4.14
Weekly Salary in Pesos by Type of Job

	Mean	SD	Cases
Total	4190.3368	1426.5801	193
Electronics maquila	3824.8636	623.2128	66
Clothing maquila	3634.3333	381.3338	57
Service sector	4987.6714	2037.3953	70

Total cases = 194; missing cases = 1, or 0.5%

floor and a ceiling for maquiladora workers' wages. Service workers revealed a much larger range of incomes: 17 percent earn less than the minimum, while 61 percent earn more.

The mean incomes presented in Table 4.14 indicate that workers in electronics firms fared only slightly better than garment assemblers. Privileged labor market status had not translated into higher income for this subsector of the maquila labor force. Service workers, on the average, were better paid than electronics or garment assemblers, although this average masks considerable variation in their incomes. While it is difficult to generalize about such a heterogeneous category of workers, it would appear that certain types of service work may be equally or more remunerative than assembly processing. This conclusion must be made cautiously, however, given the small size and indeterminate representativeness of the service worker subsample. Also, it is likely that domestic servants, who earn less than the minimum for maquila workers, are underrepresented in this sample.

A common argument is that workers seek maquiladora employment not so much for the resulting wages, but for the benefits these jobs provide (Fernández-Kelly, 1983b:216). Table 4.15 compares the average number of benefits reported by the three sample subgroups. Workers in electronics firms received only slightly more benefits than workers in other jobs. Those in the apparel industry were no better off than service workers, many of whom probably fared this well because their benefits, like those of maquiladora workers, were mandated by the state.

Perhaps the relatively low wages and job insecurity of maquiladora jobs are compensated for by on-the-job training in skills that expand a worker's employment options. A comprehensive evaluation of this question is beyond the scope of this analysis. It can be explored indirectly, however, by considering women's perceptions of the knowledge and skills they had acquired at their jobs (Table 4.16). The most notable difference is between workers in the two types of maquiladoras: Over half of the garment workers, in contrast with a third of the electronics assemblers, believed they had learned skills that would help them advance in their careers. Workers in clothing maquiladoras often felt that they had acquired sewing skills that they would be able to apply to other, perhaps better, jobs.

No doubt these perceptions mirror the reality of the labor processes in the two industries. Electronics assembly involves a Taylorized series of minutely regulated, repetitive tasks specific to a particular product, which are not easily transferred to other types of firms. Garment assembly, by contrast, involves sewing skills which vary little across firms and

TABLE 4.15
Average Number of Benefits by Type of Job

	Mean	SC	Cases
Total	3.5027	1.5295	183
Electronics maquila	3.7031	.9203	64
Clothing maquila	3.4600	1.4458	50
Service sector	3.3478	1.9765	69

Total cases = 194; missing cases = 11, or 5.7%

TABLE 4.16
Skills Learned on the Job by Type of Work

	Electronics Maquila	Clothing Maquila	Service Sector	Row Total
Nothing				
Number	28	13	20	61
Subset percentage	45.9%	25.0%	32.3%	34.9%
Skills useful only here				
Number	11	8	10	29
Subset percentage	18.0%	15.4%	16.1%	16.6%
Transferable skills				
Number	22	31	32	85
Subset percentage	36.1%	59.6%	51.6%	48.6%
Column Total				
Number	61	52	62	175
Subset percentage	34.9%	29.7%	35.4%	100.0%

Number of missing observations = 19

work assignments. The skills developed in apparel firms likely counterbalance these workers' relatively older ages and lower educational levels so that the "human capital" they bring to the labor market more closely matches that of the younger, better educated workers often drawn into electronics processing. Moreover, because many MNC subsidiaries prefer young, inexperienced workers, electronics operatives are unlikely to benefit from previously acquired skills.

To summarize, maquiladora workers in the sample, like women in service occupations, typically worked out of economic need. They were unlikely to earn above a minimum wage, however, and their benefits were not much better than those of service workers. Their jobs appear to have been more unstable than many service occupations. These findings are more consistent with the exploitation thesis than the integration thesis.

Conclusions

All conclusions drawn at this point must be highly tentative, for the representativeness of the subsamples is unknown and, especially for the service workers, indeterminable. The outlines of the emerging patterns can, however, be sketched in broad strokes.

Most women workers experience an economic imperative to support themselves and contribute financially to their households. Electronics workers are no different in this respect than seamstresses and service sector workers. They are not typically the sole supporters of their household, but instead pool their wages with those of one or more contributors. There is no evidence, however, that multinational company employees, or other women workers, work solely out of economic necessity. Instead, most claimed they would continue to work even if they did not need their incomes. Extradomestic work appears to provide many women noneconomic advantages that reinforce their commitment to their jobs. Contrary to the exploitation thesis, neither electronics workers nor other women surveyed appear to be reluctant wage earners.

Multinational companies do not appear to recruit their workers from the most vulnerable sectors of the female labor force, as the exploitation thesis would predict. Their selective hiring practices may, however, deepen the stratification of the labor force along the dimensions of age, education, marital status, and fertility (see Fernández-Kelly, 1983a:106). Electronics assemblers in the sample are more likely than seamstresses to occupy a privileged labor market position. They are on the average younger, better educated, and more likely to be single and childless than women in the apparel industry. While they are generally no better educated than service workers, they are more apt to be young, single, and childless. Their relative lack of previous employment appears to be a help, rather than a hindrance, given electronics firms managers' preference for inexperienced workers.

Yet these advantages seem to translate into few concrete gains for electronics assemblers. Their income levels, like those of garment assemblers, rarely rise above the federally legislated minimum; their benefits are not much more numerous than those of other workers; they are more likely than other workers to experience layoffs; their jobs are no more apt than others to offer long-term stability; they are less likely than other workers to believe their jobs have taught them useful skills. While they are no worse off in these respects than garment assemblers, they earn less and suffer more frequent layoffs than service workers.

There is no evidence that maquiladoras have mobilized a new contingent of workers into the Mexicali labor force who would not otherwise be there because they have no economic need to earn a wage. The vast majority of maquiladora workers in the sample, like their counterparts in the service sector, make important, if not essential, contributions to their household's economic well-being. Their decision to work outside the home reflects a collective strategy for household survival, and their incomes are integral components of the family wage economy.

These findings are more consistent with the exploitation thesis than the integration thesis. Among workers in this study, maquiladora employment does not appear to be a route to financial well-being or long-lasting job security; yet neither do service occupations. The need to help support their households typically draws these working-class women into the labor market; once there, they function as inexpensive labor. Maquiladoras do seem to take advantage of women's vulnerability on the labor market, offering them little more in the way of wages and/or benefits than Mexican law requires. Yet maquiladora workers are not without resources. Many are fairly well-educated—at least relative to women in other parts of Mexico—and some claim to be learning skills on the job that will help them advance in life. There is no evidence that, without their current jobs, they would be marginal to the formal economy, as the integration thesis implies.

Indeed, the integration−exploitation debate may be based on a false conceptual dichotomy. If one employs the orthodox Marxian definition of exploitation as the production of surplus value, then such exploitation requires integration into capitalist relations of production. But the issue underlying this debate is nevertheless real: Are women workers better or worse off because of the maquiladora program? When phrased this starkly, this question cannot be answered with a simple affirmative or negative. Maquiladoras provide jobs, minimum wages, and state-mandated benefits for women who must support themselves and their families; but these jobs are more insecure, and their wages generally lower, than many service occupations. Although the young, single, fairly well educated electronics assembler could probably find comparable work in the service sector, the more mature, less educated garment assembler might have few alternative job options. The maquiladora program may be most beneficial for women whose labor market status is the weakest.

A policy recommendation suggested by this study is that the Mexican state should play an increasingly active role in regulating multinational companies. Maquiladoras generally comply with existing legislation requiring paid vacations, financial bonuses at Christmas time, medical care, and other benefits. I found little evidence that firms avoid paying a minimum wage, despite frequent claims of such evasion in the critical literature (NACLA, 1979). It appears that maquiladoras abide by federal mandates, and that benefits, wage levels, and working conditions will improve as (and perhaps only because) worker protection legislation expands. The state is more apt to implement increasingly favorable legislation, however, if effective and representative labor unions press for it. (Female workers' organizations in northern Mexico are currently weak or nonexistent.) Yet as women are increasingly proletarianized, the conditions stimulating the establishment of unions will become more pronounced. (Maquiladora workers may eventually realize that worker protection guarantees are most likely to be effective if workers organize and demand them on their own behalf instead of depending on the government to enact such legislation for them.)

References

Abraham–Van Der Mark, Eve, 1983. "The Impact of Industrialization on Women: A Caribbean Case." In June Nash and Maria Patricia Fernández-Kelly (eds), *Women, Men and the International Division of Labor*. Albany: SUNY Press, pp. 374–386.

Barnet, Richard, and Ronald Muller, 1974. *Global Reach: The Power of Multinational Corporations*. New York: Simon and Schuster.

Boserup, Ester, 1970. *Women's Role in Economic Development*. New York: St. Martin's Press.

Bustamante, Jorge, 1983. "Maquiladoras: A New Face of International Capitalism on Mexico's Northern Frontier." In Nash and Fernández-Kelly, pp. 224–256.

Carillo, Jorge, 1980. "La Utilizacion de la mano de obra feminina en la industria maquiladora: El Caso de Ciudad Juarez." Preliminary research report, Programa de Estudios de Frontera y los Estados Unidos, El Colegio de Mexico, Mexico, D.F.

De la Rosa Hickerson, Gustavo, 1979. "La Contratacion colectiva in las maquiladoras." Professional thesis in law, Escuela de Derecho, Universidad Autonoma de Ciudad Juarez.

Ehrenreich, Barbara, and Annette Fuentes, 1981. "Life on the Global Assembly Line," *Ms.*, January, pp. 53–59.

Elliott, Carolyn, 1977. "Theories of Development: An Assessment." In Wellesley Editorial Committee (eds), *Women and National Development*. University of Chicago Press, pp. 1–8.

Enloe, Cynthia, 1983. "Women Textile Workers in the Militarization of Southeast Asia." In Nash and Fernández-Kelly, pp. 407–425.

Escamilla, Norma, and Maria Antonieta Vigorito, 1977. "Consideraciones sociologicas del trabajo feminino en las maquiladoras fronterizas." Research report, Escuela de Ciencias Sociales y Politicas, Universidad Autonoma de Baja California, Mexicali.

Fernández, Raul, 1977. *The United States–Meixcan Border: A Politico-economic Profile*. University of Notre Dame Press.

Fernández-Kelly, Maria Patricia, 1983. *For We Are Sold: I and My People*. Albany: SUNY Press.

———, 1983b. "Mexican Border Industrialization, Female Labor Force Participation, and Migration." In June Nash and Maria Patricia Fernández-Kelly (eds.), *Women, Men and the International Division of Labor*. Albany: SUNY Press. pp. 205–223.

Fuentes, Annette, and Barbara Ehrenreich, 1983. *Women in the Global Factory.* New York: South End Press.

Grossman, Rachael, 1979. "Women's Place in the Integrated Circuit." *Southeast Asia Chronicle,* no. 66 (January—February), pp. 2—17.

Hernandez, Alberto, 1980. "Politico y practica laboral en la industria maquiladora: el caso de Ciudad Juarez." Unpublished research report, Programa de Estudios de la Frontera y los Estados Unidos, El Colegio de Mexico, D.F.

Hymer, Stephen, 1978. "The Multinational Corporate Capitalist Economy." In Richard Edwards et al. (eds), *The Capitalist System.* Englewood Cliffs, N.J.: Prentice Hall, pp. 492—498.

Lim, Linda, 1983. "Capitalism, Imperialism, and Patriarchy: The Dilemma of Third-World Women Workers in Multinational Factories." In June Nash and Maria Patricia Fernández-Kelly (eds.), *Women, Men and the International Division of Labor.* Albany: SUNY Press, pp. 70—91.

————, 1981. "Women's Work in Multinational Electronics Factories." In Roslyn Dauber and Melinda Cain (eds), *Women and Technological Change in Developing Countries.* Boulder: Westview Press, pp. 181—190.

MacEwan, Arthur, 1978. "Capitalist Expansion and the Sources of Imperialism." In Richard Edwards et al. (eds.), *The Capitalist System.* Englewood Cliffs, NJ. Prentice Hall, pp. 494—498.

McCormack, Thelma, 1981. "Development with Equity for Women." In Naomi Black and Ann Baker Cottrell (eds), *Women and World Change.* Beverly Hills: Sage, pp. 15—30.

Martinez, Oscar, 1978. *Border Boom Town: Ciudad Juarez Since 1948.* Austin: University of Texas Press.

Nash, June, 1983. "The Impact of the Changing International Division of Labor on Different Sectors of the Labor Force." In June Nash and Maria Patricia Fernández-Kelly (eds.), *Women, Men and the International Division of Labor.* Albany: SUNY Press, pp. 3—38.

North American Congress on Latin America, 1979. *Beyond the Border: Mexico and the United States Today.* New York: NACLA.

Peña, Devon, 1980. "Female Workers and Trade Unionism in the Mexican Border Industrialization Program." Paper presented at the eighth annual meeting of the National Association for Chicano Studies, Houston, Texas, April.

————, 1981. *"Maquiladoras: A Select annotated Bibliography and Critical Commentary on the United States—Mexico Border Industry Program.* Center for the Study of Human Resources, University of Texas, Publication No. 7-81.

————, 1982a. "The Class Politics of Abstract Labor: Organizational Forms and Industrial Relations in the Mexican Maquiladoras." Chapter 1 of unpublished dissertation, University of Texas at Austin.

————, 1982b. "Emerging Organizational Strategies of Maquila Workers on the Mexico-U.S. Border." Tenth Annual Meeting of the National Association for Chicano Studies, Arizona State University, Tempe, Arizona, March.

Safa, Helen, 1980. "Export Processing and Female Employment: The Search for Cheap Labor." Paper prepared for the Burg Waurtenstein Symposium, No. 85, August.

Sokoloff, Natalie, 1980. *Between Love and Money.* New York: Praeger.

Tiano, Susan, 1984. "Maquiladoras, Women's Work, and Unemployment in Northern Mexico." Lansing, Mich. WID Working Papers, Michigan State University, No. 43. February.

Woog, Mario, 1980. *El Programa Mexicano de maquiladoras.* Instituto de Estudios Sociales, Universidad de Guadalajara.

II
CONSCIOUSNESS, ORGANIZATION, AND EMPOWERMENT

5

Gender Identification and Working-Class Solidarity among Maquila Workers in Ciudad Juárez: Stereotypes and Realities

Gay Young

In recent years, there has been considerable speculation on the part of both scholars and policymakers (Grunwald, 1983; Bustamante, 1983; Nash and Fernández-Kelly, 1983; Lim, 1983; El-Sanabary, 1983) about the effects of maquila work on participants in the labor force of Mexico's Border Industrialization Program (BIP). Within that general context, the specific concerns of this chapter are to examine (1) what work-related experiences enable maquila workers to expand the traditional female role, and (2) what work-related experiences enhance the development of women's consciousness of their status as workers in the new international division of labor. The larger theoretical issue on which this empirical investigation has bearing is that of the interconnections between gender relations and class processes. While class *does* structure the concrete meaning gender has for women, male−female relations also affect women's experience as workers. Following an overview of the interrelations of gender, class, and export-oriented industrialization, using Mexico's BIP as a case in point, the findings of a field experiment carried out among maquila workers in Ciudad Juárez are discussed. The conclusions highlight issues for policymakers who are concerned with furthering women's treatment as equals in society and enhancing women's capacity to author their own development.

Gender, Class, and Export-Oriented Industrialization

The theoretical foundation for the following analysis of women in the BIP is Sokoloff's (1980) examination of women's position in the labor market in the United States. She argues that the labor market is organized in the interest not only of capital but also of men, and she focuses on the interrelation of patriarchy (systematic male power) and capitalism in the whole of women's lives in advanced industrial society. That women "are recruited into low status, low-waged, female dominated occupations in industries with low capital, poor job mobility, limited job security, and little decision-making power" (1980:143) is a result of the dynamic interrelation of patriarchy and capitalism.

Sokoloff asserts that "any attempt to understand women's position in the [labor] market must relate that to her position in the home"; moreover, in her view, it is important to "investigate how patriarchal relations have been transformed and intensified within the labor market" (1980:xii−xiii). For Sokoloff, then, patriarchy is not confined to the home but is a feature of the labor market as well. It operates on two planes—"private forms of *individual* male control over women within the family" and "*collective* forms of male domination in the larger public society" (1980:166). Thus, women's entry into wage labor both weakens and strengthens patriarchal relations.

Sokoloff emphasizes that patriarchy is an independent force, having a life of its own, but it must be analyzed within the realm of a particular socio-historical period. For example, capitalism combines with patriarchy to assign home labor to women, and then uses that against women in the labor market to relegate them to sex-segregated jobs as "secondary" workers for "pin money" wages. This is the case because, being mothers, they are "unreliable" and offer only "housekeeping" skills. In other words, under conditions of patriarchal capitalism, all women enter the labor market as "mothers"—former, actual, or potential, and although they work because one income fails to support the family, the idea that only men support families remains unchallenged. Thus, women remain a powerful reserve labor force, or if active in the labor market, by spending their wages, they become somewhat bigger consumers. But they do not compete against men for higher-waged jobs. Moreover, women's market labor is also used against them in the home, where they are "punished" for not giving enough nurturance "to force them into their gender-assigned role . . . or at least to assume those home tasks as women's primary responsibility even if they are employed simultaneously" (1980:200).

Along with later Marxist feminists, then, Sokoloff (1980:198) contends that "the sexual division of production between home and market and the sexual division of labor within the market ... are the result of a synthesis of the social relations of the sexes [patriarchy] and the social relations of classes [capitalism]." Although her analysis refers to contemporary U.S. society, Sokoloff's argument extends beyond cultural region and degree of industrialization. Her thesis becomes a useful tool for examining the situation of women at work and at home in developing societies which are following an export-oriented path of industrialization.

Like women in other regions of the Third World, large numbers of Latin American women have been drawn into the industrial labor force as assembly workers in multinational corporations. Mexico's Border Industrialization Program forms a case in point. Recognizing the need to examine the interaction of gender relations and class formation, recent scholarship on Latin American women has focused on the situation of females in the "new international division of labor" (Grossman, 1979; Lim, 1978; Beneria and Sen, 1982; Safa, 1981; *Signs*, 1981; *Multinational Monitor*, 1983; El-Sanabary, 1983; Nash and Fernández-Kelly, 1983). Some scholars have even turned their attention specifically to the BIP (Carrillo, 1980; Peña, 1980; Fernández-Kelly, 1983; Tiano, 1984).

Such work reflects the position that class analysis which ignores gender remains insensitive to the causes of women's subordination. To focus on the relations through which women are incorporated in development, specifically in export-oriented industrialization, underlines the way in which Latin American women's lives are "structured by a double set of determinations arising from relations of gender and relations deriving from the economic organization of society" (IDS Bulletin, 1979:2). Taking into account the interrelationship of gender subordination and capitalist industrialization is critical, for not only does a woman's class position structure the concrete meaning gender has for her, but the reverse is also true (Beneria and Sen, 1981). Indeed, it has been through the manipulation of patriarchal relations and the sexual division of labor that young women have been drawn into the industrial labor force in Latin America (Leacock, 1981). That is, female workers' situation as workers in the new international division of labor, for example, the Border Industrialization Program in Mexico, reflects their subordination at home (Arizpe and Aranda, 1981). And the same conditions that operate, in general, to undermine Mexican women's status as workers operate in Ciudad Juárez, as well (Tiano, 1984). The aim of this chapter is to uncover what, if any, work-related experiences enable maquila workers (1) to expand the traditional sex role of the Mexican woman as well as (2) to develop solidarity with other women workers in the BIP. A few illustrations of the dynamics of the interconnection of gender relations and class processes in the BIP set the stage for that analysis.

Multinational corporations operating in the BIP did not themselves create the characteristics of the Mexican labor force, but there exists some differentiation of that labor force that makes it more profitable to employ females: The unit cost of production is lower with female labor because women are cheaper to employ or more productive or both (Elson and Pearson, 1981). Given that assembly workers in the maquiladoras are paid the minimum wage, how can one argue that maquiladoras clearly prefer young, single females because they are *cheaper* to employ than men?

First of all, women's role in the family (or women's role in reproduction) "explains" how they are less expensive to hire. Maquiladora management holds strongly to the belief that women do not *support* families; they are secondary earners whose income is "optional." Thus, it is "all right" to offer women only dead-end assembly jobs because they have limited financial responsibilities as well as limited career aspirations. Yet it is the economic need of their families that prompts young women's entry into the maquila work force (Fernández-Kelly, 1983). As members of households in which fathers, brothers, or husbands are sporadically employed or underemployed, women do not merely provide supplementary income. The conviction on management's part that they *do*, however, justifies a pattern of cyclical layoffs.

Management also counts on women's traditional marginality to work and orientation to home to prompt them to leave the labor force, and according to management, 80 percent of the turnover is "voluntary" (Van Waas, 1981). However, such high rates of turnover are in the maquiladoras' interest for at least three reasons (Fernández-Kelly, 1983). Most obvious, high turnover enables plants to adjust to fluctuations in the business cycle, and the maquiladoras commonly retrench their labor force in the winter. Second, high turnover means fewer benefits and compensations paid to workers as well as virtual elimination of claims for seniority wages. While some workers do leave the maquiladoras for marriage and motherhood (what the industry calls "natural wastage"), many others quit because they are physically or mentally exhausted. Hence, the final reason high turnover of the labor force is in the maquiladoras' interest is the infusion of fresh workers it brings.[1] Because the learning curve for tasks in both electronic and garment assembly is short, workers reach peak productivity in a few weeks. This does not mean that management does not manipulate output, however. In fact, the maquiladoras use a whole battery of methods to control women who work in the plants and thereby increase their productivity. This leads to the second "explanation" for the preference for women in the maquiladoras.

It is truly an "article of faith," as Ehrenreich and Fuentes (1981:55) put it, on the part of management in the maquiladoras that women possess "innate" capacities and personality traits that make them more productive workers. They have "naturally" nimble fingers as well as greater patience and discipline, and thus, this manual dexterity and docility makes them better suited to the tedious, monotonous routine of assembly work.

Far from being natural, these "advantages" are cultural. Through their social experiences women acquire the traits and characteristics that make them preferable. Moreover, male managers and female operators reproduce at work traditional patterns of male domination. The factory becomes family-like for young women workers—with "big brothers" and a "father" as compelling images of patriarchy in the plant (Grossman, 1979). Indeed, some plants have found that a "sprinkling" of men on the line makes women "better behaved" (Van Waas, 1981) (read "more productive"). In addition, in order to foster women's loyalty to the company, management has instituted a host of fringe benefits, most of which are geared to "feminine" interests, such as fashion and makeup classes, singing, dancing, and sports and beauty contests.[2]

However, maquiladoras make use of not only traditional values of obedience to paternal authority and passive, ornamental femininity but also "modern" values of individual incentive and competition to in-

1. With the doubling of the maquila work force—from about 40,000 employees in the early 1980s to about 80,000 in the mid-1980s—"high" turnover has become a concern for management.
2. Some plants are now emphasizing more traditional aspects of their benefits package such as savings plans and life insurance. Nonsystematic observation suggests that these are the plants where growing numbers of men can be found. The question of the connection between what management offers workers in the way of benefits and the gender of those workers is an interesting one for further study.

crease productivity. Contests of all kinds pervade assembly work. "Productivity drives" pit workers in one plant against workers in another, line against line, or the individual worker against all other workers in the plant. The prizes—cosmetics or "trips for two"—reveal management's "manipulation of 'feminine' habits and proclivities for higher productivity" (Lim, 1978:41).

Thus, while maquila work (at the government-established minimum wage and in *comparatively* good conditions) presents the means to free Mexican women from traditional economic, social, and cultural restrictions, that potential appears far from realized. First, nothing suggests that women's increased purchasing power brings significant alterations in ideas about the proper roles of men and women in Mexican society. For example, the issue of whether or not conditions in the family power constellation can be changed by women's participation in the labor force in the absence of equalitarian ideologies remains critical (see Salaff, 1976). It appears that the enhanced economic value of the daughter may lead to tighter control by males, and daughters seem to have no greater status or family decision-making power as a result of their contribution to the household. Furthermore, in the factory, management deliberately preserves and utilizes traditional paternal authority to prevent workers from realizing their potential as a class. However, wages do confer some autonomy; the maquila worker's new economic role undermines traditional family patterns somewhat. In addition, maquila work provides an escape from early marriage and motherhood. Still, this is not without cost.

Evidence also exists indicating that integration of women into the development process through assembly work increases their vulnerability to exploitation not only in the factory but in the larger society as well (Safa, 1981). Male bosses at the factory have tremendous power over female workers' lives, but they do not provide the same "protection" as do male kin; factory work is not quite respectable, and factory workers are vulnerable to sexual exploitation. The factory is also a new site for sexual objectification (in the form of promoting feminine consumerism) under the guise of boosting morale. Furthermore, there is still social stigma attached to being a "factory girl" in Mexico, and concern is widespread about the morality of maquila workers. This is used as an instrument of control both in and out of the factory.

In sum, women's struggle to participate as equals in Mexican society requires enlargement of the traditional female role. This entails consciousness on the part of women themselves of the fact of their significant involvement in the public world—the world beyond the home—and recognition by society of the importance and legitimacy of that involvement. Work in the assembly labor force provides a foundation for this process.

However, as Van Waas (1981) suggests, it would be easy to assume that centuries of machismo makes for passive, manipulable women workers. On the other hand, perhaps "docility is the *appearance* women present to men . . ." [emphasis added] (Elson and Pearson, 1981:95). The collectivization of women in the maquiladoras and women's confrontation with a common authority in patriarchal capitalism can lead to solidarity among maquila workers in strike actions and/or to formation of networks of maquila workers sharing awareness of the larger structures that shape their lives.

For example, at times, individualistic responses—"subconscious wildcat strikes" (Fernández-Kelly, 1983) are transformed into collective action. In the summer of 1983, 450 women in a garment factory in Ciudad Juárez, after experiencing a doubling of their quota, closed the plant and demanded a collective contract. The workers won the strike, and they now feel confident and powerful. But conversations with the two women leading the new union in the plant reveal how far they must still struggle to be, in their own words, "treated as equal human beings."

Another, rather different, response on the part of women to their experience as workers in the maquiladoras can be found at the Women's Center in Ciudad Juárez. Established in the early seventies, and staffed by women who themselves once worked in the maquiladoras, the center offers educational programming aimed at enhancing maquila workers' ability to analyze their situation as women in the family, in society, and as workers as well as moving women in the direction of working class solidarity. The center provides a "space" for the treatment of women as equals and for women's equal access to participation.

Both going out on strike and attending consciousness-raising classes are examples of ways in which women workers are actively confronting patriarchal capitalism in the BIP, and suggest possibilities for expanding the traditional female role and for developing solidarity with other workers. The extent to which such changes are actually occurring was examined by means of a field experiment carried out among maquila workers in Ciudad Juárez—the "shining success story" of the BIP with approximately 80,000 employees in some 180 plants.[3]

3. For a fuller discussion of the BIP in Ciudad Juárez, see Young, 1986.

The Field Experiment

Sample

Between the fall of 1982 and the summer of 1983 a Mexican colleague and I collected data from three groups of women in Ciudad Juárez on their sex role identification and on their orientation toward work and workers in the maquila industry. The sample was essentially self-selected. That is, women who had chosen to participate in a twelve-week-long consciousness-raising course (offered by an education and training organization that serves maquila workers in the city) made up the first group ($N = 102$). From late September until mid-December these women met four nights a week from about 5 P.M. to 8 P.M. for lectures, discussions, workshops, films, etc. This course was followed, beginning in January, by a training course for alternative employment, and then a course in participatory action research was offered during the summer—all in a curriculum strongly informed by Freire's philosophy of "conscientizacion." It was during the first of these, the consciousness-raising course, that the participants were surveyed.

Volunteers from women working in a garment factory (a subsidiary of a U.S.-based multinational corporation), who had recently participated in a successful strike against the company, made up the second group ($N = 32$). In July 1983, the workers closed the plant for about two weeks until their demand for a collective contract was met. They were protesting management's doubling of their quota—which had the effect of cutting wages as most of them were producing double the quota at the time. The two women who were elected to represent the newly unionized workers were among the leaders of the strike.

Finally, volunteers from the women working in an electronics plant (to which we had access and which was also a subsidiary of a U.S.-based multinational), who were involved in *no* consciousness-raising activities and *no* recent strike action, made up the third group, a "control" group ($N = 67$).

Hypotheses

In the field experiment we wanted to test a number of hypotheses regarding the gender identification and working-class solidarity of these women. The expectations regarding women's identification with the traditional female sex role focused on the extent to which women in the various groups had begun to expand that role by perceiving the significance and the legitimacy of their participating as equals in the world beyond home and family.

Thus, we hypothesized that (1) women in the consciousness-raising course would exhibit the greatest capacity to enlarge the traditional female sex role, since much of the course curriculum deals specifically with such issues; (2) women who had been on strike would also reveal, but to a lesser degree, expanded sex role identification because of that experience—which, although not explicitly "feminist," implies a larger role for women than the traditional one and certainly raises women's consciousness about their capabilities; (3) women in the control group, who were in the assembly labor force but had neither of the other experiences, would report the most traditional sex role orientations of the three groups of women.

The expectations regarding solidarity with other workers focused on the degree to which these women recognized the interests they had in common with other workers, especially in the maquilas, over and against the interests of management. This we expected to vary depending on the types of experiences the different groups had undergone and the analyses of their conditions to which they had been exposed.

On this basis, we hypothesized that (1) women in the strike group would be the least competitive with other workers because of their recent experience of solidarity in the strike, while women in the consciousness-raising course, who were exposed to theoretical analyses of the need for worker solidarity in the face of international capital, would be less competitive than the controls; (2) women in the course would be the most discontent with worker—management relations as well as most critical of dependent development in the BIP because of analyses developed in class, while the strike group, which had confronted management on an adversary basis and was in the process of negotiating a contract with a multinational firm, would be more discontent and more critical than the controls; (3) women in the strike group would commit the most support to a (hypothetical) strike and would have the most positive view of unions, having just fought for and won their strike demand for a collective contract, while the women taking a course offered by an organization that has come out publicly in solidarity with workers would be willing to commit more to a strike action than the controls and have a more positive view of unions than the controls.

Measures

The survey instrument employed was composed of several scales and a number of individual items that measured gender identification and working-class solidarity. Although the response format for some items was simply agree/disagree and for others a Likert-type format was used (categories were later collapsed), all questions were closed-ended. The vast majority of questions were taken from research conducted on other Latin American populations, although, in some cases, they were originally developed by researchers working in the United States.

In order to determine the degree of these women's identification with the traditional female role, they were asked (1) how descriptive of themselves they believed each in a set of sex-typed characteristics (some traditionally viewed as feminine and some traditionally viewed as masculine) to be; (2) which options from a series of paired-opposite value statements, concerning (a) assertiveness/docility and (b) self- versus other-directedness came closest to their own beliefs; (3) whether they agreed or disagreed with a series of statements about male—female equality.

In order to tap these women's orientation toward work and their solidarity with other maquila workers, they were asked (1) how important certain job characteristics were to them; (2) whether they agreed or disagreed with a series of statements about the importance of competition as well as with a series of statements about the quality of relations between workers and managers; (3) their opinions about foreign investment in Cuidad Juárez and about whose interests unions work for in Cuidad Juárez; (4) and which options from a list of possible actions, requiring ever-increasing commitment of self, they would take in support of a hypothetical strike by other workers.

Findings

Before discussing the substantive findings of the survey, I will present some background information on the women in the three groups— course, strike, and control. The range in age and the average age of the women in the three groups were essentially the same. Women in the course ranged in age from 15 to 40 years with an average of 22 years; the strikers ranged in age from 18 to 35 with an average of 24; the controls ranged in age from 16 to 38 with an average of 21. The women in the course, however, were better educated: 69 percent of them had more than primary (6 years) education compared to only 34 percent of the strikers and 27 percent of the controls. Less than one-fifth (17 percent) of the women in the course were married whereas one-half (50 percent) of the strikers and more than one-third (39 percent) of the controls were married or in a marriage-like relationship. A similar pattern held for motherhood. Again, less than one-fifth (19 percent) of the women in the course had children, but one-half (50 percent) of the strikers and over one-half (55 percent) of the controls had at least one child.

The average length of time at the present job ranged from a low of 2.4 years for the women in the course to a high of 3.8 years for the strikers; the controls were in the middle with an average of 3.3 years on the job. Although there was some variation, the greatest proportion of women in each group reported feeling more approval from their families since starting to work—59 percent of the women in the course, 44 percent of the strikers, and 58 percent of the controls. In addition, the overwhelming majority of women in all three groups believed that marriage/family and work were of equal importance in their lives—76 percent of the women in the course, 75 percent of the strikers, and 90 percent of the controls. Only among women in the consciousness-raising course was there any commitment to work *over* marriage/family, and although it was a very small proportion (6 percent), it is suggestive of differences discussed below among the groups regarding sex role identification.

SEX ROLE IDENTIFICATION

Looking first at the findings regarding traditional feminine characteristics (Table 5.1), the data suggest that the controls were indeed the most traditional of the three groups of women. While the vast majority of women in all three groups claimed to be home-oriented (Traditional Female Characteristic 3), considerably more of the controls saw themselves in that light. Add to this the fact that the controls as a group were the *least* complaining (TFC 2, a "negative" feminine characteristic) and the most principled (TFC 7), and the image that emerges is one of the long-suffering, morally superior mother of Mexican tradition.

A different picture appeared for the strikers. As a group, these women, who took part in the rational, systematic action (the strike) which had very serious potential consequences (loss of job/income, blacklisting), did not view themselves as emotional (TFC 5) or very much in need

TABLE 5.1
Sex-Typed Characteristics

	Percent Who Claim		
	N = 102 Course	N = 32 Strike	N = 67 Control
Traditional Feminine Characteristics (TFC)			
1. Submissive	42	25	25
2. Complaining (−)	15	13	8
3. Home-oriented	71	72	85
4. Need approval	39	22	31
5. Emotional	57	28	40
6. Indecisive (−)	38	16	16
7. Principled	62	53	78
Traditional Masculine Characteristics (TMC)			
1. Aggressive	14	19	8
2. Independent	23	13	16
3. Arrogant (−)	12	19	6
4. Competent	23	19	19
5. Ambitious	33	34	40
6. Cynical (−)	27	38	34
7. Self-confident	54	52	16
8. Superior	9	17	2

of the approval of other people (TFC 4). The practical activity of the strike and the real risks involved in terms of repercussions from management certainly figured in these women's perceptions of themselves.

Upon first examination, the results regarding traditional femininity for the women in the course appear somewhat surprising. However, a partial explanation can be found in the course curriculum itself. For example, there was heavy emphasis in the curriculum on *services* to others, especially in the form of efforts to improve conditions in the community. Moreover, the statement on submissiveness (TFC 1) was elaborated in a way that implied "doing things for others." That more of these women claimed to be submissive, then, is less unexpected when viewed in this light. This group's greater indecisiveness (TFC 6) may have been connected to the course curriculum as well. That is, in the course, women were presented with a complex social structure based on the interrelations of class and gender and how to confront this reality was hardly transparent. Thus, feelings of being overwhelmed and not knowing what to do may have resulted from women's experience with the curriculum.

However, turning next to the findings on traditional masculine characteristics, the data do suggest that the women in the consciousness-raising course were beginning to develop a sense of individualism and agency that is traditionally more characteristic of men then of women. Specifically, larger proportions of this group saw themselves as independent (Traditional Masculine Characteristic 2) and competent (TMC4).

Interestingly, it was the strike group in which the largest numbers of women claimed the supposedly "negative" masculine characteristics of arrogance (TMC 3) and cynicism (TMC 6). Whether such traits were necessary preconditions for these women to be able to organize the strike action in the first place or were perceptions of themselves that the women developed as a result of their behavior and experience on strike is beyond the data to answer. However, it does seem reasonable to speculate that the relatively larger (although absolutely quite small) number of women in this group who had feelings of superiority (TMC 8) linked directly to winning the strike because of a sense of potency that success engendered in the participants.

Of the three groups, the controls claimed to be the most ambitious (TMC 5), but one must question how far this ambition could have been carried when, as a group, the controls were the least aggressive (TMC 1) as well as the least self-confident (TMC 7). The work experience alone, then, does not appear to enable women to take a proactive stance in the world. However, the self-confidence expressed by the majority of women who experienced a consciousness-raising course or a successful strike translates into values that do promote women's capacity to act creatively in society.

The findings presented in Table 5.2 indicate that assumptions about maquila workers' "feminine" docility and obedience to authority (or other-directedness) should be questioned seriously. The overwhelming majority of women in all three groups believed that a worker should be able to challenge her supervisor's orders (Assertive Value 1). Moreover, a somewhat smaller proportion of each group, although still the majority, deemed it appropriate to point out the errors of their mothers (AV 2). In one of the two major differences among the groups regarding values,

TABLE 5.2
Assertiveness and Self-Directedness

	Percent Choosing Option		
	N = 102 Course	N = 32 Strike	N = 67 Control
Assertive Values (AV)			
1. If one thinks the orders of a supervisor are unreasonable, one should feel free to question them.	74	72	72
2. If one's mother is in error, one should feel free to disagree with her.	58	56	63
3. It is better to be able to give orders than to have to obey them.	17	25	6
Self-Directedness Values (SDV)			
1. One can change the world to suit one's needs.	77	56	45
2. I trust my judgment rather than that of others.	97	94	93
3. One makes most of one's own problems.	96	92	96

more of the women in the strike group—perhaps out of confidence gleaned from that action—value being in a position of authority above one of obedience (AV 3).

The data indicate further that virtually all these women were highly self-directed or individualistic in certain ways, trusting their own judgment (Self-Directed Value 2) and taking responsibility for their problems (SDV 3). Yet in the other major difference on values, it was the women in the consciousness-raising course, in which great value was placed on promoting social change, who had the most confidence in their capacity to reshape the world (SDV 1). One requirement for the exercise of this capacity is women's participation as equals in society. Thus, it is also the women in the consciousness-raising course who are the most adamant about equality between the genders.

As expected, on a 10-item scale measuring attitudes regarding male-female equality, both the women in the course and the strike women scored significantly higher than the controls. (For course women compared to controls, $t = 5.97, p < .001$, and for strike women compared to controls, $t = 2.46, p < .01$.) On 7 of the 10 items, the largest proportion of women taking the "feminist" stance came from the course (Table 5.3). Their attitudes about equality took some very concrete forms. For example, in their view, swearing is no more objectionable on the part of women than on the part of men (Attitude 1); educational, business and professional opportunities should be open to women on the same basis as they are to men (A 8 and A 5). On more abstract issues even greater proportions of women in the consciousness-raising course called for equality. They desired to move beyond the ideal of the sheltered female

TABLE 5.3
Male—Female Equality

	Percent Giving Feminist Response		
Attitude (A)	N = 102 Course	N = 32 Strike	N = 67 Control
a 1. Swearing and obscenities are more repulsive in women.	17	9	9
2. Men should share housework.	75	78	49
3. Either a man or a woman can propose marriage.	22	19	11
a 4. Women should worry less about rights and more about being good wives and mothers.	49	28	9
5. Women should have the same business/professional opportunities.	89	63	84
a 6. Women should not expect to go the same places and have same freedom.	71	41	46
7. Apprenticeships should be open to women.	89	90	89
a 8. A family should encourage a son's education more than a daughter's.	85	75	69
9. Economic and social freedom for women is more important than living up to the feminine ideal.	56	31	22
a 10. Men should receive preference in hiring and promotion.	39	44	37

a Feminist response is "disagree"; reverse coded for analysis.

who is a good wife and mother and claim the freedom and the right to participate fully in social life (A 4, A 6, A 9). This indicated the importance of an organizing belief system such as that developed through the course within which to evaluate one's experiences at work, in the family, and in society.

On two issues the strike group led in the proportion of feminist responses: Slightly more of these women believed men should share housework (A 2) as well as receive *no* preference in hiring or promotion in the paid workforce (A 10). They apparently came by these attitudes from practical experience. Among the three groups, the largest proportion of strikers, one-half, were married, and as full-time workers, they felt the burden of the "double day"—housework in addition to assembly work. Furthermore, having struggled and put their jobs on the line, jobs that were significant for the economic well-being of their households, the role of workers was highly salient to them. Thus, they balked at the idea of male preference for jobs.

All three groups of women were equally strong in their demand for opening apprenticeships to women (A 7). Again, very practically for these women, that was a major means for them to get ahead in the work world.

Finally, it is worth noting that, with only two exceptions, the group with the smallest proportion of women taking the feminist stance on issues of equality was the controls. On A 4 and A 5 their feminist responses surpassed those of the strikers but not of the women in the course. Such a finding suggests once again that participation in the assembly labor force is not sufficient by itself for women to begin to enlarge their traditional role and participate fully in the development of their society. This issue will be taken up again in the conclusions, but first, findings regarding orientations toward work in the maquila industry are presented.

ORIENTATIONS TOWARD WORK IN THE MAQUILA INDUSTRY

Examining work values first, it appears that women in all three groups were about equally motivated at work by opportunities for advancement and good pay (Job Characteristics 1 and 2). Table 5.4 does indicate, however, that the women in the consciousness-raising course were somewhat less concerned about social recognition or prestige (JC 3) attached to a job than either of the other two groups of women. This suggests that the women in the former group gleaned from the course some consciousness of the value of work for itself, which may be a prerequisite for working-class consciousness.

TABLE 5.4
Important Job Characteristics (JC)

	Percent Agreeing		
Important for a Job to Have:	N = 102 Course	N = 32 Strike	N = 67 Control
1. Opportunities for advancement.	96	94	97
2. Good pay.	93	94	90
3. Prestige and social recognition.	64	72	87

There were no significant differences (measured by the *t* test) among the groups on a 7-item scale measuring competitiveness. Yet on individual items composing the scale, the expected tendency of controls being most competitive, women in the consciousness-raising course less competitive, and women in the strike group being least competitive can be observed. For example, regarding the statement, "It is important to me to do the best job possible even if that is not viewed positively by my workmates," the range of agreement was control—91 percent; course—86 percent; strike—81 percent. Regarding the statement, "I believe it is important to win at games and sports and to be the best worker," the range of agreement was control—79 percent; course—77 percent; strike—76 percent. The power of cooperative action aimed at a common good was instilled in at least some of the strikers as a result of their experience.

Anticipated variations emerged when the focus was on the women's beliefs about worker–management relations in the maquilas. On a 10-item scale measuring worker "contentment," both the strike women and the women in the course scored significantly lower—more discontent with the relations—than the controls. (For the controls compared to the strikers, $t = -7.15$, and for the controls compared to the course women, $t = -8.68$; $p < .01$ for both.) The controls, to a much greater degree than the other groups, believed that management and workers share common interests (Worker–Management Relations 1 through 6). They did not seem to be examining critically their situation at work. Compared to the other two groups, the controls appeared mystified rather than conscious regarding class. On the other hand, over half of both the strikers and the women in the course asserted that they and their fellow workers had the competence to run their plant (WM 8). The basis for this belief certainly differed according to the experience of each group. Although few in either group were demanding more "say"

TABLE 5.5
Worker–Management Relations (WMR)

		Percent Giving Contented Response		
		N = 102 Course	N = 32 Strike	N = 67 Control
1.	Employers generally have concern for their workers' welfare.	26	28	49
2.	Laborers generally receive a "fair" salary.	14	28	67
3.	Labor and management have a high degree of common interest.	35	25	51
4.	Employers and workers have benefited equally from recent border economic and industrial development.	20	25	82
5.	Managers consult workers often enough in decision making.	9	3	18
6.	My fellow workers and I receive "fair treatment" from our employer.	36	28	84
a 7.	Workers in my company should be given a greater say in managerial decisions.	13	13	6
a 8.	My fellow workers and I are technically competent to manage our company.	53	56	24
a 9.	It would be desirable for workers to control my company.	25	38	19
a10.	Labor should have a greater say than it now has in economic policy.	7	16	5

ªContented response is "disagree"; reverse coded for analysis.

in decision making—at the company level or at the national level (WM 7 and 10)—over a third of the strikers did desire worker control of the company (WM 9), again rooted in their experience.

Also as anticipated, the women in the course were the least enthusiastic about the Mexican government's facilitation of foreign capital investment in the BIP, although the strike women were not much more supportive (course—57 percent; strike—62 percent). The controls—90 percent of whom supported the policy—once again exhibited a lack of critical consciousness. When it came to the question of how well *unions* represent workers' interests, the women in the course also appeared to be the most skeptical. Less than two-thirds (60 percent) of these women believed unions negotiate *for* workers compared to more than three-fourths (78 percent) of both the strike and the control groups. The fact that the latter two groups were virtually 100 percent unionized—one of them quite recently—and that the organization offering the course had, in the past, made public statements about the *non*responsiveness of unions to the needs of women workers helps explain this finding.

Finally, women in the strike group and women in the consciousness-raising course identified more strongly with the interests of other workers than the controls as measured by willingness to carry out various activities in support of a hypothetical strike (see Table 5.6). On a 9-item Guttman scale of possible actions one can take during a strike, the strike group and the women in the course both scored significantly higher than the controls. (For strikers compared to controls, $t = 7.26$, and for the course women compared to the controls, $t = 10.38$; $p < .01$ for both.) This indicated their greater commitment to solidarity with other workers.

The majority of these women were willing not only to take food to and stand watch with other workers on strike (Strike Action 3 and 4), but also

TABLE 5.6
Guttman Scale of Strike Support Action

	Percent Unwilling to Take Action		
Strike Action (SA)	N = 102 Course	N = 32 Strike	N = 67 Control
1. Gather information.	14	9	19
2. Talk with others.	11	9	40
3. Take food.	23	9	91
4. Stand watch.	32	9	90
5. Join a demonstration.	38	37	91
6. Sign a petition.	37	34	95
7. Distribute information.	34	47	97
8. Raise money.	37	45	97
9. Join a hunger strike.	67	75	91

to demonstrate and sign petitions in support of the strike (SA 5 and 6) and even promote the strike by distributing information and raising money (SA 7 and 8). In addition, fully one-quarter of the women in the strike group said they were willing to go so far as to join in a hunger strike (SA 9) to support their fellow workers' struggle. The majority of the controls, on the other hand, were at best willing to ask a few questions and discuss the strike informally (SA 1 and 2) with other workers.

Taken together, these findings especially regarding unions and strike actions, raise the issue of the need and the possibilities for alternative organizational forms aimed at advancing women workers' interests. This question is taken up again in the conclusions.

Conclusions

The findings of the field experiment can be summarized as follows: First, regarding maquila workers' identification with the traditional female role, the controls appeared closest to the stereotypical ideal for Mexican women, as expected, but the strikers, who added certain stereotypically "masculine" characteristics to their role repertoires, and the women from the course, who were making demands for more male−female equality, seem to have been enlarging their roles as women. Second, in terms of these women's solidarity with other workers, those who underwent the practical experience of a strike or who were exposed in a classroom setting to theoretical analyses of the situation of workers revealed marked consciousness of class, as anticipated, while the controls remained rather mystified about their part in the new international division of labor.

These findings suggest caution when making generalizations about the docility and submissiveness of maquila workers as a group. Conventional wisdom among maquila managers has it that Mexican women are so passive that even if they should begin to question their situation, becoming less "obedient," they will not take action to promote change. The data indicate, to the contrary, not only that some maquila workers depart from the female stereotype but also that they are far from unorganizable.

These findings also lead to two other issues—one involves directions for future research, and the other revolves around orientations for development policy. Studies such as this one are beginning to uncover the nature of the impact of assembly work on the lives of women employed in the maquiladoras, but to date, little information beyond scattered anecdotes, regarding any changes the men ____ lives are experiencing. If women's roles change, then surely men's must as well, and although this has been a topic of considerable concern in many quarters, no systematic studies have been undertaken to determine the quality of the alterations in the sex role of Mexican males.

In addition, as men's and women's roles change, the structure and dynamics of families are also revised. This phenomenon, too, has provided fertile ground for speculation, but thus far, only very limited and tentative analyses focusing on the Mexican family in the contest of labor intensive industrialization have been carried out. Both research questions are too important to the understanding of the overall social consequences of this facet of Mexico's development strategy to be left in the realm of unexamined assumptions.

As noted above, a second major issue raised by this investigation revolves around development actions. Policymakers who hold out the goal of enhancing women's participation as equals in society and enabling them to author their own development must consider what organizational forms are best suited to that endeavor. The collectivization of women in factories, by itself, does not seem to move women toward that goal. Striking is an extreme form of organizing activity and not a strategy that can be adopted easily for altering day-to-day relations and situations confronting women workers in the factory and in society. The consciousness-raising course offered by the grassroots women's organization has been able to reach only a few thousand of the tens of thousands of maquila workers in the city and has been primarily analytical and not practical in focus.

What other organizational forms exist—or can be created—to enlarge Mexican women's opportunities and capacities for full and valued participation in the development of their society? Organizing efforts that replace hierarchy with community and maintain a woman-sensitive orientation, that is, recognize that women's needs are neither the same as nor can be subsumed under men's but are instead unique in many ways, are certainly preferred, but their exact form remains elusive. Thus, this question stands as a central one for all policymakers who have an interest in women in development. A concerted effort should be made to discover with maquila workers the organizational forms most responsive to their situation in the workplace, in the family, and in society, in general, with the aim of promoting their participation as equals in all spheres of life in Mexico.

References

Arizpe, L., and J. Aranda, 1981. "The 'Comparative Advantage' of Women's Disadvantage," *Signs* 7(2):453−473.

Beneria, L., and G. Sen, 1982. "Class and Gender Inequalities and Women's Role in Economic Development." *Feminist Studies* 8 (Spring): 157−176.

Bustamante, J., 1983. "*Maquiladoras:* A New Face of International Capitalism on Mexico's Northern Frontier." In J. Nash and M. P. Fernández-Kelly (eds), *Women, Men and the International Division of Labor.* Albany: SUNY Press.

Carrillo, Jorge, 1980. "La Utilización de la mano de obra femenina en la industria maquila: el caso de Cd. Juárez." Preliminary Research Report. Mexico, D.F.: El Colegio de Mexico.

Ehrenreich, B., and A. Fuentes, 1981. "Life on the Global Assembly Line." *Ms.*, January, pp. 53−59f.

El-Sanabary, N. M. (comp), 1983. *Women and Work in the Third World: The Impact of Industrialization and Global Economic Interdependence.* Berkeley: Center for the Study, Education and Advancement of Women, University of California.

Elson, D., and R. Pearson, 1981. "Nimble Fingers Make Cheap Workers", An Analysis of Women's Employment in Third World Export Manufacturing." *Feminist Review,* Spring, pp., 87−107.

Fernández-Kelly, M. P., 1981. "Development and the Sexual Division of Labor." *Signs* 7(2):268−278.

———, 1983. *For We Are Sold, I and My People: Women and Industry in Mexico's Northern Frontier.* Albany: SUNY Press.

Grossman, R., 1979. "Women's Place on the Integrated Circuit." *Southeast Asia Chronicle* and *Pacific Review* (joint issue), No. 66/9(5):2−17.

Grunwald, J., 1983. "Internationalization of Industry: U.S.-Mexican Linkages." Paper presented at the Second Conference on the Regional Impacts of U.S.-Mexico Economic Relations, Tucson, University of Arizona, May 25−27.

IDS Bulletin, 1979. Special issue on the continuing subordination of women in the development process. No. 10(3), University of Sussex.

Leacock, E., 1981. "History, Development and Division of Labor by Sex." *Signs* 7(2):474−491.

Lim, L., 1978. "Women Workers in Multinational Corporations: The Case of Electronics Industry in Malaysia and Singapore." *Michigan Occasional Paper,* No. IX.

———, 1983. "Multinational Export Factories and Women Workers in the Third World: A Review of Theory and Evidence." In N. M. El-Sanabary (comp), *Women and Work in the Third World.* Berkeley: Center for the Study, Education and Advancement of Women, University of California.

Multinational Monitor, 1983. "By the Sweat of Her Brow: Women and Multinationals." 4(R), special issue.

Nash, J., and M. P. Fernández-Kelly, 1983. *Women, Men and the International Division of Labor.* Albany: SUNY Press.

Peña, Devon, 1980. "Las Maquiladoras: Mexican Women and Class Struggle in the Border Industries." *Aztlan* 11(2):159−229.

Safa, H., 1981. "Runaway Shops and Female Employment." *Signs* 7(2):418−433.

Salaff, J., 1976. "Working Daughters in the Hong Kong Chinese Family." *Journal of Social History* 9:439–465.

Signs, 1981. "Development and the Sexual Division of Labor." 7(2), special issue.

Sokoloff, N., 1980. *Between Money and Love.* New York: Praeger.

Tiano, S., 1984. "Maquiladoras, Women's Work, and Unemployment in Northern Mexico." Working Paper on Women in International Development, #43, East Lansing: Office of Women in International Development, Michigan State University.

Van Waas, M., 1981. *The Multinationals' Strategy for Labor.* Ph.D. dissertation, Stanford University.

Young, G., 1986. "The Development of Ciudad Juárez: Migration, Urbanization, Industrialization." In G. Young (ed), *The Social Ecology and Economic Development of Ciudad Juárez.* Boulder: Westview.

Young, G., and B. Vera, 1984. "An Extensive Evaluation: Final Report." Rosslyn, Va.: Inter-American Foundation.

6
Tortuosidad: Shop Floor Struggles of Female Maquiladora Workers

Devon Peña

Industrial sociologists and managerial consultants alike have a long-standing interest in the different forms of worker resistance and sabotage, particularly as expressed through acts of output restriction (see, e.g., Taylor, 1903; 1911; Mathewson, 1931; Roethlisberger and Dickson, 1939; Roy, 1952; 1953; 1954; 1959; Wilson, 1978; Burawoy, 1979).[1] Frederick W. Taylor, the principal founder of "scientific management," was the first to address the problem of output restriction (what he called "soldiering"). Since Taylor's time the subject of workers' informal struggle has continued to attract scholarly and managerial attention.

Recently, Marxists have developed new empirical findings and theoretical interpretations on output restriction (see, for e.g., Burawoy, 1979; Lamphere, 1979; Shapiro-Perl, 1979). Burawoy argues that industrial sociologists have largely ignored the workplace "environment" as a cause of output restriction (1979:123). Specifically, Burawoy notes that the effects of heightened supervision have not been adequately assessed. In a word, Burawoy draws attention to the key role of relations of production *in* production as key determinants of worker–management struggles on the shop floor.

In looking over the literature on output restriction, several key research gaps become apparent. First, there has been no major sociologi-

---

1. For a comprehensive review of the relevant industrial relations literature see Peña (1983: Chapter 3).

cal study of the phenomenon in a Third World (developing region) context. Yet, the current internationalization of capital involves large-scale relocation of labor-intensive assembly processes to developing regions such as Taiwan, the Philippines, and México's northern border. The export-oriented industrialization model has become a major modus operandi for the internationalization of the labor process (cf. Frobel et al., 1980; Carrillo and Hernández, 1982; Peña, 1983). Prior research suggests labor-intensive assembly processes are archetypical settings for output restriction struggles (Lamphere, 1979). A study of output restriction struggles in a Third World setting would thus seem instructive.

Second, there has been insufficient study of output restriction a-mong female workers.[2] Yet, female workers predominate in the work forces of export-oriented industries throughout developing regions (Nash, 1983; Snow, 1983). A study of output restriction among female workers should yield valuable insights on sex-specific and cross-cultural differences in the dynamics of such informal struggles.

The lack of sufficient research on other areas of shop floor struggle is also apparent. There has been no major sociological research on work stoppages, sabotage, or informal counterplanning as practiced by Third World women workers. Our study seeks to address this research gap through an empirical and theoretical analysis of shop floor struggles based on a survey of female workers in México's maquiladora industries.[3]

It is important to note that the general view of female maquiladora workers casts them as passive, unorganizable, and easily manipulated victims of transnational management (see, e.g., López, 1970; Baerresen, 1970; Van Waas, 1981; Carrillo and Hernández, 1982; Fernández-Kelly,

2. To our knowledge, the only studies which focus on output restriction among women are Lamphere (1979), Shapiro-Perl (1979), and Cavendish (1982). There has been no prior effort to study this phenomenon in the context of transnational production in developing regions like México. The other major studies of output restriction (Mathewson, 1981; Roy, 1954a, b; Burawoy, 1979) all focus on male-dominated occupations.

3. The term "maquiladora" refers to export-oriented, in-process assembly plants operating under the auspices of the Border Industrialization Program (BIP) in Mexico. For further discussion see Bustamante (1983) and Peña (1981 and 1983: Chapter 1). The terms "maquiladora," "maquila," and "border industries" are used interchangeably in this chapter.

1983). Our findings contradict this prognosis of maquila workers as women lacking the ability or motivation to engage in struggle.

Part of the reason for my disagreement with the scholarly consensus on this subject perhaps lies with the fact that most maquiladora researchers have conceptualized the process of workplace organization and labor–management relations in purely formalistic terms. Emphasis has been placed on formal union–management relations (e.g., Van Waas, 1981; Carrillo and Hernández, 1982) or on the elaboration of formal collective bargaining and arbitration procedures (e.g., De la Rosa Hickerson, 1979). One study, while providing considerable detail of informal shop floor relations, focuses on how management uses competition between workers as a means of control (Fernández-Kelly, 1983).

This essay provides conceptualization of the process of workplace organization as including both formal and informal types of relations.[4] Thus, it examines in detail the dynamics of informal shop floor networks: their formation, functioning, and impact on conditions of struggle in the workplace. The presentation which follows begins with a brief overview of the demographic characteristics of workers in the sample. This is followed by analysis of informal struggles in the maquilas, specifically, struggles focusing around output restriction. A third section recasts the analysis in light of recent theoretical breakthroughs in the comparative study of labor–management relations in Third World regions. Such theoretical analysis combines gender and class relations in the context of a transnational, cross-cultural workplace.

Worker's Demographic Characteristics

The survey sample consisted of 223 interviews with female maquiladora workers conducted in Ciudad Juárez between October 1981 and May 1982.[5] Most of the workers were from electronics sector operations

---

4. The study of informal aspects of industrial relations has a long tradition among U.S. industrial and organizational sociologists. Much of the credit for the "discovery" of the informal group in industry goes to the pioneering "Hawthorne scholars," Roethlisberger and Dickson (1939), colleagues of Elton Mayo and George Homans. See Peña (1983: Chapter 3) for further discussion.
5. For a discussion of the research and sampling techniques of this study see Peña (1983: Chapter 5). In brief, the sampling strategy involved a purposive, stratified design.

(70 percent); another proportion from garment operations (20 percent); the remaining workers from nonelectronics manufacturing and diverse service firms (10 percent).

These findings on maquila workers' demographic characteristics are in agreement with prior research (see, e.g., Carrillo and Hernández, 1982; Fernández-Kelly, 1983). Workers in the sample had an average age of 22.3 and generally workers in electronics firms were younger than those in garment plants. The respondents in this sample had an average educational attainment of 8.05 years. Again, workers in electronics firms had a higher educational attainment level compared to garment workers (see Table 6.1).

Table 6.1
Demographic Characteristics of Juárez Maquiladora Respondents

Variable	$\overline{X}$	N	Percent
Average age	22.3	223	—
Average educational attainment (years)	8.05	223	—
Marital Status			
Single		153	74.3
Married		35	17.0
Common-law		10	4.9
Widowed		6	2.9
Divorced		2	1.0
Total		206	100.0
Migratory Background			
Juárez natives		94	43.0
Migrants		129	57.0
Total		223	100.0
Rural origins		72	55.8
Urban origins		56	43.4
Total		128	100.0
Prior Occupational Experience in Other Maquilas/Industries			
Yes		58	26.5
No		161	73.5
Total		219	100.0

Source: My survey, Ciudad Juárez (1981–1982).

Over 74 percent of the respondents were single, 17 percent were married, almost 5 percent were in common-law marriages, nearly 3 percent were widowed, and only 1 percent were divorced. The origins and backgrounds of respondents also reflect demographic trends documented by other researchers (e.g., Fernández-Kelly, 1983; Centro de Investigación y Docencia Económica, 1981; Gambrill, 1981). It is generally agreed that large numbers of maquiladora workers have migratory backgrounds. Fifty-seven percent of the respondents were born in a place other than Ciudad Juárez. Most of these workers with migratory histories came from rural areas (56 percent). By comparison, close to 44 percent reported urban origins (see Table 6.1).

Prior research on maquiladora workers indicates most are working in an industrial setting for the first time in their occupational histories (see, e.g., Centro de Investigación y Docencia Económica, 1981; Gambrill, 1981). Most workers have no prior employment experience in other maquilas or factories.[6] The same is true of my respondents: Only 26.5 percent had prior experience working in the maquiladoras (Table 6.1).

There are some variables related to workplace conditions that bear mention here. For example, in the area of contracting our findings are consistent with prior research (Carrillo and Hernández, 1982). Over 95 percent of respondents had signed contracts of one type or another. However, an examination of the types of contracts signed indicates the workers' situation in terms of contract stability and length of guaranteed employment. Over 9 percent of respondents had participated in the signing of collective bargaining agreements, well below the 30 percent unionization rate of the sample.[7] Over 30 percent signed temporary contracts which guarantee employment only for a probationary 1-to-3-month period. The largest proportion of cases (almost 58 percent) signed so-called *contratos deplanta* (in-plant or "tenured" contracts). In-plant contracts do not specify the length of secure employ-

---

6. Generally, most maquila workers have little prior work experience in any occupation. However, those workers with prior work experience tend to come from private household, food service, and retail sales occupational backgrounds. See, e.g., Gambrill, 1981; Carrillo and Hernández, 1982; Fernádez-Kelly, 1983; Peña, 1983.

7. The 30 percent unionization rate is somewhat misleading. As Carrillo and Hernández (1983) have shown, most of the unionized workers are in the larger plant operations like RCA, General Electric, and American Hospital Supply/Convertors. See Peña (1983: Chapter 7) for further discussion.

ment, although the informal understanding is that a worker keeps the job indefinitely given certain productivity and behavioral standards.[8] Finally, these findings also suggest that maquila workers are subject to a veritable policy of enforced turnover or staff rotation: the average length of time on the job was 46.9 months. A large proportion of the cases had under 41 months "tenure" (49 percent). Only 21.5 percent of the respondents reported 72 months or more of tenure, which is reported as the industry average in at least two other studies (Fernández-Kelly, 1980; Carrillo and Hernández, 1982) (see Table 6.2).[9]

In sum, these findings are consistent with prior research to the

TABLE 6.2
Select Working Conditions Reported by Juárez Maquiladora Respondents

Variable:	$\bar{x}$	N	Percent
Contract Status			
Signed contract		213	95.5
No contract signed		7	3.2
Missing cases		3	1.3
Total		223	100.0
Type of Contract			
Collective bargaining			
agreement		20	9.8
Temporary contract		66	32.4
In-plant contract		118	57.8
Total		204	100.0
Current Job Tenure			
(in months)	46.9		
40 or less		109	49.0
41–80		81	36.4
81 or more		32	14.4
Total		222	100.0

Source: My survey, Ciudad Juárez (1981–1982).

8. The definitive study of labor contracting in the maquilas is De la Rose Hickerson (1979). Also see Van Waas (1981).
9. Ellwyn Stoddard, sociologist at the University of Texas–El Paso, recently completed a study of the turnover phenomenon. Dr. Stoddard estimates that turnover has reached crisis levels: 100 percent turnover (or 16,000 workers hired monthly to retain a stable work force).

extent that maquila workers (1) are predominantly young females, (2) have a higher level of education than most other Mexican workers, (3) tend to be single (never married), (4) often have migratory histories, (5) are of mixed rural and urban origins, and (6) have little or no prior experience in the industrial work setting.

Moreover, this study, in agreement with previous research, suggests that (1) most maquila workers sign contracts, (2) the majority of these are temporary and "in-plant" contracts which are associated with instability of employment and high turnover, and (3) few workers have more than 72 months of tenure in their current jobs.

A theoretical note must be added at this point. The maquiladoras, as a historically specific organizational form of the modern (international) capitalist labor process, are characterized by a system of labor–management relations known in sociological circles as "Fordism."[10] As a system of industrial organization, Fordism is best known for its use of the automated conveyor belt or assembly line. Use of the assembly line system provides management with near total control over the speed of work. The assembly line is also associated with the destruction of craft-skills in production. Workers in the Fordist factory are deskilled, that is, stripped of craft skills and subjected to a managerially determined schema involving continual fragmentation of petty job tasks and a perpetual division and redivision of shop floor labor activity (cf. Braverman, 1974; Aglietta, 1979; Burawoy, 1979; Cooley, 1980; Hales, 1980).

Thus, Fordism combines both technical and managerial modes of control over the work force. Moreover, the Fordist factory is such that the deskilled character of the work force makes possible continuous production in spite of high turnover rates. The degradation of the "mass worker" under Fordism implies deskilled laborers are easily substituted without disrupting the organization and continuity of the labor process. This represents an immense leap forward in the level of managerial control over the workers.[11] Yet, the Fordist system is also character-

10. For further discussion of Fordism, see Peña (1983: Chapters 3, 6, 7). Also see Aglietta (1979) and Hales (1980).

11. The classical analysis of Fordist control of the labor process is by Blauner, who notes:

> The essential feature of the . . . assembly line is the fact that the pace of work is determined by the machine system rather than by the worker. . . . Since the speed of the line is mechanically set . . . [components] move at a predetermined rhythm (1973:98–99).

See also Edwards (1979).

ized by high levels of absenteeism, sabotage, work slowdowns, wildcat work stoppages, and of course, output restriction (see, e.g., Braverman, 1974; Burawoy, 1979; Cleaver, 1979; Lamphere, 1979; Shapiro-Perl, 1979). Thus, any analysis of output restriction in the maquiladoras must be assessed in terms of this theoretical backdrop.

Output Restriction in the Mexican Maquiladoras

A neglected area of research on the maquiladoras concerns shop floor struggle. To fill this void, we collected data on informal networks and shop floor relations from workers in 35 different Juárez maquiladoras. A major aspect of shop floor dynamics centers around output restriction and other forms of worker sabotage and resistance. The data on output restriction produced unexpected results.

A remarkable 61.8 percent of respondents reported participation in output restriction.[12] This is an extraordinarily high level of informal struggle, particularly if one considers the general prognosis of scholars has been a lack of struggle and a persistance of "labor quiescence" (e.g., Van Waas, 1981). Motives for output restriction among these respondents varied along two dimensions: A small number or workers restricted output owing to a variety of administrative, technical, or health-related reasons ($N = 22$). However, motives related to conflicts over production standards and rules were also prevalent. In this regard, over 41 percent of the respondents reported lack of incentive pay as their underlying motive. On the other hand, over 58 percent of the respondents reported resistance to speed-up as a motive for output restriction, no doubt reflecting the constant productivity drives imposed on maquila workers by management. Speed-up, after all, is the hallmark of the Fordist organizational form.

Maquiladora workers refer to the process of resistance to speed-up as *tortuguismo* or *tortuosidad* (literally, working at a turtle's pace or working stubborn as a turtle). A closer look at our data highlights the strong association between output restriction and production speed-up.

---

12. The sample in this study is by no means representative of the entire maquila work force. Thus, we would caution against overgeneralization regarding the unusually high level of output restriction among the cases in our sample. For more discussion see Peña (1983:377−378).

The Struggle against Speed-up

A bivariate analysis of output restriction involves comparing workers reporting productivity speed-up with those also reporting output restriction. My results (utilizing a χ^2 test of significance) suggest that the association between output restriction and the incidence of productivity drives is significant at the .001 level (see Table 6.3). Of the 165 cases reporting production speed-up, over 73 percent were involved in output restriction. In comparison, among the 40 cases not reporting speed-up only 37 percent were involved in output restriction.

Utilizing a γ measure of association (which allows us to determine the direction of the relationship), the data indicate a strong, positive association between output restriction and production speed-ups ($\gamma =$ .60516). This means that positive responses on speed-up are associated with positive responses on output restriction.

Having ascertained the significance of the relationship between output restriction and production speed-up, it now becomes important to clarify the dynamics which underpin this form of worker resistance to the Fordist system. Clearly, the incidence of Fordist speed-up seems to figure prominently as an "environmental" feature of the maquiladora organizational form. However, there are a number of other "environmental" factors which merit attention. The next section focuses on

TABLE 6.3
Crosstab of Production Speed-Ups on Output Restrictions

Production Speed-Ups	Output Restriction		
	Yes	No	Total
Yes	121	44	165
	73.3[a]	26.6	100.0
No	15	25	40
	37.5	62.5	100.0
Total	136	69	205
	66.3	33.6	100.0

[a]Row percentages
Missing cases = 18
$\chi^2 = 21.56146$; 2 df; $< .001$; $\gamma = .60516$

productivity supervision and shop floor networking processes as critical aspects of the maquiladora organizational "environment."

Supervision, Networking, and Informal Struggle

Indications from recent research suggest higher levels of supervision may be closely related to conflict between workers and management and the shop floor dynamics that accompany such conflict, namely output restriction (Burawoy, 1979; Lamphere, 1979; Shapiro-Perl, 1979). A study of Canadian postal workers captures this process:

> Management, whose goal could be simply stated as increased productivity, found its implementation next to impossible. The key element in the resistance of . . . workers was the possession of the skill necessary to keep the . . . system going, and the accompanying control over the work process which that gave them. Productivity counts, counselings, and other forms of harassment (increased supervision), which had raised output prior to the 1965 strike, now had the reverse effect. No longer intimidated by these attacks . . . workers saw them clearly as provocations and thus used their control over production to slow the process down (Taylor, 1975:93).

Another study found that workers in the mass production of jewelry also resisted new forms of managerial control over output levels:

> The makeup system generates some of the sharpest struggle between workers and management. When management subtracts piecework earnings through the penalty system of the makeup, the company creates new problems for itself, because workers will consciously restrict output in retaliation (Shapiro-Perl, 1979:295).

Thus, both "skilled" and "deskilled" workers have been shown to engage in output restriction in response to increased supervision, production speed-ups, and other forms of intensification of work.

In order to understand the nature of productivity supervision in the Mexican maquilas, it is first necessary to draw a distinction between the basic types of supervision involved. In the maquilas, there are two different types of persons involved in productivity supervision. One is the group-chief, a regular assembly line operator selected by management as a leader on the basis of performance and behavioral standards (see Peña, 1983, Chapter 9, for further discussion).[13] Group-chiefs are selected from among the assembly operators who consistently produce at higher levels compared to coworkers. Such workers are otherwise known as "rate busters" because they surpass the productivity standards (rates) established by the primary work group (cf. Roethlisberger and Dickson, 1939; Roy, 1952). However, in addition to their high productivity, group-chiefs are also recruited on the basis of demonstrated loyalty to the company and subservience to male supervisors. Group-chiefs function as the first level of control over productivity standards, that is, as informants and as leaders of output rates. It is nevertheless important to note that group-chiefs are on the same status level as other assembly operators in terms of pay, benefits, control over job tasks, and personal prestige. Group-chiefs do receive certain "noneconomic" incentives for their cooptation: bonus gifts, tolerated absenteeism or tardiness, and after-work entertainment by male supervisory staff.[14] All group-chiefs in the maquilas are female.

First-line supervisors in the maquiladoras are almost exclusively male. Selection of first-line supervisors is also carefully planned by higher management. The process of selection was described to the author by a plant manager at an automotive sector operation in Juárez:

> Every Mexican has to make it in terms of productivity before we move them up. . . . The ones that are promoted are the ones that excel in our system. This produces integration of goals, acceptable behavior . . . even in engineering. They have to make it in production first. This has reduced the amount of conflict. We don't have that functional differentiation where staff fights with higher management because our supervisors have gone through production. That's where we evaluate. The production or first-line supervisor is really a long-term evaluation position. You spot your troubles there. A lot of these don't make it into higher positions. The ones that don't make it are the more political ones. . . . Because we have promoted the ones that accept measurement, they also discard those who don't fit the same profile. All appraisals on promotions are made by the older group. From production supervision they can get promoted to unit managers, the level at which these decisions are made. This in-

13. Time-and-motion studies are regularly used throughout the border industries in an effort to identify lead operators. Although such Taylorist strategies are generally in use, workers have also devised a number of tactics to resist speed-up and the imposition of higher quotas.
14. See Peña (1984) and Peña and Gettman-Peña (1984) for further discussion.

creases integration. They choose people that are more like themselves (Management interview, Ciudad Juárez, 1982).

Male workers who assume first-line supervisory positions are either promoted from the ranks of line operators, technicians, and quality control inspectors or they are recruited into the positions—usually right out of engineering schools. Few female workers break into the first-line supervisory ranks. Nevertheless, the degree of social control exerted on these male supervisors is substantial: threats of termination or blocked promotions seem sufficient to produce a high level of "integration."

My research into productivity supervision in the maquilas revealed that the relationship between female group-chiefs and male first-line supervisors is a critical conjuncture in the networks of shop floor relations (Peña, 1983: Chapters 6 and 7). In fact, given the high sex-stratified division of labor in the maquilas (generally an all-female force of operators is supervised by an all-male force of production managers), the initial contact point between workers and management is that between group-chiefs and first-line supervisors.

Our findings indicate that group-chiefs have a higher rate of daily supervisory interaction with production operators than first-line supervisors: over 70 percent of the respondents reported four or more daily contacts with group-chiefs over matters related to production standards. This compares to 50 percent who reported four or more daily contacts with first-line supervisors. Clearly, group-chiefs have greater contact with line workers than first-line supervisors.[14] My findings also suggest that this differential pattern of supervisory interaction with workers is a reflection of a patriarchal system of labor control in the maquilas. By patriarchal I refer to a system of control over work rules, regulations, evaluation, and discipline controlled by males (see Hartmann, 1976). In fact, male first-line supervisors use various forms of sexual and sexist harassment to manipulate group-chiefs into informant and rate-busting roles (see Peña, 1984).[15] By exerting pressures on

15. Once group-chiefs have been selected, sexual and sexist harassment plays a critical role in maintaining them under the control of male supervisors. I have noted:

> Essential for success in managing the productivity of female line workers . . . is participation by male supervisors in after-hour events, i.e., parties, dinners, dances and the like . . . . Women, it seems, will work harder for a supervisor who lavishly entertains them after work. . . . Wage hierarchies are also developed partly on the basis of male

a group-chief to conform to the male-dominated supervisory system, first-line supervisors extract control over the assembly line operators without resorting to direct contact with them.

This patriarchal system of indirect control results in two major dynamics: (1) It reduces the degree of "vertical" conflict, that is, direct conflict between line operators and male management. (2) It increases the degree of "lateral" conflict, that is, direct conflict between line operators and group-chiefs. In a word, group-chiefs occupy a "buffer space" between female line workers and male first-line supervisors. Group-chiefs thus find themselves in a contradictory location. On the one hand, group-chiefs are treated as assembly line workers and thus must interact daily with coworkers to keep production running. On the other hand, group-chiefs are used as a sort of "proletarianized technical supervisor" class of workers and thus must interact daily with male management under a set of expectations which requires them to accept patriarchal authority and control over the labor of women workers. This contradictory location in the constellation of shop floor networks produces erratic expressions of linkage with both line workers and management.

There are indications, in the context of a sex-stratified internal division of labor, that group-chiefs and line workers—in sharing the basic characteristic of female gender and hence in being subject to the same patriarchal relations of domination—may form specific and transient linkages in order to cooperate over matters related to shop floor organization. Group-chiefs often cooperate with operators in matters relating to productivity and output restriction (Oral Histories 1, 3, 5, 7, 9; Ciudad Juárez, 1981–1982). Oral histories revealed that group-chiefs are sometimes participants in the informal shop floor networks which facilitate output restriction. As one worker noted:

Elisa [pseudonym] is an old friend of mine. We both started work at [company name] in 1978. In 1979, she was promoted to group-chief because she was always very good about meeting standards. Then, in

---

participation in social and friendship networks. Women who join male supervisors for entertainment, put-out on the shop floor, are rewarded with wage increases, bonuses, vacation and the like. . . . And women who resist the "seduction" are ostracized or threatened with termination. Sexual harassment in this manner becomes a fundamental aspect of control in the maquilas (Peña 1984:10).

See also Peña and Gettman and Peña (1984).

1981, there were some very bad problems with the quality control supervisors. They accused her of being sloppy with her unit. The truth is that
they had consistently raised the standards until she decided it had gone
far enough. She helped us to organize ways of getting around the standards . . . by working slower, damaging components, and hiding pieces.
Eventually, management caught on to what we were doing. They fired
several workers and demoted her back to the soldering line (Oral History
12, Cuidad Juárez, 1982).

These findings are consistent with Roy (1952, 1953, 1954, 1959) and
Burawoy (1979): Both report that group-chiefs (and sometimes other
higher level production managers) often side with workers in disputes
with higher levels of plant management (see also Dalton, 1950). Moreover, they also suggest that line workers generally reject promotions to
the group-chief position. More than half (56.8 percent) of the respondents reported unconditional rejections of promotions to group-chief.
The most frequently mentioned reason for rejecting this promotion was
the belief that friendship ties may become endangered (56 percent of
the cases). Thus, the overwhelming majority of line workers based their
rejections on "interpersonal" grounds. Interpersonal relations may be
essential to the process of informal organization and struggle. Friendship ties often play a major role in the formation of informal shop floor
networks which faciltate output restriction and other forms of resistance. Thus, rejection of promotions on the basis of fear of disruption of
friendshp ties might indicate a conscious effort among workers to
preserve the interpersonal, small group basis of informal shop floor
networking and solidarity.

The process of linkage building on the shop floor proceeds on the
basis of conversations through friendship networks. But formation of
friendship networks on the shop floor is influenced as much by factory-
based work groups as by social groups in the workers' communities
(Peña, 1983; cf. Kowarick, 1983). In fact, given managerial disruption of
shop floor groups through line and workshift reassignments, workers'
use of community and social networking seems crucial. These findings
in this sense are consistent with earlier work by Shapiro-Perl (1979) and
Cavendish (1982), although the former suggests networking cannot
challenge the social relations of control in production.

Management's imposition of line and workshift reassignments must
not be seen as mere technical restructuring or managerial manipulation. It must be seen in this political light: It breaks down the unity of
primary work groups and thereby hinders the communicative and

coordinative functions of networks based on such groups. Maquila workers' networks seem to respond to this control strategy partly by carrying out "counterplanning" activities outside the factory. As one worker, a leader in the well-known Acapulco Fashions strike coalition,[16] notes:

> The group from the start was clandestine. Our action in the factory was invisible up till the time we hit with walkouts and sabotage. Sometimes it was necessary to meet after work since they watched over us closely. . . . We made little groups *(bolitas)*, had dinners and parties. We talked about the problems and made plans for the next day at work (Oral History 8, Ciudad Juárez, 1982).

This anecdote is strikingly similar to one recounted by Ruth Cavendish in her narrative on women's struggles in a British car parts assembly plant, worthy of lengthy quotation for it illustrates the critical role of "social" interaction outside the factory:

> The atmosphere on the shop floor was very good. We read at the same time as we worked, and we went to the loo [bathroom] when we pleased. There was time to chat and to talk to women on the next line whom we didn't know very well. We got up from our chairs whenever we felt like it. It was almost as if we'd taken over the place. . . . Each time a meeting was called, we got up from our benches and left [our work] half done. Chargehands and supervisors looked on helplessly. . . . In the middle of the first week of the go slow, management sent letters to each of us informing us that our pay would be cut in half. . . . Some of the women suggested a mass meeting so all the pieceworkers would be able to discuss the situation, but older women warned that there hadn't been a mass meeting in eighteen years. . . . We gathered outside the "yard" near the canteen and were joined by women from the sprocket shop. . . . she knew we were from the Main Assembly and encouraged us to stick it out. "The whole place will be 'out' on Monday if any one of you is suspended" (1982:141–143).

The point brought out by Cavendish is simply that workers provide vital information to each other outside the factory on matters related to shop floor struggles. This seems to be particularly the case whenever

---

16. Acapulco Fashions, a subsidiary of Johnson and Johnson, experienced a series of labor struggles between 1969 and 1982, culminating in the protracted strike of 1979–1982. For further analysis and discussion see De la Rosa Hickerson (1979), Carillo and Hernández (1982), and Peña (1983).

management starts to reprimand and threaten workers (e.g., wage cuts, layoffs). The same type of networking and information sharing is evident in the maquilas.

Management's efforts to disrupt primary work group networks do not always succeed. Workers in Juárez gave numerous examples of tactics they use to overcome productivity supervision, particularly time and motion study and other managerial efforts to increase workers' output. One worker described the struggle against time and motion study:

Q: Are there ever informal agreements among the line workers to restrict output?

A: Many yes. In reality the standards are much too high. We agree on this and promise not to surpass the standards. This is especially true when they are observing and timing us. We have told managers to count all the movements and not just those involved in actual assembly. Sometimes they don't count having to pick up parts or packing parts inside fixtures or boxes. We have had arguments over this.

Q: How do you arrive at these agreements to restrict output?

A: When we see an engineer with clock in hand we already know what to do through experience. We discuss tactics on the line as long as we are not overheard. It one worker is going fast and is being timed, we'll go over later and cuss her out. We'll tell her that if they raise the standards, she'll be alone in meeting them. When they fix the standard and the supervisor asks why we can't meet them, we answer that we don't all have the same capacity, the same speed or ability. They have never been able to prove otherwise with their clocks. Like right now, our current supervisor is demanding that we turn in the same level of production during our rest periods as during our regular work periods. You see, at two o'clock we get a ten-minute rest break when we can slow down or stop working altogether. She is trying to take this away from us. We only get ten minutes for breakfast and a half-hour for lunch as it is. We are not paid for time off the line. I always tell the supervisor to get someone else to work, I'm not giving up my rest period. (Oral History 6, Ciudad Juárez, 1982).

Maquila workers clearly engage in the old practice of "binging" (i.e., use of informal sanctions or threats against rate busters) in order to control output levels and preserve the solidarity of primary work groups. Use of verbal admonishments serves to restrain rate busters from surpassing standards during time and motion study and speed-ups. In this way, dynamics of informal networking and struggle among shop floor groups in the maquilas proceed along lines of development similar to those documented among workers in the mass production, labor-intensive industries of the United States, Britain, and Italy (see, e.g., Roethlisberger and Dickson, 1939; Roy, 1952, 1953; Burawoy, 1979; Lamphere, 1979; Shapiro-Perl, 1979; Cavendish, 1982; Gambino, 1972: Potere Operaio, 1972; Negri, 1980).

Accordingly, these findings suggest certain features of output restriction dynamics are "universal," that is, they occur in Fordist organizational settings regardless of national location or cultural context. If the dynamics of output restriction previously analyzed are, in fact, universal, then they should provide a basis for the development of a comparative theoretical framework. Such a theoretical framework should aim to clarify similarities and variations in the patterns of labor–management relations present in transnational labor processes in Third World and advanced capitalist settings. The final section of this chapter represents an initial step toward the development of such a comparative framework.

Women's Shop Floor Struggles in Comparative Perspective

The recent collection of studies in Nash and Fernández-Kelly (1983) offers key theoretical advances toward an understanding of labor-management relations in the new international division of labor. Generally, these studies involve various approaches to reconceptualizing the relationship between class and gender in the core and periphery regions where transnational firms operate. Much of the analytical focus is on the global electronics industry based in the U.S. Silicon Valley, on Mexico's maquiladoras, and on other "off-shore sourcing"[17] installations in the Philippines, Malaysia, and the Caribbean. In this section we first provide an overview and critique of these theoretical advances. This is followed by presentation of an alternative comparative framework for analysis of women workers' struggles in the new international division of labor.

17. The term "off-shore sourcing" is used by a number of scholars in reference to the export-oriented industries located in Third World free trade industrial zones. For further discussion see Froebel et al. (1980) and Nash and Fernández-Kelly (1983).

Women and Transnational Management:
Current Literature

Until quite recently, research on women in the international division of labor tended toward an emphasis on the changing role of women in the development process.[18] No efforts had been made to study women in relation to the actual organization of the labor process in transnational firms. Such efforts are still few and far between (see, e.g., Nash and Fernández-Kelly, 1983; Peña, 1983).

One outstanding contributor is June Nash, who examines the impact of the changing international division of labor on different sectors of the working class. While she provides a general overview of the internationalization of capital, her analysis is rich with insights relevant to an understanding of global labor—management relations. The new international division of labor is based on accumulation of capital through the employment of "defenseless" sectors of the working class (Nash, 1983:7). The theme of the defenseless condition of the working class at the global level is repeated by Nash and many other theorists.[19] As Nash argues:

> There is a strong preference for extremely low-paid, unprotected segments of the population. These may be ethnic or rural migrants without alternative employment, or women. Lacking experience in trade union or political organizations, they are vulnerable to intense exploitation. This trend is intensified as labor is forced to compete internationally (1983:11).

Nash also points out that there is no immediate prospect for organizing labor on an international scale, given the defensive posture of trade unions in the developed regions (1983:27). However, Nash also notes

18. See, e.g., Boserup (1970), Bronstein (1983), Bunster et al. (1977), Curtin (1982), Nash and Safa (1976), O'Barr (1982) and Rohrlich-Leavitt (1975). The tendency in most of this literature is analysis of women's participation in the economy and politics at an aggregate level. The macro-orientation of these studies has produced important advances in theoretical and empirical understanding of women's changing role in development. There have been numerous case studies as well. However, the phenomenon of women on the shop floor and women and industrial relations has been neglected.

19. See also, e.g., Fernández-Kelly (1983), Lim (1983), Snow (1983), and Van Waas (1981). For a detailed critique of the "docility bias" in the literature on Third World women workers, see Peña (1983: Chapters 1, 2, 9).

that it will probably be workers in the developing regions who formulate an effective challenge to transnational capital (1983:27).

In order to understand industrial relations at the global level, Nash suggests an analytical framework that will "take into account sectorial differences within countries as well as between countries" (1983:27−28). Nash proposes adoption of the "transculturation" model as an appropriate analytical framework.[20] Transculturation in the context of a theory of industrial relations involves analysis of:

> not only the transfer of culture traits from one society to another, but also the dialectical transformations in social relations within both countries that occur in the process. Whereas the dominance of multinational corporations determines much of the flow of technology, work organiza-tion, and level of production, their very presence abroad changes the character of the corporation in the home base. . . . The net effect of the transfer of capital abroad has been to reinforce managerial decision-making and weaken the control of organized labor within the plant over hiring and upgrading. . . . labor relations in the host country take on some local characteristics in response to existing rules, regulations, and cus-tomary expectations (Nash, 1983:28).

Nash's analysis focuses on changes in formal negotiations between trade unions and management and on informal relations between management and workers and among the rank and file themselves (1983:28−32). Reference is made to the process of "harmonization":

> The term harmonization as used in multinational circles is equivalent to what some anthropologists call transculturation. It refers to the process of adjusting the priorities of a powerful productive unit to the particular practices of the environment in which it becomes adapted (Nash, 1983:29).

Nash's theoretical contribution clarifies the complex nature of transna-tional industrial relations and points the way to future inquiry. How-ever, there are a number of conceptual weaknesses inherent in the transculturation/harmonization approach. The final section of this chapter offers a critique of Nash's approach and suggestions for an alternative conceptualization.

---

20. The concept of transculturation is adopted by Nash from the work of structural anthropologists.

A Critique and Alternative Conceptualization

As has been the case with most empirical studies of women in the transnational labor process, Nash's approach tends to characterize the Third World female working class as "defenseless" and unorganized. In the case of Nash, reference is made to both formal and informal aspects of industrial relations. This is a welcomed advance; however, the informal industrial relations Nash refers to basically involve a variety of control options exercised by management. Informal modes of resistance by workers are largely ignored. And yet, our research suggests that female workers in the transnational Fordist factories organize informally to resist production speed-ups and the fragmentation of primary work groups.

Thus, my research suggests that conceptualization of transnational industrial relations must involve a *two-sided* analysis of both working-class and capitalist organizational forms. Moreover, such analysis must recognize the importance of both class and gender relations in the differentiation of control and resistance on the shop floor.

This brings us to the second point of criticism. Nash suggests transculturation involves—in an industrial context—the transfer of technology, work organization, and level of production from the home base to the Third World operations. Nash also suggests that labor relations in the Third World operation take on some local characteristics in response to existing rules, regulations, and expectations. However, left unclear is an idea of precisely what types of local characteristics are integrated into the functioning and organization of the transnational labor process. This chapter suggests that, particularly in the case of the export-oriented electronics and textile sectors, the key changes capital has made are related to a synthesis between local (traditional) forms of patriarchal control and "imported" Taylorist and Fordist organizational principles. In fact, as I have suggested:

> Transnational labor processes . . . present capital with special organizational problems. Foremost among these are the extent to which local traditions of struggle impinge on capital's ability to implement changes in technical, managerial and other forms of control. Another important aspect is the degree to which capital makes adjustments in control strategies after assimilating local experiences, cultural nuances, and compositional conditions. . . . capital has adjusted to the specificities of local conditions; management did not simply import a productive apparatus and set it in motion. . . . Perhaps the most critical adjustment relates

to the synthesis between imported Fordist and Taylorist principles and native patriarchal relations. . . . capital's attempts to restructure control via changes in either technical or managerial organization is often opposed by . . . workers' self-activity. Given the limits of imported Taylorist and Fordist forms of organization . . . management has had to rely on the native patriarchal relations to exert control over workers' shop floor struggles and productivity (1983:510−513).

This conceptualization opposes the approaches of scholars strongly influenced by the work of Nash. Lim (1983), for example, argues that increasing female participation in transnational production reduces "patriarchal" exploitation but increases "imperialistic" exploitation. This approach fails to consider how capital restructures traditional patriarchal relations in Third World regions, transforming them into new modes for control over workers in the labor process. In a word, for us the synthesis between "native" patriarchy and "imported" Fordist and Taylorist principle represents precisely the type of "harmonization" outlined by Nash. Such a synthesis is exemplary of the dialectical transformations in social relations which occur whenever capital penetrates cross-culturally into new regions.

Thus, this chapter suggests that conceptualization of transnational industrial relations must involve consideration of the interaction between class and gender in the organizational setting. Moreover, such interaction must be posited not merely as involving a bidirectional transfer of "cultural traits" as per the anthropological position. Rather, changes in social relations and value systems must be seen as critical aspects of the ongoing process of *political recomposition*, that is, changes in the internal divisions of power of the working class at the global level (cf. Peña, 1984, for further discussion).

Crucial in comparative analyses of transnational labor processes, then, is understanding factory-specific power relations and managerial adaptations in the context of preexisting cross-cultural mechanisms of labor-control. In the broadest sense, there are at least two major configurations of power relations in Third World regions with export-oriented industries. In the Philippines, for example, there exists a marked "militarization" of power relations (Enloe, 1983). Given an authoritarian regime at the level of state power—and the imposition of militarized control throughout society—industrial relations in the Philippines involve strict controls over trade union activities. This involves actual or potential use of military force to control working-class organization. In contrast, industrial relations in the Mexican export-oriented sector are characterized by a Western-styled tripartite system (cf. De la Rosa Hickerson, 1979; Van Waas, 1981). The state (arbitration bodies), organized labor, and management participate in a formally pluralistic industrial relations system. The role of the military in such a setting is marginal, that is, use of military force is invoked only in times of severe crisis. However, the political reality is such that organized labor (specifically the official CTM) closely collaborates with both management and the state to control the work force.[21]

It is therefore not surprising that organized resistance by women workers under both militarized and tripartite industrial relations systems is minimal.[22] However, the absence and/or weakness of formal (trade union) oppositional tendencies should not be equated with a lack of motivation or interest and inability to organize struggle. Of interest here is the fact that in both Southeast Asian and Mexican settings, women's participation in the industrial work force is recent. This participation, moreover, is strongly influenced by paternalism and traditional patriarchal norms in both regions. Accordingly, the lack of organized resistance by Southeast Asian and Mexican women may be associated with the imposition of patriarchal controls—an issue ignored by Nash and others.

Yet, Philippine workers in the export industries have been known to participate in what one observer calls "subconscious wildcat strikes" (Paglaban, 1978). My research documents a pervasive amount of informal struggle in the Mexican maquilas (output restriction and sabotage). Thus, the existence of informal modes of struggle among Third World women in the export industries suggests: (1) organized resistance may

21. The CTM (Confederation of Mexican Workers) is the "labor wing" of the ruling party (PRI, Institutional Revolutionary Party). Interestingly, workers in our sample rejected affiliation with the CTM or other "charrista" trade unions (over 98 percent of the sample). However, workers in our sample overwhelmingly supported the formation of either independent unions or informal plant coalitions (over 60 percent preferred these organizational forms). See Peña (1983: Chapter 7). Thus rejection of traditional trade unionist organizational forms must not be equated with a rejection of worker organization in general.

22. I argue elsewhere that "organized" resistance is minimal in the maquilas if by "organized" we are referring to trade unionist organizational forms. However, if by "organized" we are referring to informal modes of organization, then maquila workers are clearly emerging as an organized force. Of the 35 plants in our sample, almost half had identifiable informal groups or semiofficial plant coalitions. See Peña (1983: Chapter 7–9).

be emerging; (2) this resistance develops informally given the constraints of militarized and/or formal tripartite controls.

Finally, it is important to qualify this conceptualization. While it could be argued that productivity drives in the long run disrupt management's ability to consistently maintain quota levels—since such pressures may create disenchantment and resistance—the unique circumstances of the export-oriented labor markets strengthen speed-up efforts. High productivity pressures do create problems for management: the incidence of output restriction and other forms of resistance represents a challenge to managerial control. The short length for training also strengthens managerial policies based on high productivity. In a way, the problem faced by production supervisors in the export-oriented industries is short-term: Output restriction may disrupt production during brief periods. In the long-term, such resistance may not really affect management's ability to meet production goals. And in those rare cases where worker resistance becomes intransigient and effective, geopolitical mobility offers an escape. However, it may also be that women's experience with informal modes of struggle constitutes a form of political socialization, preparing the way for higher levels of struggle.[23]

To conclude: A comparative approach to the study of women in the transnational labor process must incorporate (1) a two-sided analysis of working-class and capitalist organization forms that considers both formal and informal aspects of organization; (2) an analysis of both class and gender relations as aspects of the process of transculturation/harmonization.

Women's shop floor struggles—whether the output restriction struggles in the maquilas or the "subconscious wildcat strikes" among Philippine workers—represent a relatively unexplored dimension of industrial relations in the transnational export-oriented industries of the Third World. The significance of a study of such struggles resides in the clarity it may bring to an understanding of the emerging changes in the global capital—working class relation.

---

23. For example, in an earlier study we found that workers involved in output restriction networks were also more likely to participate in general work stoppages ($\chi = 70.41008$; df 4; $p < .001$). See Peña (1983: Chapter 7). For more on women's struggles in the export-oriented sectors see Pacific Research (1979 and 1980); North American Congress on Latin America (1976).

References

Aglietta, M., 1979. *A Theory of Capitalist Regulation*. New York: New Left Books.

Baerresen, D., 1970. *The Border Industrialization Program of Mexico*. Lexington: Heath-Lexington Books.

Blauner, R., 1973. *Alienation and Freedom*. University of Chicago Press.

Boserup, E., 1970. *Woman's Role in Economic Development*. London: St. Martin's Press.

Bronstein, A., 1983. *The Triple Struggle: Latin American Peasant Women*. Boston: South End Press.

Bunster, X., et al. (eds), 1977. "Women and National Development: The Complexities of Change." Special Issue, *Signs: Journal of Women in Culture and Society* 3:1 (autumn).

Burawoy, M., 1979. *Manufacturing Consent*. University of Chicago Press.

Bustamante, J., 1983. "Maquiladoras: A New Face of International Capitalism on Mexico's Northern Fronter." In June Nash and Maria Patricica Fernández-Kelly (eds), *Women, Men and the International Division of Labor*. Albany: SUNY Press.

Carrillo, J., and A. Hernández, 1982. "La Mujer obrera en la industria maquiladora: el caso de Ciudad Juárez." Professional thesis, Facultad de Ciencias Politicas y Sociales, Universidad Nacional Autonoma de México, México, D.F.

Cavendish, R., 1982. *Women on the Line*. London: Routledge and Kegan Paul.

Centro de Investigacion y Docencia Economica (CIDE), 1981. "Los Limites del programa de industrializacion fronteriza para el abatimiento de las tasas de desocupacion y la calificacion de la fuerza de trabajo." Unpublished research report, CIDE, Mexico.

Cleaver, H., 1979. *Reading Capital Politically*. Austin: University of Texas Press.

Cooley, M., 1980. *Architect or Bee? The Human/Technology Relationship*. Boston: South End Press.

Curtin, L. B., 1982. *Status of Women: A Comparative Analysis of Twenty Developing Countries*. Washington, D.C.: Population Reference Bureau.

Dalton, M., 1950. "Unofficial Union—Management Relations." *American Sociological Review*, 15 (October).

De la Rosa Hickerson, G., 1979. "La Contratacion colectiva en las maquiladoras." Professional thesis, Escuela de Derecho, Universidad Autonoma de Ciudad Juárez, Chihuahua, Mexico.

Edwards, R., 1979. *Contested Terrain*. New York: Basic Books.

Enloe, C., 1983. "Women Textile Workers in the Militarization of Southeast Asia," in Nash and Fernández-Kelly.

Fernández-Kelly, M. P., , 1980. "Chavalas de Maquila: A Study of the Female Labor Force in Ciudad Juárez' Offshore Production Plants." Ph.D. dissertation, Rutgers University, New Brunswick, N.J.

———, 1983. *For We Are Sold, I and My People: Women and Industry on Mexico's Northern Frontier*. Albany: SUNY Press.

Froebel, F., et al., 1980. *The New International Division of Labor*. Cambridge: Cambridge University Press.

Gambino, F., 1972. "Workers' Struggles and the Development of Ford in Britain." *Bulletin of the Conference of Socialist Economists* (March).

Gambrill, M. C., 1981. "La Fuerza de trabajo en las maquiladoras: resultados de una encuesta y algunas hipotesis interpretativas." *Lecturas del CEESTEM: Maquiladoras*. Mexico, D.F.: Centro de Estudios Economicos y Sociales del Tercer Mundo.

Gettman, Dawn S., and D. G. Peña, 1984. "Women, Mental Health, and the Workplace: Research Issues and Challenges in a Transnational Setting." Paper presented at the National Association of Social Workers, National Conference on Health and Public Policy, June, Washington, D.C. Forthcoming in *Social Work: Journal of the National Association of Social Workers*, Fall 1985.

Hales, M., 1980. *Living Thinkwork*. London: CSE Books.

Hartmann, H., et al., 1976. "The Unhappy Marriage of Marxism and Feminism: Towards New Union." Unpublished paper. Author's files.

Kowarick, L., 1983. "Identity: The Hidden Side of Social Movements in Latin American." In W. Pansters and A. Ramdas, "CEDLA Workshop 1983: The State and the New Social Movements in Latin America." *Boletin de Estudios Latino-americanos y Del Caribe* 35 (December).

Lamphere, L., 1979. "Fighting the Piece-Rate System: New Dimensions of an Old Struggle in the Apparel Industry." In A. Zimbalist (ed), *Case Studies on the Labor Process*. New York: Monthly Review Press.

Lim, L., 1983. "Capitalism, Imperialism, and Patriarchy: The Dilemmas of Third-World Women Workers in Multinational Factories." In Nash and Fernández-Kelly.

Lopez, D., 1970. "Low Wage Lures South of the Border." *American Federationist* (June).

Mathewson, S., 1931. *Restriction of Output Among Unorganized Workers*. New York: Viking.

Nash, J., 1983. "The Impact of the Changing International Division of Labor on Different Sectors of the Labor Force." In Nash and Fernández-Kelly.

————, and M. P. Fernández-Kelly (eds), 1983. *Women, Men and the International Division of Labor*. Albany: SUNY Press.

————, and Safa, H. I. (eds), 1976. *Sex and Class in Latin America*. New York: Praeger.

Negri, A., 1980. *Del Obrero-masa al obrero social*. Barcelona: Editorial Anagrama.

O'Barr, J. F. (ed), 1982. *Perspectives on Power: Women in Africa, Asia and Latin America*. Durham, N. C.: Center for International Studies, Duke University.

Pacific Research, 1979. "Changing Roles of Southeast Asian Women: The Global Assembly Line and the Special Manipulation of Women on the Job," *Pacific Research* 9:5 – 6 (July – October).

————, 1980. "Delicate Bonds: The Global Semiconductor Industry." *Pacific Research* 11:1 (Spring).

Paglaban, E., 1978. "Philippines: Workers in the Export Industries." *Pacific Research* 9:3 – 4 (March – June).

Peña, D. G., 1981. *Maquiladoras: A Select Annotated Bibliography and Critical Commentary on the U.S.-Mexico Border Industry Program*. Bibliography Series 7-81, Center for the Study of Human Resources, University of Texas at Austin.

————, 1983. "The Class Politics of Abstract Labor: Organizational Forms and Industrial Relations in the Mexican Maquiladoras." Ph.D. dissertation, University of Texas at Austin.

————, 1984. "Between the Lines: Toward a New Perspective on the Industrial Sociology of Women Workers in the Transnational Labor Process." Paper presented at the Annual Meetings of the National Association for Chicano Studies, University of Texas-Austin (March). Forthcoming in National Association for Chicano Studies Editorial Committee (eds). *La Mujer: The 1984 Proceedings of the National Association for Chicano Studies*. Austin: Center for Mexican American Studies and University of Texas Press.

Portere, Operaio, 1972. "Porto Marghera: An Analysis of Workers' Struggles and the Capitalist Attempts to Restructure the Chemical Industry—A Workers' Inquiry." Unpublished report (translated from the Italian manuscript by Big Flame, London). Author's files.

Roethlisberger, J., and W. Dickson, 1939. *Management and the Worker*. Cambridge: Harvard University Press.

Rohrlich-Leavitt, R. (ed), 1975. *Women Cross-Culturally: Change and Challenge*. The Hague: Mouton and Co.

Roy, D., 1952. "Restriction of Output in a Piecework Machine Shop." Ph.D. dissertation, University of Chicago.

———, 1953. "Work Satisfaction and Social Reward." *American Sociological Review* 18.

———, 1954a, "Efficiency and the Fix: Informal Intergroup Relations in a Piecework Machine Shop." *American Journal of Sociology* 60.

———,1954b. "Quota Restriction and Goldbricking in a Machine Shop," *American Journal of Sociology* 57.

———, 1958. "Banana Time': Job Satisfaction and Informal Interaction," *Human Organization* 18.

Shapiro-Perl, N. 1979. "The Piece-Rate: Class Struggle on the Shop Floor—Evidence from the Costume Jewelry Industry in Providence, Rhode Island." In A Zimbalist (ed). *Case Studies on the Labor Process*. New York: Monthly Review Press.

Snow, R. T., 1983. "The New International Division of Labor and the U.S. Workforce: The Case of the Electronics Industry." In Nash and Fernández-Kelly.

Taylor, F. W., 1903. *Shop Management*. New York: Harper and Brothers.

———, 1911. *The Principles of Scientific Management*. New York: Harper and Brothers.

Taylor, P., 1975. "The Sons of Bitches Just Won't Work: Postal Workers Against the State." *Zerowork: Political Materials* 1 (December).

Van Waas, M., 1981. "The Multinationals' Strategy for Labor: Foreign Assembly Plants in Mexico's Border Industrialization Program." Ph.D. dissertation, Stanford University.

7

Programming Women's Empowerment:
A Case from Northern Mexico

Kathleen Staudt

"The personal is political" seems a mainstay phrase of the international women's movement. Women share many personal experiences, conditioned in large part by the economic, political, and ideological structures in which they live. Women's near-universal subordination to men ultimately reflects women's political powerlessness compared with men. In the political process, decisions are made about the allocation of resources and values. Men dominate decision making in the formal political process in organizations which have institutionalized male interests.[1] Women's devaluation, limited access to, and control over resources originate in political inequalities. Any redistribution of values and resources between men and women requires increased power for women as a group.

During the rapidly changing development process, women's disadvantage compared with men's has often been noted. Under conditions of dependent capitalist development, such as that of Mexico, this female disadvantage is complex to unravel, given the different circum-

I am grateful to Beatriz Vera and Gay Young for their comments on this chapter, their evaluation of the center, and their supply of its curriculum to me; to the U.S. Interamerican Foundation for its support of the evaluation which made the interviews possible; and to the work of the center staff and director, without whom these activities would not exist. The center will remain nameless in this chapter.

1. This idea is developed by Staudt, Chapter 8.

stances of women in various classes. Elsewhere, observers have noted the primacy of politics in explaining people's disadvantage (Uphoff, 1980). While development projects pay lip service to political participation via the development process, rarely is the commitment genuine, planned into project activity, or even measured. Advocates of participation base and, if successful, realize their claims largely on the grounds that people's involvement will both ease administrative implementation and bring better information into decision making.[2] Instead of participatory development, activities tend to be individualist, economist, and/or service oriented. Governments and international development agencies are reluctant to alter the political status quo, and nongovernmental organizations avoid potential risks associated with this activity.

Development can be defined as empowerment, a process by which people acquire the ability to act in ways to control their lives. More specifically, empowerment involves advances in people's critical capacity and skill acquisition to influence material and political circumstances of themselves and members of their group and to alter power relations in society. For women, empowerment means consciousness of female subordination and collective solidarity to achieve the solutions implied by the causes attributed to subordination. To restrict the conception of empowerment to individuals would deny both the significance of the gender structure in shaping people's lives and the efficacy of collective action to achieve group goals. Empowerment goes beyond consciousness raising, or attitudinal change, to attitudinal *and* behavioral change. "Reform" or "revolution" is not the issue here, as goals are best determined by people themselves, but rather consistency between analysis and action.

Empowerment contains three levels—personal, network, and organizational—each distinguished by progressively greater capacity. Personal empowerment involves critical intellectual capacity, along with language to define and explain one's collective reality, and increasing self-esteem and personal communication skills. Personal empowerment is the foundation on which the next two forms of collective and thus politicized empowerment rest. Network empowerment involves informal, temporary, and ad hoc efforts to achieve individual and col-

2. For example, see Cohen and Uphoff (1977).

lective goals and thus to put newfound consciousness into practice with other members of one's group. That network empowerment is conscious, goal-oriented behavior distinguishes it from interpersonal influence, though clearly interpersonal influence represents a bridge from individual consciousness to activation of that consciousness with others. Finally, organizational empowerment represents the most advanced form of empowerment in its reliance on formal, relatively permanent, goal-oriented activity based on conscious collective action. This threefold conceptualization operationalizes the transcendence of the personal toward political.

The size and complexity of Mexico's cultures almost defy a traditional characterization of women. Still, the idealized conception is one of the sacrificing wife and mother, supported by husband and father. Clearly subordinate to men in public political life and the economy, she nevertheless exercises legitimate influence in the domestic, or household, sphere, as spiritually superior to men (Stevens, 1973:91). While these cultural features do not challenge the conception of empowerment, they do suggest the challenge that personal empowerment poses and the special constraints to realizing network and organizational empowerment.

This chapter analyzes the extent to which female participants in a women's center in Ciudad Juárez, Mexico, have undergone personal, network, and organizational empowerment. First, it describes the center, the female clientele, and recruitment strategies, and analyzes the center's curriculum. Finally, it examines empowerment in interviews developed for an extensive evaluation conducted of the center. In the conclusion, the chapter delineates these findings in terms of organizational design, the center recruits, and the Mexican political system.

The Women's Center

The women's center analyzed is a rare example of an organization committed to women's empowerment. The center is dedicated to increasing the ability of working women to be aware of and to act upon the structural factors that impinge upon their lives. Now a decade old, the center began as factory women joined with relatively privileged professional women to facilitate self-awareness and basic skills learning. As one of its founders and later staff member expressed in 1972 to the woman who was to become director:

> Our greatest problem is that we lack a sense of self. . . . If you really want to help us, then you must teach us to know ourselves, so that we can take pride and demand that others value us in the same way that we do (cited in Fernández-Kelly, 1983b:42).

The center's women's program consists of more than a year's training in consciousness raising and skill building. Participants first complete ten weeks devoted to the topics of women, work economics, politics, and labor problems. Following that, they enter skill courses for twenty weeks, and finally, they complete a ten-week internship, where ideas are applied to practice. In the 1980–1981 course, there were 56 participants studying to be nurse's aides; 28 teacher's aides; 23 social workers; and 6 in personnel administration. This breakdown has continued in subsequent years. In previous years, the center has offered secretarial training, modern dance, crafts, baking, and open secondary school.

The vast majority of center participants are industrial assembly workers, employed in one of the 144 (1984 figures) *maquiladoras*. Maquiladoras are labor-intensive, export-processing subsidiaries of largely U.S. multinational corporations initiated under the supportive wing of Mexico's 1965 Border Industrialization Program. Primarily electronics and textile assembly plants, these firms take advantage of low-cost Mexican labor and of limited government safety regulations to do partial processing of their products and thus benefit from U.S. Tariff Codes 806 and 807, which require tax on only the value added. Although originally designed to address high rates of male unemployment, the firms recruit an overwhelmingly female labor force, approximately 80 percent (Fernández-Kelly, 1980:8). The result of successive Mexican currency devaluations was that, by 1983, approximately a *day's* minimum wage of under $4 in Ciudad Juárez for plant workers was equivalent to an *hour's* minimum wage labor in the United States. Young women between the ages of 16 and 24 are recruited into factories through word of mouth, newspapers, and catchy radio ads. For example, to background music of Frank Sinatra's "Strangers in the Night" (in English), an enthusiastic Spanish-speaking male voiceover calls for young women, age 16 and above, to apply for factory work amid good working conditions with various fringe benefits.

Rather than actively seeking labor force opportunities, these women represent a first generation leaving the domestic sphere or probably paid service work for paid factory work. Though working out of economic need, they are viewed as a purely temporary, or reserve labor force, creating inevitable contradictions in how these women view themselves and how the larger society views them.[3]

One hundred and two center participants were surveyed before the 1982−1983 course. Their average age was 22 and three-fourths of the 70 percent who were employed worked in electronics plants with an average job tenure of just over two years. Less than 10 percent were recent migrants to the city; 83 percent were single, and 19 percent had children. Almost all participants had some secondary schooling (Young and Vera, 1984:29−30). Although one-fourth belonged to a union [less than the one-third figures cited in an earlier study (Fernández-Kelly, 1983a:144)], these women workers generally expressed skepticism about union leaders and their commitment to workers, rather than to themselves, employers, and/or political parties (see also Peña, 1980).

Recruitment for center courses is unsystematic, but far-reaching. Notices appear in the newspaper and on the radio, but more usually, participants hear of the center through word of mouth, such as from friends who have completed the course. Center staff have no routine lines of communication to workers in different factories. This somewhat haphazard style of recruitment means that courses begin with a broad mix of orientations and motivations among participants. Still, results of a comparison of 102 center participants in the 1982−1983 course and of 67 similar, though slightly less educated women factory workers, revealed center women to be less traditional in sex roles, more nationalistic in solutions offered for Mexico's development problems, and more willing to commit fully to strike action (Young and Vera, 1984:30).

Center Curriculum

When the center first opened, it was loosely and informally addressed to women's health and family problems. Initially more philanthropic than consciousness raising in its approach, its director and staff (most

---

3. Beatriz Vera, personal communication.

of whom are former *maquila* workers) later developed a curriculum shaped to represent students' voices (Fernández-Kelly, 1983b:43).[4]

The first ten weeks of the center's 1980–1981 curriculum were analyzed,[5] focusing on the content, cues, and political skills conveyed to participants and on participants' reactions to that curriculum in their workshops and feedback. All center participants, whether in social work, teacher's, or nurse's aide courses, are exposed to this very intensive experience. The curriculum consisted of, for each session, an overview of goals, themes and their subgoals, descriptions, workshop tasks, workshop reports, and participants' evaluations. Missing in this otherwise very thorough document are transcripts of the expositions for the collective sessions. Still, the material permits an analysis of the coherence and consistency of the design, and as important, of how participants understood the material, in what proportions, and in their own voices.

Center general curriculum goals are ambitious. First, the curriculum aims to help women analyze their condition in the family, work, society, and politics. Second, it teaches techniques for participants to locate personal problems in their structural contexts. Next, it promotes consciousness of group solidarity and the identification of class interests. Fourth, it provides technical training for community service. Finally, it provides settings in which participants can put theory into concrete action.

A fundamental principle upon which the center is dedicated, the "personal as political," carries over into the center's education methodology. Sessions begin with a short, orienting lecture; then participants break up into small groups for role play, sociodrama, problem-solving tasks, or discussion sessions on questions posed in lecture; and finally, the groups reunite to compare findings. Meeting from approximately 5 to 8 P.M. every day, and after a full day's work for most, participants are expected to make a heavy energy commitment to their training experience. The center's teaching methodology should increase the absorbability of the massive amount of material participants are exposed to. Only occasionally are there reading assignments, which range from feminist magazine articles to selections from *Das Kapital*. Ideas or theory are applied to reality or practice, later implemented in the

---

4. Ibid.
5. This curriculum served as a foundation for subsequent years.

internship experience as well. Means and ends are thereby to be inter-connected. Staff commitment toward building a more participatory and egalitarian society reflect these same means in the learning process, and thus, barriers between students and teachers are minimized.

Given the diverse mix of participants, the center's curriculum is designed to establish a common foundation from which participants will be oriented. During the initial two-week introduction, labeled the "promotional course," participants consider seven themes: what it means to be a woman; dating, marriage, and family; work; society; and the center's methodology. Session by session, participants move from the personal to the political, hearing and discussing how larger struc-tures impinge upon themselves as women and as workers. After that, theme six is devoted to explicit consideration of the personal as politi-cal. In the final theme, participants pledge themselves to the level at which they are disposed to commit themselves.

Center Worldviews

The center experience calls upon participants not only to reorient their worldview, but also to act on that worldview. Not all participants are prepared to invest the necessary energy to fulfill this obligation; a worrisome attrition rate, increasing over the years to more than half in the 1982–1983 course, tends to occur after the two-week session or somewhere in the next eight weeks of similar course intensity. For the majority of those women who remain, commitments are fulfilled at a personal rather than network or organizational level, as a later section describes.

But what is this worldview? Is it one in which class-conscious indus-trial workers act on their common interests under conditions of depen-dent capitalist development? Taken to its logical implications, such a worldview invites skepticism about the prospects for change within the given political–economic system, and thus prompts ideologically one inspired activism toward transforming that system. Or is the worldview in which socially conscious women organize themselves to ameliorate their conditions and solve local community problems? The implica-tions of this worldview would require skill building for reformist politi-cal action. The center curriculum contains mixed messages of both worldviews, diluting the effect of either one, as developed in the follow-ing sections on content.

Still, other consistent themes cohere in the curriculum. First, the

conception of politics as structured power inequalities permeates discussions of history, work, and family. Also, data collection is impressed
upon people as a necessary complement to social action. Further,
participants learn to look sociologically beyond blaming individual
victims for their problems to the social structure. Finally, constantly
stressed is how women are and should be active social actors; hereto-
fore their activities have been undervalued. Finally, group action is
promoted as more effective than individual care.

Curriculum Content

Despite the consistencies, the fundamental contradiction between
radicalism and reformism remains, as outlined below. After the initial
promotional course, participants maintain the same pace of concentrated, action-oriented learning for eight weeks in what is called the
"basic introductory course." It is divided into eight sections, in the
following order:

I. WOMEN AND WORK:	Men and the Transformation of Nature
	History and the Modes of Production
	Salaried Work and Valuation
II. WOMEN AND WORK:	Political Economic Divisions of the World
	Capitalist Expansion and Transnational Production
III. WOMEN AND FAMILY:	Family: Reproductions of the Labor Force
	Domestic Work Subsidizes Salaried Work
	Sexual Relations Equal Power Relations
IV. WOMEN AND COMMUNICATION METHODS:	Public Transmission of Models of Consumerism
	Movies, TV, Radio, and Magazines
	Communication Methods in Capitalist Structures

V. WOMEN AND EDUCATION:	Capitalist Societies Capitalism, Socialism, and Popular Education Education in Mexico
VI. WOMEN AND POLITICS:	Participation of Women in Politics Analysis of the Mexican Political System Marginalization and Democracy
VII. WOMEN AND SOCIAL CHANGE:	Macro-Structures of Women's Participation in Social Change: Gender and Class Violence and Nonviolence as Struggle Strategies
VIII. LABOR RIGHTS:	Associations Unions Strikes

REFORMISM

Key parts of the course contain a reformist thrust, which suggests that participants need to identify community problems, analyze their causes and solutions, and work in groups to solve them within the given system. For example, two workshop exercises involve group discussion aimed at developing solutions for such problems as unemployment, education, drug addiction, family planning, abandoned children, minimal municipal services, malnutrition, and the exploitation of domestic and industrial workers. In workshop reports, participants attributed the causes of the problems to a lack of money or to some vague structure. Solutions invariably involve the formation of committees, although in some workshops there was skepticism about success in being heard by the corresponding authorities. Beyond creating a group, little insight exists on how to make the system work for people faced with such problems. In another exercise on women and communication, participants analyzed local newspaper articles on group action to explore motives, causes behind cases, action methods, and local solutions; later in collective sessions, comparisons were made of workshop reports. In that section as well as in the section on women and education, participants concluded that only solutions agreeable to the capitalist class are possible. The interests of the dominant class are discussed as fundamental barriers to a liberating education or to a free press. As such, does it really make sense to pursue reformist strategies? Why bother trying?

RADICALISM

Other parts of the curriculum emphasize large, distant, and abstract structures which make group action essential, however much such action pales in power compared with these structures. The two sections on women's work are analyzed in terms of women's domestic and salaried work and women's reproduction of the labor force in the context of historical changes in the mode of production. Participants learn about capitalism and socialism. After discussing capitalist expansion, rich and poor nations are compared, and participants judge the merits of the New International Economic Order (NIEO). Once in small groups discussing how to make NIEO a reality, participants grope with this complex issue and come up with idealistic goals and ultimately feeble strategies, citing "no more wars," "military money to be used to help humanity," and "more communication, education, and agreement between countries." Participants also learn a new language to explain their experiences in sessions on women and global corporations. They draw pictures in workshops of octopus-like corporations with tentacles stretched all over the globe. They sit in classrooms with maps covering the walls and sense the vast internationalism of their experience. The maquila industry is discussed in terms of the search for cheap, young female labor; industry mobility to other countries and thus the insecurity of employment; the U.S. tariff codes; the risks workers face in organization; and the government's supportive posture of foreign industry. The enormity of it all surely immobilizes some participants. The determinism with which topics are introduced suggests a certain folly in trying to penetrate this leviathan, particularly when strategy discussions do not go far beyond calls for forming groups and analyzing problems. Indeed, participants expressed fears after the global session with such questions as "What will we do if they [maquilas] go?" "Why do they fire older workers?" "What's the solution?" In this worldview, the long-term solution to problems would entail short-term tragedies that participants well recognize.

POLITICAL ACTION

Ultimately, the explicit sections on politics could bring this all together with solid information on what is the current status, what strategies work and don't work, and how women workers fit into the process of influencing the system. Only twice is the women and politics theme addressed in the curriculum, first in the promotional section, and later, toward the end of the introductory course. Each time, explicit female political action is described in terms of suffrage and equal rights politics. Participants hear about European and Mexican suffragists who struggled for equal rights and involved themselves in social reform. Presumably here, rather than in the later abstract, and as participants criticized, poorly understood "gender and class" session, participants could have developed insight into class-based women's politics. The political feminism described is a "rights"-oriented, class-based, national feminism, seemingly rather distant from local industrial workers. Details of the Mexican political system are not outlined, nor are strategies for influence. Still, popular marginalization as well as the basic rights to participate are stressed. Follow-through on these themes was, however, limited to a discussion of nonviolence over violence as general political strategy.

The political section promotes reformism without suggesting tools for effective reformism, but it still reminds participants of a larger structure to induce skepticism about prospects for reformist success. This is revealed in the following examples of comments from workshop reports, as answers were laid forth for questions posed in the lecture. Vagueness and confusion are apparent.

In response to the question, "What do you understand by politics?" three reports refer to politics as the social structure that influences all; while another, that politics are rules imposed over time; and still another, the art of governing. One group reported that they used to think it referred only to the upper class and the president; as such, the curriculum legitimizes politics as "mass" rather than "elite" activity only. Two groups interpreted politics as mass participation, involving everything and important to one's personality. Two more spoke of women's equal rights, with one making reference to a woman governor. Reports generally concluded that it was as important for women to participate as men.

In another session, groups were divided to answer questions about the Mexican political system. In the group which addressed the question of whether there was democracy in Mexico, three-fourths said no, owing to the absence of a free press. Another group, considering the question of what characteristics the future President should have, declared that he should be honest, just, and conscious of his responsibilities to help the public and make common cause with peasants and workers. On a question about their level of interest in party politics, almost half supported greater national interest in the humble people. One-third had little or no interest, while just under one-fifth expressed interest in viewing parties critically and pressuring them. Finally, on the question posed about how people define their participation in party politics, almost half said they were passive spectators, while the rest voted with varying degrees of interest. These sessions appear to maintain an image of a system which acts on people rather than one which encourages people to act on the system.

In a later session on women's participation in social change, workshop participants concluded in response to a question about the real possibilities for women's participation that they have the same rights and capacities as men to take part in decision making. But where to go from here? And toward action on which worldview? Participants would still have great distance to cover. Not surprisingly, many women do not move beyond empowerment once completing the course, as the next section reveals.

Course Participants

To trace the center's effects on women's empowerment, two samples of in-depth interviews are drawn upon. The first consists of an approximate 20 percent sample of 165 past participants of center courses who attended a 1982 Christmas reunion after contacts through letters, media notices, and word of mouth. These 31 women were selected to provide representative responses from participants in the various courses from different years. Approximately a third each participated in the social work and teacher's aide courses, thereby underrepresenting the nurse's aide trainees who typically constitute about half of the participants. The second consists of a 10 percent sample of the 1982–1983 participants, resulting in 9 of the 40 who finally completed that year's high-attrition course of 102. Transcripts of taped interviews were analyzed for the changes in consciousness and action that participants attribute to involvement with the center.[6]

Personal transformation does not occur immediately, during or at

6. This emphasis on attitudes *and* action avoids the common limitation of studies on the
   effects of consciousness raising, which tend to examine attitudes alone. See the review
   of results in Nassi and Abramowitz.

the end of a course, but becomes integrated in people's life experiences over time. Past participants, while older and less educated,[7] are more seasoned in work and organizational experience. As such, the priority emphasis on past participants avoids the usual problem of impact studies which do not give participants sufficient time to integrate change (Nassi and Abramowitz, 1981:381). Of the younger, current cohort, only two had primary education and all lacked organizational experience. Indeed, when queried about organizations they would like to belong to, only three mentioned labor-related groups.

Personal Empowerment

Virtually all women in both samples were personally empowered as a result of their course experience. The women view themselves as autonomous, responsible actors. Some say they now "have words" for their experiences. Others see their experience as linked to that of other women, and group solutions are posed for problem solving. Virtually all report the center's positive effect on their daily lives and can give concrete examples of that. One said she used to be intimidated and was later able to face up to a boss who harassed her. Others said they now understand better how things work and are linked together. Still others read, watch, and analyze the news more critically as a result of the course. For several, participation literally "opened their eyes," as they put it. Survey results comparing 1982–1983 course participants with a similar group indicate statistically significant advances in assertiveness and more independence (Young and Vera, 1984:32).

For current participants, this personal growth meshes with acceptance of and identification with feminism. Participants define feminism alternatively as male–female equality, women's liberation, the progress of women, and the advancement of women's rights. Although questions about feminism were not asked of past participants, interviews concluded with respondents outlining their view of the "ideal woman." Participants commonly responded that an ideal woman is in control of her life, that she makes decisions, solves problems, is interested in improving herself, and is equal to a man. For many, an ideal woman is educated and intelligent, she works and contributes, and she is aware and responsible, involving herself in causes. One said an ideal

---

7. Two fifths of these older participants had no education beyond primary.

woman does not look at herself as male or female, but as a complete person, with or without a man. Some respondents even rejected the question altogether, claiming all women are ideal in their own way.[8] For the current group, a different but similar question on the type of woman they admired revealed similar characteristics.[9] Such views are clearly feminist, defined in a broad way.

An autonomous, more aware, and self-assured style serves as a foundation for other forms of empowerment. Identification with feminism provides a framework into which women fit, explaining and legitimizing their goals. Yet participants adhere to a traditional sex division of occupational labor, raising questions about the thoroughness of their feminism. When asked what other courses they would like to see offered, all—even the most politically conscious—called for traditionally female skill courses, ranging from cooking, sewing, and pastry making to secretarial training. Several others called for courses that are gender-neutral in the Mexican context, such as communications, journalism, accounting, and English. Courses now train women for occupations toward which they aspire, but none challenges the given sex division of labor in Mexico.

Not only do participants by and large accept the sex division of labor, but they also seek training in either the domestic sphere or in a semi-professional field, suggesting individualist-oriented career mobility orientations. When asked about job preferences, virtually all aspired to semiprofessional work in, primarily, teaching, social work, and nursing. Their dissatisfaction with industrial labor, clearly reality-based and possibly their motive for seeking the center experience, was perhaps aggravated in their course experience. Yet when queried about their opinion of the maquila industry as a whole—as were current, but not past participants—only one of the nine expressed absolutely negative views. While recognizing the low pay, stress, and exploitation, the others judge the industry as capacitating people and providing jobs which women and single mothers need. The center's goal to promote group mobilization around the identification of class interests has little

8. For exceptions, one past participant of a modern dance class expressed the traditional ideal of a good cook and housewife who helps her husband and children. Another said she had no idea how to answer the question, but said in response to a question about where she thought she'd be in five years, "perhaps married."

9. One exception was a participant who admired a woman who makes sacrifices for her family.

concern for these women. If now, however *temporarily*, part of the working class, these women seek escape as soon as possible. Yet the likelihood of such flight is dim.

Network Empowerment

As a result of the center, some women are now involved in informal organization or solidarity networks of working women.[10] For these women, the center experience extended beyond the interpersonal relationships of individual and family life to workplace friends.[11] Women use their consciousness to struggle for better conditions even if on temporary, ad hoc, and informal bases.[12] These, and the following more fully empowered women, are politicized.

Judith, aged 28 and from the teacher's aide course, led an informal group of a dozen or so women to protest air contamination at the factory where they work. For this, as well as for arguments with her supervisor, she was fired. Now that she is what the industry would call a "troublemaker," her job tenure at factories lasts no longer than a year. For her, personal improvement over the last five years is measured by her increased consciousness and her ability to make others conscious.

Luz, aged 32 and a member of an evangelical church group, now acts as a spokesperson for workers at her plant. Since the administration and teacher's aide courses, she says she has been able to recognize violations of workers' rights. Recently she was named a member of her plant's Committee on Security and Hygiene, and she feels she has been able to make changes.

Sylvia, aged 32, is a plant supervisor of thirty employees and likes her work. In an evangelical church group in which she has influence, she believes her center experience, first in social work and then in open secondary, helped to infuse her work with better human relations and to see workers as people rather than instruments. She criticizes the tendency for some maquila workers to quit after the course—as did

10. Religious participation is not included when it predates course experience and when groups concern themselves solely with proselytizing.

11. Young and Vera (p. 49) judged one-third of the women to have experienced increased interpersonal influence.

12. See Peña's (1980) review of literature on the militancy of women factory workers, which contrasts with images of them as docile.

several at her plant—and then be unable to move into jobs the course trained them for.

Rosalia, aged 27, had been in contact with the center even before taking the modern dance course she was unable to complete. She has always been interested in exploitative conditions at work, such as low pay, restrictions on the use of the bathroom, and fumes in the plant. The labor speaker at the center helped her in work protest activities, for which she was eventually fired. But she is now married to a man who won't permit her to work.

Several past participants lacked the same intensive involvement as those above. Rocio and Raquel, both aged 27 and from the social work course, volunteer at the center. Lorenza, aged 27 and a confidence employee at her plant, sympathizes with, but is not trusted by, union members at her plant. Two others, Rita and Magda, cite union affiliation but interview transcripts were unclear as to whether the course inspired such activity. Seven of the thirty-one past participants now have employment as a teacher's or nurse's aide. Whether these jobs empower women depends on the degree to which they infuse their work with the social consciousness stressed in the courses.

Organizational Empowerment

Only the unusual course participant goes beyond informal networks to establish organizations or work within existing organizations. These women commit themselves regularly to social action, but face the stiff, risky challenge of creating organizations or penetrating them from within. The already experienced flourish, others flounder in frustration, while still others are virtually immobilized.

One woman, Leticia, aged 26 and trained as a social worker, was fired for organizing workers around labor problems. Working hours were to be cut for the factory workers, but supervisory personnel were to continue full time. Leticia worked with others to form an independent union and was then laid off, but the group achieved their principal goal and those let go got severance pay. Leticia is the only one of the politicized women to secure a job for which center courses prepared her; she is now a teacher's aide.

Juana, aged 44, who took the nursing course, was a long-time neighborhood leader even before the course experience. A local PRI voter activist and neighborhood group leader, she has helped her predominantly female group secure piped water and electricity. The course has infused her political activity with new qualities. For example, she says she now realizes the health problem in her neighborhood, which lacks even a drugstore, and is working with others to get a dispensary located nearby. She has intricate knowledge of how to make municipal government work for the neighborhood.

Asacia, in her mid-twenties, belongs to both the Confederacion Trabajadores Mexicanos and to a socialist party. She's disgruntled about the prospects for change in the existing political system, but views her party as offering some solutions. For her, the center lacks an ideology: It critiques capitalism, but offers no solutions.

Consuelo, aged 22 and from the teacher training course, belongs to a union at the plant and serves on committees relating to transportation and labor problems with bosses. As for moving into leadership, she is disillusioned with the union. She is tired of listening to male leadership; she says the union, rather than really defending workers' rights, works closely with supervisors and promotes sports activities.

Conclusions

Although women are empowered by the center experience, most are personally empowered but not politicized and involved in networks or organizations. However, course participants now have the personal foundation for other types of empowerment which require major behavioral changes, not to mention risks and energy commitments.

Why, even with the center's dedication to women's empowerment, do only a minority of participants move beyond the personal to politicized network or organizational empowerment? The reasons for this vary. First, the center has not identified past politicization to recruit participants for existing follow-up courses. Several characteristics of the politicized women stand out. They average 28 years of age in contrast to the nonpoliticized, who average 22. Education has little bearing on participants' likelihood of becoming politicized. If anything, politicized women's education is limited to primary.[13] Recruiting an older, more experienced group may produce more politicized women. Finally, politicized women tend to come through the teacher's aide course or

---

13. This conclusion, though, must be tempered with their higher age and the more limited educational facilities during their adolescence.

social work course more often than the nurse's aide course. While the older, politically effective Juana received nursing training, she came to the center with many years of political experience behind her.

Second, the mixed reformist—radical signals of the curriculum create confusion and even immobilization among participants. Ultimately, though, the preprofessional training and internship stacks the deck of course time toward reformism. Messages from the first ten weeks may undermine satisfaction with reformist activity, however.

Third, in its attention to larger structures, the center's *political* thrust takes a back seat to its *economic* emphasis. Indeed, participants' political efficacy, or perception of their ability to influence the system, is perhaps hindered more than helped. Participants secure limited knowledge of political channels, personalities, and strategies to foster change.

Yet the challenge represented in a political empowerment approach cannot be underestimated. An organization like the center would be hardpressed to cope with this challenge, *even with* curriculum and recruitment changes.

Unless women's informal organizational empowerment develops—whether in autonomous revolutionary groups or in pressure groups and institutionalized parties and their affiliated organizations (including unions)—female powerlessness is unlikely to be altered. Yet this point reveals the special challenges of empowerment in Mexico.

In Mexico, autonomous revolutionary organizations are tolerated while they are weak, but ruthlessly repressed once they gain strength. The incorporation of marginal groups into mainstream politics, power-enhancing as it may be for groups *prior* to formal incorporation, results in a rigid reinforcement of the status quo and its dominant class. Contrary to accepted wisdom in participation studies, vertical *linkage* as strength-enhancing (Uphoff and Esman, 1984:xii, 13) may ironically signify impotence for marginal sectors in the Mexico context, as various studies document (Anderson and Cockroft, 1966; Eckstein, 1977:33; Velez-Ibanez, 1983:23). Once "integrated" into the existing system via pressure group or union reformism, participants were controlled rather than empowered.

This big picture of Mexican politics poses a dilemma for organizations like the center. Whether consistently reformist or revolutionary, marginal groups challenging the political system face stiff challenges. All this points to the fundamental importance of personal empowerment, an activity in which the center excels. Resilient, personally empowered women *choose* whether to act or not in networks and organizations. By so doing, they have acted on their personal i.. , the most basic of political actions.

References

Anderson, Bo, and James Cockroft, 1966. "Control and Cooptation in Mexican Politics." *International Journal of Comparative Sociology* 7 (March): 11–28.

Cohen, John, and Norman Uphoff, 1977. *Rural Development and Participation: Concepts and Measures for Project Design, Implementation and Evaluation.* Ithaca, New York: Cornell University, Center for International Studies.

Eckstein, Susan, 1977. "The State and the Urban Poor." In Jose Luis Reyna and Richard Weinert (eds), *Authoritarianism in Mexico.* Philadelphia: Institute for the Study of Human Issues.

Fernández-Kelly, María Patricia, 1983a. *For We Are Sold, I and My People: Women in Mexico's Frontier.* Albany: SUNY Press.

———, 1982, 1983b. "Alternative Education for Maquiladora Workers." *Grassroots Development.* 16(2): Winter 1982; 7(1): Spring 1983: 41–45.

Nassi, Alberta, and Stephen Abramowitz, 1981. "Raising Consciousness About Women's Groups: Process and Outcome Research." In Sue Cox (ed), *Female Psychology.* New York: St. Martin's.

Peña, Devon, 1980. "Las Maquiladoras: Mexican Women and Class Struggle in the Border Industries." *Aztlan* 11 (Fall): 159–229.

Staudt, Kathleen, 1985. *Women, Foreign Assistance, and Advocacy Administration.* New York: Praeger.

Stevens, Evelyn P., 1973. "Marianismo: The Other Face of Machismo in Latin American." In Ann Pescatello, (ed), *Female and Male in Latin America.* University of Pittsburgh Press.

Uphoff, Norman, 1980. "Political Considerations in Human Development." In Peter Knight (ed), *Implementing Programs of Human Development.* Washington, D.C.: World Bank Working Paper No. 43.

Uphoff, Norman, and Milton Esman, 1974. *Local Organization for Rural Development: Analysis of Asian Experience.* Ithaca, N.Y.: Cornell University, Center for International Studies.

Velez-Ibanez, Carlos G., 1983. *Rituals of Marginality: Politics, Process, and Culture Change in Urban Mexico, 1969–1974.* Berkeley: University of California Press.

Young, Gay, and Beatriz Vera, 1984. "Extensive Evaluation of ——— in Cd. Juárez." Unpublished report submitted to the Inter-American Foundation, 1984. (Referencs to the name of the organization have been removed.)

III
CULTURE, CREATIVITY, AND RELATIONS OF REPRODUCTION

8

Shipwrecked in the Desert:
A Short History of the Mexican Sisters
of the House of the Providence
in Douglas, Arizona, 1927–1949

Raquel Rubio Goldsmith

In 1930 one of the sisters of the Company of Mary, remembering their arrival in Douglas, Arizona, wrote, "The House of the Divine Providence as our beloved Reverend Mother calls it, and in truth it deserves this name, as it has come sailing like a little boat in the infinite ocean; having as its pilots and guides, the Sacred Heart, Our Miraculous Virgin, the Immaculate Mother, St. Joseph and Our Blessed Virgin Mother, whose protection we have felt at all times, in the spiritual, as well as in the material (Archive).

The House of the Divine Providence was not established in the infinite ocean by these Mexican sisters, but in the inhospitable desert of the southeastern corner of Arizona, forced there by another of the political upheavals in Mexico, where the government and the Catholic Church were engaged in one of their periodical accommodations. (Meyer and Sherman, 1983). Fortunately these sisters were far from the patriarchal centers of power in their own church and felt only the results of the government's offensive. President Plutarco Elías Calles had "confiscated and taken their properties." (Archive). All those schools and convents. Who knew what would come next?

After the Church protested the government decrees by announcing the end to all rites and the closing of the churches, one of the Catholic

This chapter was previously published in *La Chicana/Mexicana*, The Renata Rosaldo Lecture Series, Monograph No. 1. Tucson: University of Arizona Mexican American Studies Center, 1985. Reprinted by permission.

families in Agua Prieta, Sonora, worried that the "terrible persecution
and the dangers" would reach their niece, Sister Mercedes Barceló,
offered to seek asylum for her in the United States. Sister Barceló was in
Pachuca, Hidalgo, where she had traveled to follow her vocation when
she received the letter. The offer to intercede with American authorities
in Douglas, Arizona, in order to arrange for her safety, was well received
by her superiors. Upon being apprised of the offer, the mother provincial in Mexico City saw the guiding hand of the founding mother trying
to save the general novitiate. The Company of Mary had establish its
General Novitiate for the Americas in the city of Aguascalientes. It was
from here that the teachers for their schools in Mexico and Cuba went
forth after their long formation. Undoubtedly, these fine people on
the border with the United States, including the relatives of Sister
Barceló and the Knights of Columbus, would allow the Company of
Mary to continue the work of its novitiate in safety and tranquility.
Surely the founding mother had interceded and opened the path to the
temporal salvation of the Order.

    And so it was that when the small group of fourteen sisters arrived in
Eagle Pass, Texas, the Sisters of the Divine Shepherd there were glad to
open their doors to them while the final arrangements were approved
for the move to Douglas. Bishop Daniel J. Gercke of the Diocese of
Tucson received two members of the group who sought a haven for
their religious community, and decided that the decision on housing
was not his, but rather that of the parish where the sisters were asking to
be housed, the parish of the Immaculate Conception. The Reverend
Fernando Rousselle, a French priest who understood the difficulties of
working in a foreign land, gladly received the sisters. He soon found a
temporary shelter for them at the Convent of the Sisters of Loretto.
Within a month, a small house on H Avenue had been located for them
through the help of the Knights of Columbus. This retreat, away from
religious persecution in Mexico, was surrounded by Mexican families
who worked for the copper smelters in the town. Most of these families
were also refugees from the revolutionary chaos and violence of northern Mexico.[1]

    So it came to be that in their search for tranquility and safety, far from
government antireligious sentiment, they found a tiny corner on the
earth—Douglas, Arizona—where they could "occupy themselves with

---

1. The oral history project I conducted included unstructured interviews with Rebeca
   Gaitán, María Luisa Elizondo, and Refugio Burguess from July 1978 to June 1980. These
   three women spoke extensively about the Company of Mary.

the tasks proper to their state" (Archive). Their harbor, that high desert community of Douglas, Arizona, was an American industrial boom town and the apex of a mining triangle that the mining company Phelps Dodge had created on both sides of the Arizona—Sonora border. The area encompassed to the west the mines in Bisbee, Arizona, and to the south the mines in Nacozari, Sonora. Douglas, designed with broad streets so that the mule-drawn ore carts could easily turn, was 260 miles west of El Paso, 250 miles southeast of Phoenix, and 550 miles east of San Diego, California (Douglas Chamber of Commerce, 1929). The mother provincial may not have received the information distributed by the Douglas Chamber of Commerce during these years, but if she had, she would have learned that by 1929, Arizona was the largest copper-producing state in the country, and that in the area north of Douglas, the Sulpher Springs Valley, could be found some of the best stock-raising country in the state, as well as fertile soil with enough ground water to become a top producer in alfalfa hay, alfalfa seed, cotton, winter wheat, and cantaloupes. The 15,800 souls, some Anglo, some Mexican, some Chinese, and some black, used the three city parks. The brochure did not say it, but their children went to eleven schools where they were segregated—except in the Catholic school of Loretto—according to ethnicity or color (Elizondo, 1978—1980). (The few Yaqui children were sent to the Mexicano schools.) According to the town boosters, the future was filled with promise of "ample opportunities to the men of wealth, the large, and small ranchers, to sportsman, dairyman, poultry raiser, businessman, professional man, trained worker, and to all who want to improve their health and add ten years to their lives (Douglas Chamber of Commerce, 1929).

An economic thumbnail sketch reinforced the optimistic forecasts made by the Chamber of Commerce. In 1928, it was not absurd to think that Douglas would become the greatest copper-smelting city in the West. The smelters had a combined output of 271,400,00 pounds of copper, 5,970,118 ounces of silver, 105,641 ounces of gold, and 14,500, 000 pounds of lead in that year. Other large industries listed were the Arizona Gypsum plant, Paul Lime's Quarry and Brick Plant, and the railway shops. All Douglas industries employed a combined total of about 2200 people with a payroll of $310,000 a month. The banks boasted of deposits totaling $5,261,839.44. This carried promise of great prosperity for all (Douglas Chamber of Commerce, 1929).

Economically and commercially, Douglas compared favorably to Aguascalientes. Surely the provincial was right in sending the general novitiate to Douglas in 1927. The Company of Mary would also prosper, and prosper in familiar surroundings. The gateway to Sonora resounded with Spanish in the southern and western barrios. It was heard in all those places close to the border, going north from First to about Seventh Street and then west of the downtown area. These were the barrios close to the smelters where large numbers of Mexican workers found employment. Rarely was Spanish heard on the other side of town, in places considered to be important, or centers of power in the community; places such as the immigration office, the court, the post office, the church, the police station, and the schools where only English, written and spoken, dominated. The sisters discovered that in Douglas, as in Aguascalientes, it was American mining companies that controlled dominant positions, while providing a wealth of jobs at the bottom scale for Mexicanos (Bernstein, 1964:56–59). But unlike Aguascalientes, Douglas was the total creation of the copper companies in a country that was Protestant. The majestic churches and convents that stood over central Aguascalientes were constant testimony of the importance most Mexicans attributed to their Catholicism.

Meanwhile in Douglas, the sisters faced the stark reality that with the exception of the Immaculate Conception, the Loretto School, and the small Mission of St. Bernard in Pirtleville, all other churches were Protestant. While most Catholics appeared to be Mexicanos, mass was said in English; the priest was French. There was of course the imposing yellow brick convent built for the Sisters of Loretto. The convent, an elementary school, and a high school were housed in its two stories. However, it seemed to serve the English-speaking Catholics more than it did the Spanish-speaking ones. Yes, the sisters had found a new and different world in Douglas (Gaitán, 1978–1980).

In this Protestant, English-speaking ocean, their little house on H Avenue became a welcome retreat. Every evening in the chapel, prayers to St. Joseph and the Sacred Heart chanted Spanish intonations to the star-studded desert heavens, thanking God for the help of those Mexican families that never abandoned them, for the support of Father Rousselle, and all others who helped them find a new home in this ocean of desert and dust. But not for one moment did they fail to face the new reality that they were religious and political refugees, foreigners in an alien land of Protestants who spoke English. The obstacle that loomed incessantly was that of language. The problems arising from lack of space, scant funds, and even scant food appeared insignificant in comparison with the lack of knowledge of English. After all, the main temporal purpose of their order was education of a caliber and excellence that had been unrivaled in Spain, France, Holland, or Mexico

(Vásquez et al., 1981; Foz y Foz, 1981:96). The best possible education for young women, both the rich and the poor, was their overriding task. But without English, how could they carry it out?

Since that day in 1607, when Pope Paul V approved the order established by Jeanne de Lestonnac, with the same rules as that of the Company of Jesus, every sister that entered the novitiate knew that her life would be devoted to the principles of excellent education for young women (Foz y Foz, 1981:96). Their founding mother not only had given the second half of her life to this purpose, but had also committed a good portion of her fortune to it (Foz y Foz, 1981:67–71). For religious women from Mexico, this commitment was further determined by the woman who established the order in Mexico, María Ignacia Azlor, daughter of the governor of Texas and lieutenant general of the Spanish army of the New Spain (Foz y Foz, 1981:53). In 1926, Mother Guadalupe Rizo deemed it most fitting that the order should find a home in the deserts in the far north of what had once been Mexico, because it was from here that María Ignacia Azlor had traveled to Spain to enter the Company of Mary. She knew that by bringing this order to New Spain, young women in Mexico would have a chance of getting a good education (Foz y Foz, 1981:83).

This wealthy, noble *criolla* grew up on the Hacienda de Los Patos in Coahuila. She is described by historian María Foz y Foz as an eighteenth-century woman enriched by an uncommon culture, who worked and struggled all her life to bring education to all young women of New Spain. She was endowed with a refined religious sensibility and imbued with ideas of the Enlightenment regarding the value and social function of education. So it was that on the eleventh of January, 1755, through the Company of Mary, she opened the first public school for women in Mexico City. Her entire inheritance was put into this enterprise (Foz y Foz, 1981:218).

Throughout Mexico, the graduates of the schools of the Company of Mary soon became known for their scientific training, as well as for their spiritual and moral teachings. Following the principles of the time meant educating the needy as well as the rich (Foz y Foz, 1981:265–267, 359). Education for the ones who could not pay the tuition had to be supported by those families who could easily afford it. The wealthy not only sent their daughters to the Company of Mary, but also contributed handsomely to the financial needs of the religious community. They did so because the schools not only provided excellent intellectual training, but also developed an environment proper to the elevated status of their pupils. To be *bien educada* in the Mexican and Spanish sense of the words demanded the formation of proper ritual behavior and demeanor, along with the development of high moral character. All this, the sisters of the Company of Mary did for their charges. And as long as this purpose was carried out successfully for the wealthy, they were able to offer free education for the less well-to-do. Girls from poor families could also aspire to admission to the schools. The pedagogic commitments made by the order were to be fulfilled and not set aside when times were difficult. The compliance with its social and cultural responsibilities were important and not insignificant even if the religious and moral training they provided had a primary place. So it was in their schools in Europe and Mexico (Foz y Foz, 1981:359).

So it would be in Douglas, Arizona. The House of Divine Providence was bound to carry out the goals set by their order, that is, to establish a convent and a novitiate for the Americas. The education of young women, another primary purpose, would have to be reexamined in light of the lack of funds, diocesan approval, and the lack of knowledge of English. But the first worry was finding suitable quarters for the novitiate. Their order had strict rules governing the use of space. To have a community of nuns that could fulfill their spiritual growth and at the same time be actively involved as teachers with both boarding and day students required special accommodations that responded to the varying needs. The Company of Mary had developed a building code for all its convents and schools, outlining the delineations and requirements needed for good spiritual and academic development. This had to be considered (Foz y Foz, 1981:240−244).

The little house on H Avenue was small. That was one of the first challenges—to find larger accommodations. Every spare penny from each donation was saved, and the vegetable garden was used to provide as much of the food as possible. Saving the meager earnings from the new kindergarten gave them hope that soon they would find something larger. One of the sisters remembers, "Clearly we could see that St. Joseph was the active agent from our Heavenly Father, that made us start to buy four lots that were next door to this building, without even dreaming that very soon this building would become our property" (Archive).

Mr. and Mrs. Packard, owners of the large house adjoining the four lots, decided to sell it to the nuns. They were known to have said, "We never would have been moved to sell the house if it hadn't been for the Religious of the Company of Mary" (Archive). Father Rouselle expected Mr. Packard to request an exorbitant sum for the house and was very surprised to hear that it would sell for $12,000. "Upon knowing this, we fell apart with gratitude to our Good Father, which, through the certain mediation of St. Joseph, was assuring our most desired grace, that of owning our own residence, which could be adequately adapted to the needs of a novitiate in this an advantageous place" (Archive).

By 1936, despite persistent economic crises, Sister Ana Serrano, a visionary and an optimist, initiated a remodeling plan. After the chapel had been remodeled and enlarged, a large refectory and two classrooms were built on the first floor, all facing a wide corridor leading to the chapel. This area proved useful for catechism classes and for the kindergarten children. On the second floor a dormitory was added, which had enough room for ten roomettes and two protruding terraces, one facing east, the other west. This remodeling made the final appearance of the house that of a dovecote. A gallery with baths and a staircase leading to a second patio, which was the most common passage to the novitiate were built. That year, 1938, the Feast of Christ the King included the dedication of the new additions. The benediction of the house and the chapel added to the solemn festivities.

The acquisition of this large house and the adjoining lots, as well as the corresponding remodeling, culminated in a residence worthy of the presence of two imposing wood-carved statues, one of the Sacred Heart and the other of St. Joseph. For twelve years, these saints had stood over the chapel of the provincial house in Mexico City. Their vigilance brought hope and serenity amidst turmoil and threats in anticlerical Mexico. The mother superior feared for the destruction of such holy objects, and when Sister Serrano and Sister Aceves arrived from Douglas in 1938, she allowed them to return with the statues.

The dovecote provided space for all the activities of the House of the Divine Providence, but it did much more than that. For Mexicanas in Douglas, the convent symbolized a Mexican world; the way of life left behind on the other side of the border. For many years after its completion, no other building in Douglas housed Mexican culture so grandly. The functional beauty of the convent of the Company of Mary, known as *El convento de las madres Mexicanas* stood proudly for that which was pushed into corners in the rest of the town. There, Mexican culture found a home, and Mexicanas in Douglas reveled in its existence, feeling pride along with comfort (Gaitán, Elizondo, Burguess, 1978–1980).

For Mexicanas torn from their churches in Mexico, the convent became the center for comfort and solace as the sisters reinforced the way of life and beliefs these women wanted for themselves and their young ones. Mexican mothers, in agreement with the nuns, could insist their children's behavior show respect for the church, the family, and all elders. *Saluda, mi hija, despidete, no retobes.* Modesty in dress and respect in behavior were virtues not to be left in Mexico. But if some customs stressed serious and quiet demeanor, others reveled in the joy of celebrating religious feasts and Mexican national holidays with processions, *actos*, and hymns in Spanish.

The chapel, with its Virgin de Guadalupe, offered hope not available from the saints and images at the Immaculate Conception. In the chapel, with the *madres mexicanas*, the women could enjoy those customs familiar to them in Mexico. They also delighted themselves in the using of bright colors and real clothing for their saints. These Mexicanas were certain the communal prayers uttered in Spanish reached heaven sooner (Gaitán, Elizondo, Burguess, 1978–1980).

Not only had the House of the Divine Providence acquired a large building, and remodeled it to meet the specifications of their order, they had given Mexicanos and their families a grand Mexican symbol uplifting their spirits and reaffirming dignity of being Mexicans in Protestant Anglo Arizona. Yes, Mexicans also could have a place of their own.

With the building ready for more novices, the order could proceed with the training of those young women devoted to the service of God and to the education of the young. Vocations thrived in surroundings conducive to the spiritual and temporal development of each young woman who entered the novitiate.

Since the time of foundress, Jeanne de Lestonnac, through the times of María Ignacia Azlor and on to the twentieth century, the nuns had attracted outstanding women to their communities. The history of the order in Mexico demonstrated the dynamic, intelligent, and spiritual leadership initiated by María Ignacia (Foz y Foz, 1981:503). But in Douglas, where would they find the young women for their novitiate, if they had no schools in the United States or even in Douglas from where vocations could emerge and grow? How could they attract the best families in Douglas to support their work, when the "best" families didn't even speak Spanish? Their daughters attended Loretto school or public schools. The wealthy ranching families of Sonora who wanted a better education for their daughters sent them to Catholic boarding schools in El Paso or Tucson (Gaitán, Elizondo, Burguess, 1978–1980). The sisters realized that their new environment would not bend on certain issues.

How did they meet these challenges? How were they able to attract young women to their order?

The novitiate is of prime importance in every order. After all, it is the only way it can survive as a community and fulfill its purposes. Without new postulants it would cease to exist. Knowing this, the Company of Mary made great efforts to attract the best young women in the communities they served. But the times had brought both political and economic difficulties, constantly challenging the best efforts of the order. The problem also struck at the very essence of their order. Whom could they educate in their new country? How could they bring in the daughters of the wealthy into their school to help pay for the poor? Where could they begin?

New strategies had to be formulated if the order was to survive and comply with its pedagogic goals. This has been the reality for political or religious refugees at all times. From that first moment they realized this, the sisters began to weave step by step the new with the old, the Mexican known and comforting, with the new and often puzzling American ways. They contributed what they knew, and learned how to live as part of a Mexican working-class community in an Anglo town, and to live and to serve a Mexican community that was on the lowest rungs of the social and economic ladder.

Upon examination it appears that the nuns of the House of Divine Providence followed several roads in resolving the problem of the recruitment of new novices. Ideally these young women could be found in their communities in Mexico and in Douglas. However, events, some national and some local, presented obstacles to that ideal goal. There is no doubt that their reduced number concerned the religious community intensely. "At the end of 1931 there were six novices and four professed. A number truly insignificant for a general novitiate!" (Archive). This same year, the mother superior asked Sister Barceló, who was on her death bed, to intercede when she reached heaven, for more vocations, but 1932 began even worse. One of the novices professed, reducing the novitiate further. The anxiety was such that "we would each say to ourselves, 'My lack of fervor must be the cause that God does not hear our prayers.' " (Archive). But lack of fervor was not the only obstacle. The anticlerical activities in Mexico made it difficult for Mexicanas to recognize and nourish their vocations, while the economic crisis in the United States had resulted in severe restrictions on Mexican immigration (Cardoso, 1980). These two calamities translated into serious difficulties because it was from Mexico that the order had always found its members. The House of the Divine Providence found itself facing strict immigration requirements on the part of the United States government. In 1927, the year after their initial arrival, the religious community had lost Mother Jesusa Seuscun, the energetic director of the novitiate and the founder of the catechism classes. After a year, despite the clear indications of the dangers that awaited her in Mexico, she had to return to Mexico because it was not possible for her to normalize her residence status in this country (Archive).

Over the years the sisters were seen literally walking hundreds of miles through the streets of Douglas, soliciting letters of recommendation to present before the office of immigration or the American consulates in Mexico. One letter after another was requested, some from the parish pastor, some from the various members of the Knights of Columbus, who were in a position of respect, and some from other prominent members of the community (Elizondo, 1978–1980).

If 1933 is proof of a successful year, the intercession of Sister Barceló in heaven seems clear.

> But the intercession of Sister Barceló must have reached St. Joseph, because it was on the 19th of March, on the feast of St. Joseph, that the consulate in Mexico gave the passport to two; and on the 21st of the same month, the consul in Sonora approved a passport for a third; also on the 13 of April four postulants in the chorus and one co-helper received passports; and in August a ninth entered. She was the niece of Mother Guadalupe Rizo (Archive).

The sisters found different problems when they tried to recruit novices in Douglas. In the first place, the total number of Catholics was not large in comparison to the pool of Catholic young women in Mexican towns and cities. Anglo young women who considered monastic life were not attracted to the Mexican order. Their interest directed them to the Loretto Sisters. But even more disheartening was the fact that many of the Catholic Mexican families were from northern Mexico, where the religious monastic tradition was almost nonexistent. The imposing religious complexes present in central Mexico never flourished on the northern frontier. Under these conditions the sisters found their task difficult and their efforts scantly fruitful. Some Mexican mothers in Douglas who had daughters also found convent life unattractive. They felt life there was too difficult. And it was.

The sisters had to cultivate infrequent vocations in order to transport the novices into a spiritual status of grace required to become a bride of Christ. Those years of spiritual preparation, as well as the road to perfection in the virtues of discipline, humility, and especially obedience, had to take place under persistent supervision and vigilance. The sister encharged with the novitiate was selected for her virtue because she was not only a guide, but a model that coaxed her disciples over all the obstacles of pride, egotism, and the lack of piety and spirituality. These master nuns had to know how to discipline and guide without rancor, lighting the darkness and struggles of the soul with love and charity. And, the *novicias* had to be trained in the pedagogic arts so that they could also comply little by little with that obligation of the order (Archive; Foz y Foz; 1981:99; Bernstein, 1976:74−76).

After the longer period of initiation the novice examined her conscience, the purity of her soul, partook of long reflection and prayer, until she could take her vow of obedience and dedication to Christ. It meant that all else was left behind, even family responsibilities (Gaitán; Bernstein, 1976:41−55). Young daughters grasped this freedom, even if their mothers had their doubts.

For many centuries in the Christian world, in many Catholic societies similar to the Mexican one, the convent and the veil of the bride of Christ were one of the few places that allowed a woman to live outside the family with a status of respect. For women who wanted a life of study, the monastery was the only place where that opportunity was available to them. Even with the limitations imposed by the patriarchal church, the convents of the Company of Mary opened more intellectual doors than almost any other institution open to Mexican women.

In reality, monastic life was such a revolutionary notion, that many families, perceiving that they would lose control over their daughters, tried to prohibit their entrance into the convent. A story is told of one of the sisters who arrived in Douglas in 1929 who had faced family opposition. Mother Guadalupe Rizo remembered:

Being a young girl, she aspired to the contemplative life in order to give herself totally to God, ignoring men and the brilliant future that awaited her after having completed an excellent professional career and being the object of the special love of her own. In spite of the great opposition that she encountered in her family to enter the religion, she did not dismay nor lose her will until she achieved it, happily suffering the sorrow that some of the family members—those she loved best—never even spoke to her again. It was not until her nieces, going to the school and loving her dearly, became the liaison that newly reunited [sic] the loved ones. In spite of having great family sorrows, she always presented a happy and resigned face; always forgetting herself in order to comfort others (Archive).

The convent was seen by young Mexicanas, daughters of workers, as one of the few places, maybe the only one, where Mexican women were in charge legitimately; women who had no husbands or fathers, or brothers, or children tying them down. For example, many of the young women studied under Mother Ana Serrano, the nun with a vibrant and picturesque look who never appeared restricted by her order. On the contrary, they viewed her life as one of travel and adventure. She was constantly off to Los Angeles, Mexico City, even Rome. It appeared to the young Mexicanas that the world was hers. There were no other Mexicanas in Douglas, within view of the young women, whose circumstances came close to comparing to Mother Serrano's life of glamour (Elizondo and Burguess, 1978—1980).

Mother Serrano was a pianist. She taught piano lessons in the formal receiving room of the house. There, the advanced students were efficiently scheduled around her other duties, and often the most interesting part of the lesson was the wait in the entrance lobby, sitting on a highly polished oak bench, listening to her subdued conversations behind a wooden frame screen. Not only did she demand musical perfection, she was unbending in her practice requirements, and she also made certain that parents were kept well apprised of their children's progress. Student recitals were organized once a year.

Her recital room was a model of high-quality housekeeping. Well-placed vases abounded with freshly cut flowers from the *jardín*, and the window panes shone brilliantly. The floors, waxed to perfection, reflected the gleaming white walls. Flowers were not enough to overcome the odor of waxed floors, and only the slight spring breezes, mixed with the sulphur smelter smoke and the fragrance of blooming roses whisking through open doors, kept a balance of aromas. The four-foot statue of the Immaculate Conception dominated the salon, watching over all while it received the anxious petitions from performers for her assistance in execution of the musical selection. In those moments, Madre Serrano was the ruler of the universe, or at least so she seemed to her students and maybe even to their mothers. Here was a place, in a town of inferiority, where their children were important.

She disciplined without accusations. She made demands with reasons. What a woman! What young Mexicana seeking to find a bigger world would not see the service to Christ as the most marvelous opportunities. "After all, God gave so much and was in all places" (Elizondo, 1978—1980).

These Mexican sisters dressed with long heavy black habits that gracefully fell from the waist to their ankles. The white still wimple outlined their faces while covering the neck with a semicircular frame for the lively and always dark eyes. But most attractive was the long heavy rosary that fell, wrapped in the folds of the long skirt, hanging from the waist, then rising halfway up, hooking to the large crucifix at the waist. This elegance almost succeeded in covering up the shining black shoes, of leather made soft from wear, that showed several layers of soles held together only with the coaxing of shoe wax (Gaitán, Elizondo, and Burguess, 1978—1980).

Furthermore, the young souls were impressed upon hearing the sacred litanies under the gaze of St. Joseph of the Sacred Heart. While singing those mesmerizing Gregorian chants on First Fridays in a chapel filled with light, happiness, and joy, young Mexican women found themselves breathing air heavy with perfume incense. The oxygen was made scarce by the many burning candles. It even seemed that the multicolored embroidery on the altar cloth ran and jumped, almost coming to life (Elizondo, 1978—1980). How could any young woman remain closed to this assault on her senses in a time when radio or an occasional Hollywood musical were the closest she came to this stimulation? There was no other place in the dusty desert town where she could legitimately recognize the passionate feelings of her being; only in the love of God was it permitted for a woman who was not married, and had no children, to recognize such profound feelings. For the young Mexicanas, the House of the Divine Providence not only was a sacred place but was also a place of magic. It fed the spirit and the imagination like no other place in their lives.

But then, why were there not numerous postulants for the novitiate from among the Mexican young women who took lessons at the convent? One answer involves the mothers of the young women. Older women looked at a reality that escaped the mesmerized and inexperienced young women.

> Look, my daughter, do anything you want as long as you don't go into a convent. Because with anything else, you can stop or change and end it right there. But if you go into the convent, well, there you have to stay until you die. Because even if you leave the convent, you leave with those ideas of guilt. Those ideas don't fit in the outside world. The first thing they teach is that . . . guilt. Even if you leave, you leave with no hope (Gaitán, 1978—1980).

These mothers understood that while the lives of their daughters were circumscribed by many limitations, an education and a bit of luck could provide more opportunities for them than had ever existed in the rancherias and the isolated pueblos of Sonora and Chihuahua. Those were the kinds of opportunities that did not exist in the convent. Of course it was difficult for them to find jobs in Douglas where Mexicanas did not seem to fit the specifications for teachers or nurses. But there was always the possibility of going somewhere else. These mothers saw changes around them that their daughters did not see as changes. The world in Douglas belonged to the modern era, while the convent was closer to the old life of the pueblos in Sonora and Chihuahua.

There was another problem. In 1940, as it had been for centuries past, women needed a dowry if they were to enter the service of God. Few were the young Mexican women in Douglas who could possibly put together a dowry in those years. Those who did not have it could enter, not as teachers-to-be, but rather as the scrubwomen of the convent. That was not at all attractive in comparison with the possibilities of even domestic work in town (Gaitán, Elizondo, and Burguess, 1978–1980).

Consequently, despite the attractions many young Mexicanas and Chicanas felt for religious life, they were not able to overcome the obstacles presented by their families and the lack of a dowry. But even if they did not join, the experience was unforgettable. For the rest of their lives they would remember the strength and pride that nourished their spirit as they worked at the side of those marvelous Mexican nuns. There were one or two young Mexicanas from Douglas who postulated, but from 1926 to 1949 the majority of the novices came from Mexico (Archive).

The problems with the recruitment of novices were closely related to the other new challenge that confronted them. The Company of Mary was dedicated to education. How to provide this was another question. They found that numerous changes were necessary if they were to fulfill this purpose in English, in this Protestant Anglo desert town that was now their home.

The impossibility of establishing a school for girls such as they had in many parts of Mexico became obvious. The parish already boasted of a magnificant parish school in the hands of the Sisters of Loretto. This order had been invited to this mission land by the first Bishop of the Dioceses of Tucson in 1907. Since that time the Sisters had provided an excellent education to the Catholic community that could afford to pay the tuition. It was used by families both in Douglas and in Agua Prieta, but it tended to be for the well-to-do. If there were scholarships, they must have been few and rarely given, because no one knew anyone who had received one (Gaitán, Elizondo, and Burguess, 1978–1980). For the majority of Mexican families in Douglas, struggling economically even before the Depression, this parish school was not an alternative. Yet, at the same time, it was precisely by serving these well-to-do families that the Company of Mary in Mexico had been able to offer a free education to poor girls in Mexico.

A regular elementary or high school was out of the question, not only because of the lack of economic support, but also because the sisters could never acquire the teaching credentials required by the State of Arizona. They debated whether to eliminate their dedication to education and devote themselves exclusively to the formation of novices. But it was precisely through their work of educating the young that they trained the novices in pedagogy and supported themselves financially. The vegetable garden, as big as it was, was not an economic solution. They were not a mendicant order. It was through their paid pedagogic tasks that they developed new vocations. The financial success they had in Mexico was a result of their excellent teaching.

In Douglas this challenge caused a redirecting of their purpose. If their pedagogic temporal purpose was not feasible by being Spanish-speaking Mexicans in an Anglo community, they would adapt to the needs of the Mexican Catholic children. Here was a group that needed their service and dedication. Surely it was "divine grace" that pointed out the path and the solutions. During the next fifteen years they implemented a series of educational activities, some traditional and others innovative to meet new needs of Mexican families.

They taught kindergarten with a complete Spanish curriculum. In 1940, it became bilingual. This was the first bilingual school in Douglas. Second, they started an academy for needlework and painting, going back to the oldest tradition of female education in convents. It was something they could implement for Spanish and English speakers who happened to be interested. Third, they offered piano lessons, English instruction, and business courses. For the older young women there were lessons in morality and religion. There was also the continuous teaching of catechism and preparation for First Communion (Archive).

Catechism for Catholic children in Douglas had been taught by the parish. However, Immaculate Conception priests, usually non–Spanish speakers, found that most children spoke little or no English.

So in the summer of 1926, when Father Rouselle heard that the sisters of the Company of Mary on H Avenue were teaching catechism, he was more than pleased. He quickly proceeded to ask the Mexican nuns to assume the responsibility of catechism for all the Mexican children in the parish.

Mother Seuscun had proposed the classes to her superior because "the poor little Mexican children have no school and no occupation other than to wander around their barrios causing trouble and playing pranks that are sometimes costly" (Archive). Mother Seuscun defended the unorthodox proposal to the superior, saying that the novices had to be trained in pedagogic methods, and if there was no school attached to the convent, they could at least teach catechism. The sisters of the Company of Mary had never taught catechism in isolation from a total curriculum, but in this new land, it was catechism these children needed. The sisters would serve God in this way. However, catechism was taught with lessons that included the history of Mexico. They taught the Mexicanitos Bible history with numerous allusion to Mexico and its culture (Gaitán, Elizondo, and Burguess, 1978–1980). Here again the nuns brought the Mexican past into the desert Anglo town.

Father Rouselle quickly invited the mother superior to help the parish. He explained that he was very busy and that at this time he was alone. One of the sisters wrote, "Father Rouselle explained that although there were some very nice young women who helped him out, they could not maintain the necessary discipline with the children that in their majority were of people of . . . humble beginnings" (Archive).

The parish children needed to learn proper behavior. The sisters took over the new catechism classes and slowly "domesticated" the little boys and girls. "But the worst of all was the deterioration of the pretty pews that are in the church for the use of the faithful. . . ." And so it was that "during the hour of catechism we had to be on top of them exhorting them not to scratch the pews with their feet or hands" (Archive).

When Reverend Davis was pastor, the parish was remodeled due to a fire on the altar. The master sister wrote, "It occurred to these priests that we could occupy ourselves more freely with the catechism if the children were brought to our house and that way the church would remain in a better state" (Archive).

Once the decision was approved, the sisters began teaching catechism in their house on October 2, 1934. In eight short years the nuns had redirected their educational services to the needs of the Mexican children of Douglas. In addition, they even expanded it to Pueblo Nuevo, a community of Mexicanos outside of Douglas.

As a result, in May 1935, the Douglas parish held Holy Communion for 130 children and in Pueblo Nuevo for 70 children. This, despite the fact that the majority of the children were so poor that their mothers could not buy them white dresses, suits, or shoes. Many people, especially the Anglos, gave them what they needed to participate in such an important ritual.

After 10 years in their new land, the changes in their *apostolado* were clearly seen. The reality of serving a Mexican community was translated into fundamental changes in the type of education they offered. By 1945, the result of about 20 years in Douglas showed they had developed a "civilizing" institution for a community with a short history, even though they never established a girls' school.

For 20 years they "tamed" the children in kindergarten; they opened the ears of those boys and girls to the rhythms and harmonies of Bach and Mozart; and they prepared hundreds of children for the moment at the altar for their Holy Communion. For 15 years they organized, each time bigger and better, the procession of Corpus Christi, filling the Mexican spirit and imagination of each child with inspiring hymns and prayers (Elizondo, 1978–1980). The celebration of the well-known Mexican rituals, all in Spanish, elevated each and everyone to God in their own language; the language of the Mexicanos.

The sisters of the Company of Mary created a tiny world whose center filled the Mexican feminine soul with pride. It was a refuge, where in the tranquility of the entrance lobby and under the watchful protection of the statue of the Virgin of Fátima, Mexicanas could come, to ask for everything from advice to food, to shelter, or simply come to share some good news. It was a refuge created by women for other women and their families. Never did the sisters battle the patriarchal church that determined their limits. Rather, they created a Mexican world for women inside this system of men and its male goals within an Anglo Protestant society. The patriarchal ideas reigned, but these women found ways to ignore certain rules and adapt them to the needs of the women they served. Theirs was not a female ideology. Nevertheless, they recognized the two aspects of their female world, the feminine and the feminine ruled by patriarchal ideas. And they sought to accommodate both.

But it was in 1949 when the sisters gave their maximum gift to the Mexican women of Douglas. After years of negotiation and efforts, they honored that most important feminine symbol of the Mexican culture. Overcoming the obstacles, Mother Ana Serrano was able to arrange the placement of the image of the Virgin of Guadalupe among the other saints of the parish church. The Mexican Virgin would leave her niche of honor in the chapel of the House of the Divine Providence and take her new home in the parish of the Immaculate Conception. On February 12, 1949, starting with a procession from the chapel, led by Father Francisco Ramos, the Mexican Virgin arrived to adorn the walls of the wood-paneled altar and the walls of the Immaculate Conception. One of the sisters recalls:

> Once the image was blessed, she received the honors of the children of the city who let their emotions show, some with the silent language of tears and others with fervent *plegarias* which came from the most intimate of their hearts. For us, religious, who live in foreign lands, it is the love of the Virgin of Guadalupe, with which we count in order to take souls to God. Through experience we have learned that Mexicans living in this region whose faith seemed extinguished, [sic] when we speak to them of the love of our Excellent Lady and Mother and help them up the road to her devotion, their faith awakens. It is with those Mexicans that have spent some time in some corner of the Mexican homeland that the lively scenes of the filial love to the Virgin are most clear (Archive).

Conclusion

This community of religious women accepted their new *apostalado* at the side of the sons and daughters of Mexican women. Children of the Mexicans who worked for the mining companies and for the railroads were brought to the civilization of Mexico. After several centuries of occupying a privileged place in the societies they served, these nuns had to share the lower rung in the Anglo world, sharing the discrimination with those they served. The community of religious experienced it, adapted to the new town, and created a Spanish-speaking oasis of comfort, and glory in the *Vírgen de Guadalupe*, all with prayer, tranquility, and *paz* amid the hostility.

References

Archive, 1928—1950, Company of Mary—House of the Divine Providence. Unpublished manuscript. Douglas, Ariz.

Bernstein, Marcelle, 1976. *The Nuns: A Firsthand Report*. Philadelphia and New York: Lippincott.

Bernstein, Marvin, 1964. *The Mexican Mining Industry, 1890—1950*. Albany, N.Y.: SUNY Press.

Burguess, Refugio, interviewed July 1978 to June 1980, by Raquel Rubio Goldsmith. Author's personal manuscript.

Cardoso, Lawrence, 1980. *Mexican Emigration to the United States 1897—1931*. Tucson: University of Arizona Press.

The Catholic Encyclopedia, 1910. Vol. IX, Robert Appleton Co.

Elizondo, Maria Luísa, interviewed July 1978 to June 1980, by Raquel Rubio Goldsmith. Author's personal manuscript.

Foz y Foz, Pilar, 1981. *La Revolucíon Pedagógica en Nueva España: 1754—1820*. Vol. I. A.C. México. Madrid: Instituto de Estudios y Documentos Históricos.

Gaitán, Rebeca, interviewed July 1978 to June 1980, by Raquel Rubio Goldsmith. Author's personal manuscript.

Douglas Chamber of Commerce, 1929. *Land Anytime in Douglas, Arizona by Plane, Train or Auto.*

Meyer, Michael C., and William L. Sherman, 1983. *The Course of Mexican History*. New York: Oxford University Press.

Vásquez, Josefina Zoraida, Dorothy Tanck de Estrada, Ann Staples and Francisco Arce Garza, 1981. *Ensayos Sobre Historia de la Educacíon en México*. El Colegio de México, México, D.F.

9

Changes in Funeral Patterns and Gender Roles among Mexican Americans

Norma Williams

The main objective of this chapter is to investigate the funeral ceremony— a crucial life cycle ritual—as a means to understanding some of
the changes in gender roles that have taken place among Mexican
American men and women in central and south Texas. As we will
observe, the roles played by men and, in particular, by women, in
carrying out their activities during funeral ceremonies have undergone
important revisions during the past few decades. And these shifts in
gender role expectations and behavior during funeral ceremonies are
indicative of broader changes in gender (or sex) roles that are taking
place among Mexican Americans.[1] Overall, our effort adds to the very
limited information on gender role changes among Mexican Americans, especially among women (e.g., Melville, 1980; Mirandé and Enríquez, 1979; and Baca Zinn, 1980).[2]

I wish to thank all my respondents, who spent many hours helping me understand the
changes that have occurred in an important aspect of Mexican American life. I am
especially grateful to my mother's sister, Mrs. Casimiro Naranjo, Jr., who lives in
Falfurrias, Texas, for going over the manuscript with me so carefully and making many
helpful suggestions.

1. The terms of "gender roles" and "sex roles" are not used consistently in the literature.
   Nowadays many social scientists advocate the use of "gender roles" when referring to
   biological ones. Still, such prominent sociologists as Davis (1984) continue to use the
   term "sex roles" when discussing cultural factors.
2. The sociological literature on contemporary Mexican American women, or Chicanas, is
   limited. In addition to the literature cited, a number of articles focus on decision

Although our focus is upon changing gender roles, an examination of funeral patterns provides a highly useful means of getting at certain significant changes in gender role relationships. Therefore, we shall first discuss traditional funeral ceremonies, and the particular roles carried out by women and men, and then look at the changes in these ceremonies that have been occurring in recent years. As far as can be determined, this forms the first effort to study changing gender roles among Mexican Americans by looking at a central life cycle ceremony—that relating to death.

The Data Base for the Study

This investigation relies upon a number of data sources. First, I drew upon my field research on changing family patterns in Austin, Texas. One aspect of this research was to examine the relationship between changes in such life cycle ceremonies as *compadrazgo* (baptism), marriage, and funerals and changes in the conjugal and extended family structures. Herein we focus upon funeral rites, in part because the breakdown of traditional patterns in this particular ceremony seems to have been associated with dramatic shifts in gender role patterns. The effects have not been quite so striking in the case of other types of rituals.

In my research in Austin, in-depth interviews were conducted with 22 working-class couples and 21 couples from the professional/business group. A deliberate effort was made to focus upon those groups within the Mexican American community in which social and cultural change is most likely to be apparent. (Most research on Mexican Americans to date has been upon the poor.) At the same time, we sought to take account of variations among status groups. Occupation and education were the two criteria employed to differentiate the working class from the professional/business group. Among the professional/business couples at least one spouse had a college degree and the other at least some college education; in most cases both spouses had college

---

making by husbands and wives in the family context. See, for example, Ybarra, 1982. However, these recent studies on decision making, which typically emphasize equality between men and women, must be used with caution. For empirical data that bear on this issue as well as a review of relevant literature, see Williams (1984).

degrees. Most of the working-class couples interviewed had completed high school but had not attended college. (A detailed account of the design of this research appears in Williams, 1984.)

The respondents (typically in the age group 25 to 50) were asked, for example, to describe what they recalled about traditional funeral rites—including the wake, the service at the church and at the graveside, and the social gathering afterward. They were also asked to describe the changes they perceived to have taken place. The formal interviews were supplemented by data from participant observation involving many respondents.

Second, I took data from published accounts—by, for instance, such social scientists as Rubel (1966) and Moore (1970)[3]—that describe traditional funeral ceremonies among Mexican Americans. Third, in the summer of 1982 I carried out in-depth interviews with five persons in the Corpus Christi–Kingsville area who were in their seventies and eighties. In particular, I asked the respondents what they recalled about funeral rites in the 1920s and earlier. Fourth, I conducted a number of informal interviews with Mexican Americans from different parts of south Texas. Fifth, I observed as a participant many Mexican American funerals in the Corpus Christi–Kingsville region. I observed over a number of years many of the patterns and changes described, although I have used these observations only when they have been confirmed by the accounts of a number of other respondents.

Theoretical Background

Little, if any, research conducted by American sociologists has taken life cycle rituals as a point of departure for analyzing gender roles. Thus, some recognition of the place of these rituals in traditional social orders, including Mexican American social life, seems necessary. Also, the general perspective we employ regarding social and cultural change needs to be made explicit if the resulting data and analysis are to be understood.

If we examine the work of van Gennep (1960) and Fried and Fried (1980), we find that life cycle rituals have been an integral aspect of many

3. Joan Moore is one of the few sociologists who has recognized the importance of studying Mexican American ceremonies surrounding death. For an account of funeral ceremonies in Mexico see, for example, Osuna and Reynolds (1970).

traditional societies in different parts of the world. The patterns within traditional Mexican American culture are no exception. Although life cycle ceremonies, such as those associated with a young woman's fifteenth birthday *(quinceañera)* have been observed, it has been the rituals relating to birth, marriage, and death that have been central to the lives of traditional Mexican Americans. *Compadrazgo*, in particular, continues to be singled out for special attention by social scientists, though they provide few details about it. What is apparent is that these markers of life cycle transitions have been closely connected with family and community activities.

The importance of rituals in creating and maintaining social solidarity has been recognized by scholars such as Durkheim (1915), Geertz (1973), and Eliade (1957). With respect to Mexican Americans, life cycle rituals have been a significant aspect of the religious belief system and, as such, a key element in the folk Catholic heritage that is part of the Southwest. Life cycle rituals have played an important role in integrating the individual into the conjugal and especially, the extended family system, as well as into the broader community. These life cycle transitions also serve to highlight certain kinds of gender role relationships among Mexican Americans. We shall give special attention to the "separate domains" participated in by men and by women, and to changes in these domains over time.

If we follow Eliade, the leading present-day authority on comparative religion, sacred rituals have been a means by which people recapture and maintain the past. It is through sacred ceremonial activities that the members of a community attempt to recreate the past (cf. Turner, 1981), although people's memory of what the past is may shift over time. In a more general sense, it is through rituals that persons seek to maintain continuity with past role expectations and social relationships. Because of the importance of rituals in maintaining a stable conception of the past, we can begin to perceive how a decline in the social demands of these rituals might affect people's everyday life—gender role expectations in particular.

When we discuss changes in the nature of rituals and gender roles, we face the question as to why these changes have taken place. One source of disagreement relates to the controversy among sociologists regarding assimilation (e.g., Portes, 1984). One group of sociologists assumes that we can most adequately explain what is taking place among minorities such as Mexican Americans by adopting an assimilationist perspective. Gordon (1964), among others, has been prominent in advancing this orientation. It is, however, inadequate for understanding, for example, changing funeral ceremonies and the accompanying modifications in gender roles among Mexican Americans. The respondents in my formal interviews as well as the persons involved in my participant observation do not conceive of themselves as assimilated. We must take account of their perspective. In fact, changing funeral rites and the associated changes in gender roles serve as an avenue for raising serious questions about the assimilationist perspectives.

·Although we can not dwell upon the problem in this chapter, we shall examine the matter of how Mexican Americans, as part of a broader social order (cf. Lieberson, 1982), are responding to social forces—urbanization, industrialization, and bureaucratization—that are bringing about changes in values and social structure in the society as a whole.

Traditional Funeral Patterns

In studying traditional Mexican American patterns in the Southwest, particularly in the "border area,"[4] we should be aware of the problems of determining what is "traditional" in Mexican American patterns. When most social scientists speak of traditional Mexican American gender roles and family arrangements—as well as traditional life cycle patterns—they focus upon data from the 1940s, 1950s, and early 1960s (an example is Alvirez, Bean, and Williams, 1981). However, if we take Paredes's (1958) work as a guide for our research, we come up with somewhat different results, for he is describing patterns that held for the early part of the ceremony.

When describing traditional funeral ceremonies, we will most often refer to patterns from the 1940s and 1950s (the historical period for which we have the fullest data). However, some attention must also be given to patterns insofar as data are available concerning funeral cere-

---

4. The changes in rituals as one moves from preindustrial to industrial (or modernizing) societies is a complex one. In the Western world, for example, new rituals seem to have been created as older forms have disappeared. For a general review of some of these patterns see the discussion by the historian Payne (1984). He also provides a survey of various scholarly works on this topic.

monies prior to the 1940s—before the widespread industrialization and urbanization of the Southwest.[5] Also, we should be aware of the fact that there have been variations according to social class. Unfortunately, the information regarding these variations is inadequate.

As to traditional funeral patterns it was the custom in small towns and rural communities in Texas to distribute *esquelas* to announce a death and subsequent funeral arrangements. These printed announcements gave the name of the deceased, the time and place of the wake (or rosary) and the funeral service, and the names of the immediate family members as well as sons-in-law and daughters-in-law. These formalized public announcements were delivered to the homes of friends and relatives. The *esquela* reproduced in Figure 9.1 provides an illustration. Also, a *corona* (wreath) or a purple ribbon was hung on the front door of the home of the deceased. This served as an announcement to the community that someone in the family had died.

Traditionally the body was viewed in the home, and some other preburial activities, including the wake *(velorio)*, were held there. Some of my respondents in the Corpus Christi region remember a time when a local carpenter would make wooden caskets. These were reportedly decorated with purple satin if the deceased was an older person. The color blue was used for a little boy and pink for a little girl.

5. One question that comes to the fore in any study of the traditional patterns of Mexican Americans concerns the relationship of the Mexican American culture to that in Mexico. This is a difficult problem area that has not, in my judgment, been adequately discussed by social scientists. It seems necessary to sort out conceptually and empirically the ''cultural,'' ''political,'' and ''economic'' spheres and to examine carefully the interaction among these spheres.

Although Mexican Americans share certain patterns with persons in Mexico, it is also apparent that the ''border area'' on the U.S. side differs appreciably from that in central Mexico. For example, the Catholic Church seems to have historically exerted less control in the border region than in central Mexico (e.g., Weber, 1981). Thus, the social and cultural patterns relating to religion, and to some degree life cycle rituals, seem to have diverged in these two areas.

In this chapter it is not possible to examine the similarities and differences between Mexican Americans living in the Southwest and Mexicans living in Mexico. Also, it is not feasible to examine the differences among Mexican Americans in the United States, for there is considerable diversity within this group. Some persons might even question whether Austin, for instance, should be viewed as part of the border area. It is at least on the edge of the general border area, if for no other reason than that the Austin respondents have strong cultural and social bonds with south Texas.

Derramad sobre su alma el perfume santo y salvador de las oraciones.

Haz, Señor, que sonriente contemple tu Faz divina, gozando de eterna dicha.

Hoy

a las 3:50 A. M. falleció en el Seno de la Santa Iglesia Católica Apostólica Romana la

Sra. Braulia G. Williams

a la edad de 77 años, 11 meses, 10 días.

Su esposo D. J. Williams, sus hijas May W. Pineda, Lola Williams, Bessie W. Villa y Velia W. Cruz; sus hijos Robert Lee, Allen, Walter, Delbert J. Jr., y David H. Williams; hermanos José G. Cantú, Catarina G. Byington y Tomasa G. Zárate; hijos políticos Pedro Pineda, Gilberto Villa, Lucía C. Williams, Lupita M. Williams, Basilia C. Williams y Lola V. Williams, nietos y biznietos y demás familiares, profundamente apesarados participan a usted tan triste acontecimiento y le suplican eleve a

Dios Nuestro Señor

las oraciones q' su piedad le dicte por el eterno descanso del alma de la finada y se sirva asistir a la inhumación del cadaver que se efectuará mañana, a las 5 de la tarde, partiendo el córtejo fúnebre de la casa número 110 de la calle W. Noble a la Iglesia del Sagrado Corazón donde tendrán lugar las honras fúnebres y de ahí al Panteón de esta ciudad, donde se despidirá.

El Rosario será en la Agencia Funeraria Howard-Williams hoy a las 8 de la noche y después el cadaver será velada en la casa de la finada.

Falfurrias, Texas, Marzo 8 de 1954

Imprenta LA VERDAD Falfurrias

FIGURE 9.1

According to the older respondents, the body was prepared by the women for viewing in the home. Apparently in the 1920s a person's body was placed on top of a table covered with white sheets. White candles were set at four points around the body so as to form a cross. In addition, the body was placed so that the feet of the deceased faced the door. The body was not embalmed. Therefore, large blocks of ice were set underneath the table to keep the body cold, and a coal iron (made of heavy cast iron) was placed on top of the stomach of the deceased to keep it from becoming bloated. The body was kept in the home for only one night, and the burial was the next day.

In more recent decades (the 1940s and the 1950s), the body typically was embalmed in a funeral home and then taken to the house where the wake was to be conducted.[6] The casket was left open. The upper half of the body was shown and the hands were crossed with a rosary between them. It was not uncommon for the wake to be held for one night. In most cases, during the wake a rosary was held for an hour or so. The rosary was led by a priest or, if a priest was unavailable, by an older woman closely identified with the church. If a rosary was not held, the family and relatives would attend church on Sunday and pray for the deceased.

During the wake, people spoke softly out of respect for the deceased. The people also prayed, the women more than the men. Some of the women cried loudly. The women also took care of the children and the home. In other words, they worked very hard during the wake.[7] While the women were in the house working and crying, the men typically stood outside the home reminiscing about the deceased, eating *caldo* (vegetable soup), drinking black coffee and beer. These contrasting patterns symbolize the separate domains of men and women.[8] Yet it should be emphasized that both men and women gained their sense of identity and self-worth by carrying out these routines and rituals, as well as others associated with the familial−religious sphere.

---

6. See, for example, "Death in Austin" (1984), p. 65.
7. Silva (1984), writing in the *Falfurrias Facts*, observes that young men "would dig the grave while the wake was going on in the home of the deceased. Often we would dig the graves at night because people died one day and were buried the next. The cemetery there is very old and it was not unusual to dig up bones and skulls." Silva's observations, though brief, lend support to the patterns discussed in this chapter.

During the wake a few friends and/or relatives stayed with the body all night as a sign of respect. Early in the morning neighbors, friends, and relatives brought homemade food, especially *pan dulce* (sweet rolls), for the mourners, who included out-of-town guests. Again, it was the women (including those in the extended family and friends in the community) who cooked and served the food.

Funeral rites also called for the wearing of somber colors. Women typically wore black and covered their heads with a black veil (even in the home). The men had a black band on their upper left arm and usually wore white shirts and black trousers only during the funeral rite. (Gray clothing, particularly for women, seems to have become accepted a few decades ago.) The somber colors were a sign of respect for the deceased and stood in sharp contrast to the bright colors worn during the marriage rite and the *compadrazgo* ritual, which were viewed as festive occasions.

Funeral ceremonies played an important role in the lives of the participants for several reasons. For example, funerals were a means of heightening social solidarity among friends and, in particular, among extended family members. Funerals were highly emotional events at which grief was publicly displayed. But it was the women, not the men, who would cry loudly when friends and relatives came to the home to offer condolences. And it was the women who cried loudly at the funeral service, and especially at the graveside. This overt public display of emotion provided a strong integrative support system for the grief-stricken members of the immediate family, and this kind of activity also forged a strong bond among extended family members, such as grand-parents, grandchildren, uncles, aunts, nephews, nieces, and cousins. In other words, the women played a central role in the expression of emotional solidarity within the extended family and among close friends.

The funeral ceremony was carried out within a Catholic Church (when a church existed in the community). Otherwise it was conduct-

8. The concept of "separate domains" for men and women has been emphasized by certain scholars studying gender (or sex) roles in traditional cultural settings. This pattern emerges from the work of Smith and Wiswell (1982) on a traditional Japanese village. This conceptual framework also seems to be important for understanding patterns in Muslim society. See the work, for instance, of Papanek and Minault (1983) and the lengthy review of relevant literature by Papanek (1984). I am indebted to Andrée F. Sjoberg for calling this body of writings to my attention.

ed at home or at the graveside. The Catholic religious tradition or, more accurately, the folk Catholic heritage that evolved in the border region provided the setting within which the funeral ceremony was conducted.

In the early part of this century, after the funeral service, the casket was carried on the shoulders of six men to the graveyards. In later decades wagons were used. These were covered with white sheets and pulled by two horses. A few respondents mentioned the use of carriages resembling stagecoaches with hearses arriving later.

Typically there was a ceremony at the graveside (supplementing that in the church). Some of the loudest crying by women occurred as the body was lowered into the grave, for this act symbolized the finality of the separation from the living. A significant aspect of the service at the graveside was the presentation of the crucifix (which had been placed in the coffin with the deceased during the rosary) to a member of the immediate family. The widow or widower (or other close family member) would then display the crucifix in the home, and it became an important symbol of respect and remembrance of the dead. Also, immediately after the graveside service the family members and guests completed the funeral rite by walking past the grave and made the sign of the cross as they sprinkled a handful of dirt on top of the coffin.

After the funeral ceremony, friends and relatives convened at the home of the deceased and continued to express their grief. On the evening of the burial, members of the conjugal and the extended family, as well as close friends, assembled at the house of the deceased to pray. Once again, the praying was done primarily by the women. According to the religious practice known as the *novenario* (novena), one should pray for the soul of the deceased for nine consecutive nights, beginning with the evening of the first rosary. An older woman considered close to the church led the prayers, which lasted for half an hour. The recitation of the rosary was to ensure that the soul of the deceased would rest in peace and attain salvation. Afterward, friends stayed and visited for an hour or two.

But this was not the end of the mourning period. Family members typically mourned for a year or longer. They were not expected to listen to music or to attend dances. In other words, they were not to participate in festive activities or engage in behavior or display emotions that would suggest that they were happy. Often, weddings would be postponed until after the mourning period. This period of sadness symbolized respect for the deceased, and those friends and relatives provided themselves with ongoing emotional support during this period of loss.

For a year the women—that is, the wife, mother, and sisters of the deceased—would wear black clothing at all times. In practice, even in the 1940s, 1950s, and 1960s, women stayed at home except for attending church or visiting the grave site. I have been told about—and I have known—women who never went shopping during the period of mourning. And some women widowed during the 1940s, 1950s, and early 1960s wore black for the rest of their lives. This attire symbolized respect for the deceased spouse. But it also emphasized that the wife's identity was closely intertwined with, and dependent upon, that of her spouse. It was assumed that the widow would not remarry. In a fundamental sense women had no independent status outside of the familial—religious sphere. There they found emotional support in interaction with other women (or perhaps with close male relatives).

Mourners also visited the grave frequently, bringing flowers to place on the grave.[9] On the first anniversary of the death, a member of the family would ask that a mass be dedicated to the deceased. Members of the extended family would be asked to attend this mass, thereby reinforcing family solidarity.

Mexican Americans have also traditionally celebrated November 2, the Day of the Dead, at which time family members, particularly women, would go to the grave site not only to place flowers but also to clean up the area. Some persons in Falfurrias and Kingsville took their lunch and spent the entire day at the cemetery. It appears that the practice of placing food on the grave, which is widespread in central Mexico, has not been a common practice in many parts of Texas. (We should remember that in many of these Texas communities Mexican Americans were buried in segregated graveyards, though this segregation is not as fixed in some areas as in others; cf. Jordan, 1982.)

In summary, we find that in the traditional Mexican American culture women played a more important role than men in sustaining religious and family traditions, as well as the very strong emotional bonds associated with these rituals. Although both sexes expressed grief after the death of a family member, it was the women who prayed

---

9. Flowers were important in the traditional funerals. They were brought to the home during the wake and then were taken to the graveside.

the most, who cried the most, and who served as the chief mourners. Women, then, were crucial in maintaining the familial—religious heritage.

Present-Day Funeral Ceremonies and Emerging Gender Roles

This discussion of traditional Mexican American funeral patterns has sketched the main features of these ceremonies; it does not seek to present all the details. I intend to facilitate an understanding of certain basic changes in funeral rites that have occurred among Mexican Americans during the past few decades, especially as these changes relate to gender role expectations and behavior.

On the basis of my research, it seems apparent that prior to the 1940s, 1950s, and early 1960s, changes were occurring in some aspects of funeral ceremonies—for example, with respect to embalming. However, during the past few decades dramatic changes have occurred, and these changes have had considerable impact on gender role patterns. In general, only persons in their mid-thirties or forties or older remember some of the typical features of the traditional funeral rite. Persons in their twenties and thirties or younger do not recall the body being viewed in the home, they do not remember the mourning patterns of women, and they are unfamiliar with the use of *esquelas*. A number of the younger persons whom I interviewed have never heard of *esquelas*, and thus we must assume that a number of the older funeral traditions are not mentioned to younger Mexican Americans.

We would expect the use of *esquelas* to have more or less disappeared. A few persons whom I interviewed remembered seeing them used in small communities in Texas as late as the mid-1970s to announce a death, the wake, and the funeral. Today, however, they have been replaced by announcements via the mass media such as newspapers and radio.

Also, today the body is no longer viewed in the home, and the all-night wake is no longer practiced. One of my respondents in the professional/business group in Austin had viewed a body in the deceased's home in a small community in south Texas (which had no funeral home) in the 1970s, and one might expect this tradition to survive in a few outlying districts. But the increased role of the funeral industry, along with the heightened formalization (or bureaucratization) of funeral activities, has meant that the deceased is no longer in the care of a family member.

The wake, and the accompanying rosary, persists among most Mexican Americans (except for the small but growing number of Protestants). However, the wake and the rosary are circumscribed to a considerable degree by the rules and regulations of the funeral home. People no longer stay with the body all night, and this means that the intensive interaction that accompanied these rites in the past has diminished.

The funeral rites—from the wake to the ceremony in the church to the graveside service to the *novenario* afterward—seem to be in the process of simplification. (A similar pattern has taken place in society as a whole; cf. Engel, 1984.) My respondents observed that fewer flowers are being sent than in the past. Today, some people donate money instead of sending flowers. Moreover, the loud crying that accompanied the wake, the church ceremony, and especially the graveside service has perceptibly diminished. Today, women still express grief more openly than men, but their emotional responses are more quiet and controlled.

One factor in this change is the bureaucratization (including commercialization and formalization) of the overall funeral rite. As the funeral home has taken over most of the arrangements, it has brought about significant changes. My respondents have remarked on—and I have personally witnessed—situations where the funeral home director or his assistants, strongly criticized family members and friends who were sobbing loudly. The mourners were told that it disturbed other persons in the funeral home. If the loud crying did not stop, the offenders would be asked to leave the premises.

Many of my Austin respondents (as well as persons whom I talked to in the Corpus Christi—Kingsville area) have complained about the impersonal nature of funerals today. They have expressed concern that the traditional, highly personal ways of expressing grief and respect are being undermined by the formal demands of the funeral homes. Although they do not use the terminology of sociologists, they are upset by the current bureaucratization and commercialization of the funeral process. Moreover, a number of respondents are disturbed that the bereaved are taken advantage of financially during a period of great emotional vulnerability.

The depersonalization and simplification of funeral rites are also associated with basic changes in the role of religion in Mexican American funerals. All my respondents in the working class and professional group in Austin, even one or two who claimed to be non-religious, expected the funeral to be conducted under religious auspices. However, the professional/business group, on the whole, was much less devout than members of the working class. The professional group, in particular, adheres to a generalized view of what it means to be religious. They hold to what might be termed a "generalized belief system." For some persons, this has meant a greater sense of religion as a private matter. But for most it has meant a sense of religion as something more general, more abstract than that defined by traditional orthodox religion. It is apparent, on the basis of my observations, that the changes within the professional group have been much greater than within the working class and among the poor. Even for these latter groups, however, the religious belief system, as reflected in the funeral rites, has lost some of its influence. For example, the traditional *novena* lasted for nine nights in succession. Individuals may participate for a few nights but not for all nine. In this sense, women no longer sustain traditional religious patterns. Social and geographical mobility, and the demands of modern urban life, make it difficult for people to do so.

Certain other changes in funeral patterns must also be taken into account. According to my interviews in Austin, considerable change has occurred in the nature of the social gathering after the graveside service. One obvious pattern is that the women do not spend their time preparing food. There appears a much greater reliance upon fast foods. Also, during these gatherings there has been some breakdown in the separate domains between men and women, especially within the proessional/business groups. The most striking pattern is that the social gathering appears much less solemn than in the past. For many of the respondents in the professional group, the postburial get-together at the home of the family turns into a festive occasion. A number of respondents were uneasy about this trend, and a few complained that respect was not being shown the deceased as in the past. However, for a number of respondents (especially in the professional group), funerals form the last link they have to many members of the extended family. It is one of the few times that people visit with cousins, aunts and uncles, nieces and nephews. It is a time to reminisce and catch up on the news about distant relatives.

To highlight the nature of these social gatherings, I quote from the statements of my respondents in the working class and in the professional group in Austin. One working-class person observed:

After my brother-in-law died, people came over to my house. The men were playing dominoes. They were laughing and drinking. I thought it was terrible. But then I thought we needed to do something to forget [the death]. It was a little reunion. We were happy to see people—relatives we do not usually see.

Another comment:

[At funerals] you see a lot of friends and relatives you have not seen in quite a while. What starts out to be a sad thing turns out to be a joyful thing. The neighbors bring food, and pan dulce. Everything is ready for people from out of town.

Similar responses were in evidence among members of the professional/business group:

The funeral was pretty solemn. Then, after we ate, it became more festive. There were cousins, aunts, and uncles we hadn't seen in years. They came from San Francisco, San Diego, and San Antonio, and it was fun to see them. My mother didn't like it at first, but the funeral was over. We came and paid our respects.

The aforementioned patterns bear, directly or indirectly, upon what I consider the most important change in the funeral ceremony among Mexican Americans—the mourning patterns of women. From my research in Austin and in the Corpus Christi–Kingsville region it is obvious that fundamental changes have taken place within the past two or three decades with respect to the manner in which Mexican Americans mourn the dead. In the Austin study, none of the respondents had observed the traditional pattern in their own family. None expected women to mourn and wear black for a year. Although some of the older respondents remember their grandmothers following this tradition, it definitely belongs to the past.

It used to be wearing black and no music or dancing for the whole family. Now it is different; life must go on. Everything is changing.

Or:

I remember the women wearing black for a year. My grandmother wore black for years. We don't mourn anymore.

Consider some comments from the professional/business group:

My mother stopped the traditional mourning pattern when I was in high school.

The only significant death was that of my father. I didn't have any mourning. It was a sad and difficult time for me. I was going through a lot of changes myself.

One professional man noted: "My mother never had any mourning patterns." Another commented, "Mourning is not used anymore. I feel that rather than mourn we should pray."

These comments should not be taken to mean that women do not still carry out more important roles in funeral rites than do men. However, the traditional mourning patterns associated with Mexican American women have disappeared before the very eyes of many persons living today. The rapidity of this change should always be kept in mind, for many persons under 30 do not recall the traditional forms.

Implications

This chapter has examined certain aspects of changing gender role patterns among Mexican Americans in central and south Texas by studying these within the context of basic shifts in the nature of funeral ceremonies. Although examining only one facet of changes in gender roles, this particular approach has the advantage of placing changes in men's and women's roles within a concrete social and cultural context—that relating to funeral rites. Changes in the familial—religious sphere, though, as I suggest, are affected by, and are responsive to, broader political and economic forces.

If using traditional rites of Mexican Americans as a standard of evaluation, then significant changes have taken place with respect to the manner in which men and women are expected to act. The change for women has been more dramatic than that for men. Although they still play a very important role in present-day funeral ceremonies, many of the traditional role expectations have undergone fundamental revision. For example, women are no longer expected to express their devotion and life-long commitment to men, particularly their husbands, through a long period of mourning.

In a more theoretical sense, rather separate domains for men and women seem to have been characteristic of traditional Mexican American culture. These separate domains can be clearly observed during funeral rites. (Women did not serve as significant functionaries in religious and political life, but they played a major role in sustaining everyday familial and religious beliefs or values.) Although separate domains for men and women in traditional Mexican American culture were not as well defined as in some traditional agrarian societies, they were nonetheless present. Today this separation appears not as marked or compelling as it was a few decades ago.

In examining the disappearance of many aspects of traditional rites, I follow Eliade (1957), who contends that rituals are a means of recapturing the past, and that, through participation in them actors are able to maintain a stable set of role expectations. Thus, fundamental changes in funeral ceremonies have been associated with the demise of traditional social and cultural constraints on the manner in which men and women carry out their roles. Among the Mexican Americans who were studied, the women, in particular, are no longer anchored in role expectations reinforced by intense interaction with the extended family, strong community bonds, or traditional religious beliefs.

It seems quite apparent that persons, in carrying out funeral rites, are responding to social and cultural changes in the broader society. Women today are more likely to work outside the home in jobs that discourage mourning practices. Davis (1984) contends that the pattern whereby women work outside the home (instead of in the household settings or in the field with their husbands) has had a far-reaching impact upon sex roles in all industrial societies. Moreover, the extended family, an integral part of older funeral rites, has been undermined by social and geographic mobility. Many Mexican Americans have extended family members scattered throughout the Southwest and beyond. But even when extended family members live in the same area, the demands of the work world do not permit women or men to carry out traditional funeral roles. In addition, religious beliefs have undergone considerable upheaval, as the Catholic Church, especially in the United States, has been struggling to redefine its doctrine (cf. Friedrich, 1985). All these changes are associated with industrialization, urbanization, and bureaucratization (Goode, 1970).

Within this context Mexican American men and women carve new roles for themselves, and in the realm of life cycle rituals, for example, funerals, prove no exception. Many of the respondents in Austin, in both the working class and the professional/business sector, were reflective about the fact that they could not (and did not wish to) act as people did in the past. In effect, many persons said, when discussing traditional role expectations, that "life is different today." When talking about the way in which their parents or grandparents acted, they stressed that "life was different then." The stereotypical conception of Mexican American women as passive and docile is not supported by my observations. Many of those I interviewed, or observed, are consciously striving to make adaptations to, or to create, new social environments for themselves. They are, in Turner's words (1962), engaged not simply in role taking but also in role making. And it should be noted that most of the male respondents did not expect, nor did they want, their wives to act as did their mothers or grandmothers with respect to such an activity as mourning. In fact, no male respondents in Austin indicated that their wives should grieve as did their mothers and grandmothers.

This leads us to consideration of tensions or strains that have arisen as a result of changes in funeral rites. A number of my respondents expressed concern about the changing patterns, but no sharp tensions seem to exist. A number of respondents seem concerned with the impersonality and commercialization of funerals arranged by funeral homes, and some persons (especially in the working class) had serious reservations about the social gatherings after the funerals. Most persons were aware that the social world seemed in a state of flux. Older Mexican Americans (those in their sixties and older) expressed concern that there will be no one to pray and grieve for them at their own funeral (a comment I have heard on a number of occasions in the Corpus Christi region). Even these Mexican Americans, however, do not wish to revive the traditional funeral rites in their entirety. I speculate that the lack of major tensions results from the fact that changes in the cultural (or belief) sphere have gone hand in hand with changes in social structure. The rise, for example, of a generalized religious belief system permits the acceptance of rapid change. Finally, changes in the role of women, which involve a breakdown in the pattern of "separate domains" for men and women, do not pose a challenge in the authority of men, particularly in the public sphere. Changes in women's roles relating to life cycle rituals, such as the funeral, have not directly threatened the authority structure of the family.

The data in this chapter also bear, in several ways, upon the use of the "assimilationist model" to interpret changes among Mexican Americans. Most social scientists seem committed to view that Mexican Americans are striving to be like Anglos. The data collected raise several questions about the assimilationist world view.

First, almost all the respondents in Austin, as well as persons whom I have observed in the Corpus Christi area, have a strong sense of ethnic identity, and they do not perceive any contradiction between this identity and the changes taking place in gender role patterns associated with funeral rites. Most advocates of the assimilationist model discount the actor's perspective. However, not only do these Mexican Americans maintain their own ethnic identity, they also do not view themselves as being accepted as equals by members of the majority society. In general, they view themselves as excluded from the major society because of their ethnicity or racial background.

Second, the data on changing funeral rites and the resulting changes in gender role patterns raise an even more subtle issue about the assimilationist model. One assumption of this model, as noted above, is that members of the minority group adopt the patterns (or model) of the dominant group in society. But if we look at funeral rites in the United States, we must ask, What is the Anglo model? It, too, has undergone major changes in recent decades. It too, has become bureaucratized, commercialized, and impersonal. And many segments of the Anglo society are moving toward a simplification of funeral activities (Engel, 1984).

If this is true, how then can Mexican Americans be viewed as assimilating into patterns that themselves are undergoing major revisions and about which there appears great uncertainty? The majority sector is in the process of inventing new social and cultural forms. Instead of adopting an assimilationist perspective, it appears far more realistic, given the empirical data, to assume that Anglos—as well as Mexican Americans—are responding to basic cultural and structural changes in the broader society. Both groups are undergoing basic revisions in their funeral rites and gender role expectations. However, this does not mean that Mexican Americans strive to become Anglicized. Both groups respond to patterns associated with such basic processes as industrialization, urbanization, and bureaucratization—or more specifically to higher educational attainment and the rise of the service economy. Although a detailed criticism of the assimilationist model lies beyond the scope of this chapter, I hope that the data and brief analysis will raise questions about the adequacy of this theoretical orientation for attempting to understand an important aspect of change—that relating to funerals and gender role expectations in Mexican American life.

References

Alvirez, David, Frank D. Bean, and Dorie Williams, 1981. "The Mexican American Family." In C. Mindel and R. Haberstein (eds) *Ethnic Families in America: Patterns and Variations*. New York: Elsevier.

Baca Zinn, Maxine, 1980. "Employment and Education of Mexican-American Women: The Interplay of Modernity and Ethnicity in Eight Families." *Harvard Educational Review* 50 (February):47–62.

Davis, Kingsley, 1984. "Wives and Work: The Sex Role Revolution and Its Consequences." *Population and Development Review* 10 (September):397–417.

"Death in Austin," 1984. *Third Coast* 3 (June):65–77.

Durkheim, Emile, 1915. *The Elementary Forms of the Religious Life*. New York: Free Press.

Eliade, Mircea, 1957. *The Sacred and the Profane*. New York: Harcourt, Brace and World.

Engel, Margaret. 1984. "Those High-Priced Funerals Are Dying." *The Washington Post National Weekly*.

Fried, Martha N., and Morton H. Fried, 1980. *Transition: Four Rituals in Eight Cultures*. New York: Norton.

Friedrich, Otto, 1985. "Discord in the Church." *Time* (February):50–63.

Geertz, Clifford, 1973. *The Interpretation of Cultures*. New York: Basic Books.

Goode, William J., 1970. *World Revolution and Family Patterns*. New York: Free Press.

Gordon, Milton, 1964. *Assimilation in American Life*. New York: Oxford University Press.

Jordan, Terry G., 1982. *Texas Graveyards: A Cultural Legacy*. Austin: University of Texas Press.

Leiberson, Stanley, 1982. "Stereotypes: Their Consequences for Race and Ethnic Interaction." In (eds) Robert M. Hauser, Archibold O. Haller, David Meehauser, and Taissa S. Hauser (eds.), *Social Structure and Behavior: Essays in Honor of William Hamilton Sewell*. New York: Academic Press.

Melville, Margarita B. (ed), 1980. *Twice a Minority: Mexican American Women*. St. Louis: C. V. Mosby.

Mirandé, Alfredo, and Evangelina Enríquez, 1979. *La Chicana*. University of Chicago Press.

Moore, Joan, 1970. "The Death Culture of Mexico and Mexican-Americans." *Omega* 1:271–291.

Osuna, Patricia, and David K. Reynolds, 1970. "A Funeral in Mexico: Description and Analysis." *Omega* 1:249–269.

Papanek, Hanna, 1984. "False Specialization and the Purdah of Scholarship—A Review Article." *Journal of Asian Studies* 44 (November):127–148.

———, and Gail Minault (eds), 1983. *Separate Worlds Studies of Purdah in South Asia*. Columbia, Mo.: South Asia Books.

Paredes Américo, 1958. *With His Pistol in His Hand*. Austin: University of Texas Press.

Payne, Harry C., 1984. "The Ritual Question and Modernizing Society, 1800–1945—A Schema for a History." *Historical Reflections/Réflexions and Historiques* 11 (Fall): 403–432.

Portes, Alejandro, 1984. "The Rise of Ethnicity: Determinants of Ethnic Perceptions among Cuban Exiles in Miami." *American Sociological Review* 49 (June):383–397.

Rubel, Arthur, 1966. Across the Tracks: *Mexican-Americans in a Texas City*. Austin: University of Texas Press.

Silva, Marcelo, 1984. "Matter of Fact." *Falfurrias Facts*.

Smith, Robert J., and Ella Lury Wiswell, 1982. *Women of Suye Mura*. University of Chicago Press.

Turner, Ralph, 1962. "Role-Taking: Process Versus Conformity." In A. Rose (ed) *Human Behavior and Social Processes*, London: Routledge and Kegan Paul.

Turner, Victor, 1981. *The Drums of Affliction*. New York: Cornell University Press.

Van Gennep, Arnold, 1960. *The Rites of Passage*. University of Chicago Press.

Weber, David J., 1981. "Failure of a Frontier Institution: The Secular Church in the Borderlands under Independent Mexico." *The Western Historical Quarterly* XIII (April):125–143.

Williams, Norma, 1984. "Changing Patterns in the Mexican American Family." Unpublished Ph.D. dissertation, University of Texas at Austin.

Ybarra, Lea, 1982. "When Wives Work: The Impact on the Chicano Family." *Journal of Marriage and the Family* 44 (February):169–178.

10

Oral History and La Mujer: The Rosa Guerrero Story

Vicki L. Ruiz

> *I want people to read what my thoughts are. I can dance it all the way; I can jump it all the way; I can sing it all the way; but if I write, then it stays in the world.*
> ROSA GUERRERO

Oral history, at its best, not only offers insight into past events and experiences but also provides a window into another person's soul. An individual's attitudes and values color and give meaning to his or her memories. This personalization of the past brings vibrance, sensitivity, and understanding of preceding generations. The story of Rosa Ramírez de Guerrero chronicles the life of an extraordinary Mexicana, reared in a barrio tenement, who became an internationally renowned choreographer. It is also a tale of growing up "brown" during the decades following World War II in El Paso, Texas, a traditionally conservative border community.

From 1880 to 1940, Mexicans in El Paso rarely advanced beyond blue-collar occupations. Perceived as cheap labor by Anglo businessmen, Mexicans typically received low pay, inferior education, and limited economic opportunities. After 1940, increasing numbers of Spanish-surnamed persons began attaining lower white-collar positions. Professional posts, however, eluded most Mexican Americans. For example, in 1930, 1.8 percent of Hispanic workers held high white-collar jobs, a figure which remained constant until 1960, when 3.4 percent obtained these top-level occupations (Garcia, 1980:64–104; Martinez,

1980:9−10).[1]Rosa Guerrero's life mirrors the modest, though important, gains achieved by Mexicanos in El Paso. She taught at Austin High School during the 1960s, when approximately 15 percent of all public school teachers had Spanish surnames. Ten years later, she taught part-time at the University of Texas at El Paso, part of the 8 percent Hispanic professoriate and administrative staff (Martínez, 1980:26−27).

Although the 1980 census has classified 63 percent of the city's population as having "Spanish origin," ethnic differences in occupation and income levels continue. For instance, 40 percent of Hispanic workers hold blue-collar jobs while 47 percent of Anglo employees fill high-level professional positions (Copeland, 1983a:12). It is within this context of past and present disparities and discrimination that the life of Rosa Ramírez de Guerrero assumes telling importance. She serves not only as a role model but as a teacher to hundreds of border children.

In addition to directing the award-winning Rosa Guerrero International Ballet Folklorico, she produced the film *Tapestry*, a dramatic, moving affirmation of Mexican American culture. Currently, she supervises the folklorico group that bears her name and teaches dance at the Houchen Community Center in El Segundo, the poor. predominantly Mexicano, section of El Paso. In return for studio space at the neighborhood center, Guerrero offers free classes for barrio youth (Ligon, 1983). The following edited bilingual oral interview, chronicling her early years, captures the warmth, compassion, determination, and courage of this mujer de la gente.[2]

My name is Rosa Guerrero and I will tell you a little bit about my family background. I was born in El Paso, Texas, in 1934 and my parents came from Mexico. I remember my grandparents, my mother's side only; I never met my father's parents. My grandfather (my mother's father) was from Jalapa, Veracruz, and my grandmother from Toluca. They were beautiful people. They were divorced or separated a long time because my grandmother followed Pancho Villa during the revolution. She wanted to really follow in his footsteps and she was a cook for

---

1. For more information on the history of Mexicans and Mexican Americans in El Paso, see Mario T. García, *Desert Immigrants: Mexicans of El Paso, 1880-1920*, and Oscar J. Martínez, *The Chicanos of El Paso: An Assessment of Progress*.
2. This bilingual interview with Rosa Guerrero was conducted by Paulina Aldrete April 12, 1983. On file at the Institute of Oral History (IOH), University of Texas at El Paso, Texas. The interview was edited by Vicki L. Ruiz, former IOH director.

him. Since my father worked for the railroad, we would go to Mexico and be with the family over there. My mother says I was about eight months old when she first took me to Mexico, so that was about 1935. Every year from then on, I've gone to Mexico and have immersed myself en la cultura.

It was a very beautiful treat to go to Mexico City and be with my grandmother and go to Jalapa and be with my grandfather. Both of them were hard, hardworking people. I remember my grandmother getting up at five in the morning and watering the patio, the hierbas, and all the plantas; then starting her soups, frijolitos, tortillas, and the comal being ready by six. Everything on the table was ready. The mole that my grandmother made was the most authentic mole that I have ever tasted because she used to get on her hands and knees and start from scratch. There was no Doña María, no jars at the time. There was the ajonjolí, and the different types of chiles; chile chipotle, chile colorado, chile de esto y otro, cacahuate, chocolate—we'd mix it all up. I remember doing it. When I tried, I used to smash my finger with the metate. I wanted to follow her. I remember making tortillas de maiz and they used to come out crazy, longer or fatter, funny or whatever. But at least I said, "Yo quiero aprender, abuelita; yo quiero aprender." I always wanted to learn.

I never saw her sick until I found out that she was dead. She used to cure herself like my mother does, with hierbas (home remedies). She never saw a doctor, never in her life stepped into a beauty shop, never saw the part of what we call "civilization" because she was very, very much an Indian at heart and very traditional. Her rebozo de bolitos, I have it. She had it with Pancho Villa and her metate and her molcajete are my heirlooms.

Now, in my childhood, I remember my mother telling me all these stories. We didn't have enough books, and the magazines we had were the *Continental*, the *Fronterizo*; the papers from Mexico: *La Prensa, El Diario, El Pepin, El Chamaco*. We did learn English and Spanish at home and read it. One thing about mother was when she used to get our piojitos out, espulgarnos, which is part of the culture too, whether we like it or not. She used to tell us stories about La Llorona and cuentos de Juan Pirulero y las historias de diferentes fantasías románticas de Bellas Artes—por ejemplo, Literatura Infantil Universal, things like Cinderella, Sleeping Beauty, the Seven Dwarfs, the beautiful Snow White, La Blancanieves. You immediately start stereotyping as white being very beautiful and at that time you wanted to be white like Americanas and like Snow White. Then you had piojitos, so I remember Snow White not having piojitos. She was too beautiful to have piojitos.

My mother used to tell us stories, especially about my grandmother. Then my grandmother would come from Mexico and continue the same thing. It was nothing but oral history that was taught to us. She told us about the ghosts, the haunted places, the different types of witches and creencias, and about tradiciones and customs in Mexico. To me, it was such a beautiful, exciting, story because I didn't have to go and open a history book; it was told to me at home. I thought I had very poor parents, but very exciting parents. The school system would teach us everything about American history, the colonists and all of that. Then I would do a comparison in my mind of where my grandparents came from, what they did, and wonder how was I to be evolved and educated.

My grandmother gave us so much, especially during the revolution, how she suffered and how the family came to Juárez and then eventually to El Paso. My mother had to work as domestic help because she didn't know English and she didn't have an education as such. She met my father here in El Paso and married him.

After she got married, she continued working, because the Depression came, and then my dad didn't have a job. She was the one that worked and my father stayed at home. He was the one that made us sopita, frijolitos, arrocito, and beautiful capirotada; and he played El Papalote con nosotros. Nos bañaba because he had to take the part of the woman because there were no jobs. During the Depression, everybody in the neighborhood wore these relief-type overalls, everybody. It looked like the whole prison was there. I lived at 620 N. Santa Fe, at the end of Sunset Heights. We lived there twenty years.

My relationship with my parents, my brothers, and my sisters was just beautiful. My happy sisters Enedina, the eldest, and my beautiful younger sister (may she rest in peace), Hazel. I was the favorite of my father, but Hazel was the favorite of the whole family, including myself. She taught at Bowie High School, down in South El Paso. She died about fifteen years ago—she was just gorgeous. I used to go to Juárez on the streetcar and on the bus and take her as a friend and companion. Tenía que ir conmigo como de chaperone. Then I took my niece Martha; Martha, Hazel, and I were very, very close. My favorite brother was Daniel; but all of them are my favorite. As you grow in years, you even learn to love them more. I think that the family in the Mexican culture, la cultura Hispana, the family (the immediate family, the extended family) is the greatest contribution that mankind can have. My eldest sister Nadine was called "la gallina," not because she laughed like a chicken, but because she guided everybody. She was la gallina de todos los pollitos; we were the pollitos. There were seven of us. I didn't have a lot of chores as a child because I was my father's favorite. My brother Bill and my brother George used to wash the dishes and used to do this and that. I don't think my brothers had an easier time than I because they were also given more responsibilities.

I love my family. They were just super. We were so poor though; we had that one bathroom. I remember that we had to share it with about thirty people and everybody was constipated.

There were arguments in the family—financial, especially when my father drank. I used to take care of my father when he was drunk, pobrecito. I used to sing to him, take care of him, and I was the only one who could guide him. My mother would get mad with him because he would spend the whole check. It is a very sad feeling in the cultura Mexicana that the machismo element is there, so evident en la borrachera, which I hated most with a passion. I can still see it in the eighties, the cycle of poverty, the cycle of borracheras, the cycle of machismo is still there. This is the irony; it's still there. You think your father and your mother are God or godlike. Even though my dad drank a lot, I didn't judge him; I loved him. When you love somebody, you don't judge. You love and you forget and you forgive.

Yes, my family was different from my neighbors, very much so, because my mother was a fortune-teller and people used to look at her. So my home was not a regular home. It used to be like Grand Central Station, everybody visiting my mother. All of her friends, all her patients, her clientas would come to see her. I never had my own room, never, until I got married—really, because I had to wait until the clientas left and then the sofa was made into a bed. It was kind of sad because we didn't have the right studying facilities or anything like that. How we made it; I don't know, by the grace of the Lord.

One time, one of my friends, Carmen Rodríguez, said to me, "My mother doesn't want me to play with you." And I said, "Why not?" "Because she says your mother's a witch. She's a fortune-teller and a witch!" And I said, "No, my mother's not a witch; and if she's a witch, she's a good witch. She's a beautiful lady and she's my mother. She won't hurt you."...I remember those little things that people would say.

My mother's a beautiful person. She has a different gift from God—to psychoanalyze people, to question them, and through her cards and her way she helps them. That's what she has been doing for a long time. She brought us up and she gave us food from that. I cannot judge and I cannot condemn. She is my mother and a very gifted lady. She worked outside the home. Yes, she worked very hard. For a dollar a week, she used to work and scrub by hand, wash all the linen and boil them.

I also remember my mother being very much a fiestera. Oh, to this day (she's going to be eighty-one on March the nineteenth), she is so alive. She's like an eighteen-year-old. She feels like one, and she acts like one. She's amazing. She's Indian, pata rajada; that will never change. I adore her for it and the more years that pass, the more I adore her.

My father was unique, he was el Castellano. All of my life style involving culture, dance, music, traditions, folklore, language was due to the upbringing he gave me at home; the escuelita he gave me. We would sit and conjugate verbs in Spanish, just for the love of it. We would go over geography; we would go over history; we would go over dances, operas, waltzes. He was just a beautiful Socratic man. I loved it! I loved relating with my dad because I thought he was the smartest man in the world. My favorite childhood memory, of course, is my father, dancing with him, getting on his feet, dancing the corridos, the paso dobles, the mazurkas, the varsovianas. I used to get on his feet and dance. I thought I was tremendously great. And then seeing my mother and my father dance—that was such a joy.

I can't remember the family not going to Juárez every Sunday. I don't remember going to a restaurant in El Paso. Ciudad Juárez was our life. We would go to the bullfights, seeing the greatest of toreros. I saw Manolete, Silverio Pérez, David Luciano, Carlos Arruza. I saw Conchita Cintrón, la Regionadora, a beautiful bullfighter on horseback. Anytime they killed the bull, I would turn around. But I would live the art, and the olé, and the music, and tan tara ta tan, when the clarín would come out and announce that the bull was going to be dedicated to the mayor or to whoever. That was exciting!

That's when I was starting to get confused inside because I didn't know if I was Spanish or Indian or Mexican because I liked all types of music. The Indian would come out when the matachines would dance; the Spanish would come out when the pasos dobles would play; and the Mexican when the jarabes would play. So I was confused. I thought, "What am I?" And here I was in the United States, a pocha—Lord, have mercy! But I loved the music and the dance. I just enjoyed it. I loved going with my mother and father to "La Fiesta Taurina." From there we would go out and eat.

From the restaurante, we used to go to the Lobby, or the Trivoli, or the Casanova. The Casanova was one of the most elegant places in Juárez. My parents would take the family, especially me, because I love the dancing. These exclusive nightclubs would bring the greatest musicians, concert pianists, opera singers, flamenco dancers. I saw the greatest flamenco dancer in the world, Carmen Amaya. I loved her. She danced with all that glory. I wanted to be right with her, to be like her. I started to see the evolution of dance then. I saw Veloz and Yolanda do the beautiful ballroom dancing, the great Antonio Triana, and on and on.

Aprendí yo la música jarocha, las bambas, las contrabambas, la media bamba, el zapateado, los danzones. Mi tío Rufino, hijo de mi abuelito y hermano de mi mamá, era el campión del danzón del estado de Veracruz. Una gente muy culta, los Veracruzanos. Todos saben tocar instrumento, a cantar, a tocar la guitarra; una gente que es muy culta. En Aguascalientes tambíen aprendí mucho con mis tías. Mi tiá Chita, Felisa, era directora de escuela. Entonces yo tenía que prepararme en español lo mejor porque ella me iba a poner un exámen allí y evaluar mi Castellano. Gracias a Dios que mi padre me dio todo eso para poder prepararme ambos, en los Estados Unidos como in México. Los deseos de mis padres para mí eran muy liberales. Mi madre quería que fuera bailarina. Ella creía que me iba a ver en el teatro y de bailarina como Carmen Amaya. La danza y la música y la cultura en la identificación de mi sangre y de mi cultura fue inspirada por mi padre; mi madre también; pero más mi padre; porque él me decía, "No se deje, mire esto y ándele esto y ándele pa' adelante."[3]

When I came home from school or from work or whatever, I used to just dance all the time, *all* the time. I remember taking care of my

---

3. My uncle, Rufino, my grandfather's son and my mother's brother, was the dance champion of the state of Veracruz. A very cultured people, the Veracruzanos. They all know how to play musical instruments, to sing, to play the guitar, a very cultured people. In Aguascalientes I also learned a lot from my aunts. My aunt, Chita, Felisa, was the director of a school. So I had to prepare myself as well as I could in Spanish because she was going to give me a test there and evaluate my Castilian [Spanish]. Thank God, my father helped me prepare myself, in the United States as well as in Mexico. My parents' hopes for me were very liberal. My mother wanted me to be a dancer. She thought she'd see me in a theater as a dancer like Carmen Amaya. Dance and music and culture in the identification of my blood and of my culture was inspired by my father; my mother, too; but mostly my father because he used to tell me, "Don't let others get the better of you. Always move ahead."

homework, to get it out of the way, so I could start dancing. All during the summer months I danced and danced and danced. My profesora used to charge me fifty cents for the lesson. But then I could stay the whole day because I could teach other children. So it was a treat for me to stay all day long with my profesora Rosita and then later on professor Aguilar. It was such a challenge because I was a little girl, and I was teaching others. All of my life I've been teaching; all of my life every since I was ten or eleven years old.

Later, I got a job that paid ten dollars a week, after school with Dr. Hartrick; he had a little grocery store. I wanted to work because I wanted to dress nice, to be like the other girls and all that. I kept that job for a year or so and I did teach dancing. But ten dollars a week was a lot of money. And you know what I would do with that money? I would buy peanut butter. I love peanut butter and I would buy my own personal things. Shampoo to me was a luxury. I had to buy shampoo so I wouldn't have to wash my hair with the old dirty Oxydol. I used to wash my hair with the soap for the clothes. So to me, shampoo was great. And then the rest of the money, I gave it to my mother. I bought food for the family; I wanted to help my family. It wasn't just for me. I've always wanted to help other people.

I also worked as a—would you believe I cleaned houses when I was ten or eleven years old? I didn't mind it. On Saturdays, I cleaned for Mrs. Collette and I used to get fifty cents for the whole day. I remember going in at seven or eight o'clock in the morning and cleaning five bathrooms, getting on my hands and knees, scrubbing, putting wax, polishing, and all that. And there were no machines as such, polishing machines or anything like that. But it was joy—those fifty cents were mine! You know, if I earned fifty cents right now, I wouldn't mind. Compared to what I'm earning; if I get one hundred dollars a day as a consultant or one hundred dollars an hour or—to me, I'm still the same person. It hasn't changed me.

I loved school although at the very beginning I didn't. I was kind of fearful of it. I went to the old Vilas School; it's still there in Sunset Heights. I remember being punished for speaking Spanish. Nos daban unos coscorrones, pero coscorrones, o nos daban unas zuribandas con un board. Tenían un board of education por hablar español. Yo no entendía lo que me decian, ni jota, ni jota. Pero por eso estoy tan cercana, y mi corazón y mi espíritu al programa bilingue, porque yo sufrí unas cosas horribles. Yo no fui la única; fueron miles de gentes que sufrieron en Arizona, en Colorado, en Nuevo México, en Texas, en

California; que nos esteretipaban horriblemente.[4] "Don't you speak that ugly language, you are an American now, you Mexican child." They degraded us horribly, but uno se hacía valer.[5]

Fui a la Morehead School, el old Morehead School que está en la calle Arizona donde está the [UTEP] School of Nursing right now. Y ahí gradué en 1948. Me gustaba mucho la música. Y me acuerdo que nos ponían la música de *Peter and the Wolf*.[6] My favorite subject, of course, was music. We didn't have any Spanish at all. I would have loved Spanish if we would have had it. I didn't have it until my freshman or sophomore year in high school. But I loved music and social studies. I liked reading, even though I knew I had an accent and my "ch's" were horrible. There were many, many teachers I liked. Miss Hignett, my gosh, I learned English with that beautiful Mary Hignett in my homeroom class in the sixth and seventh grade. What a teacher! She used to teach every part of speech in English—just drilling it into us. And because of her, I learned good English grammar. I didn't like Miss Eason. She used to hit me with a ruler for speaking Spanish or hide me behind the closet. I know she hated Mexicans because she would tell the other teachers, "These typical Mexican girls; they stink, blah, blah, blah."

Yo me hacía valer en ese sentido, porque tenía que tener competencia con unas personas tan inteligentes, como los Judíos y todos los Americanos que íbamos a El Paso High; iban a El Paso High. Y nosotros los Mexicanos, pues, teníamos que hacernos valer en otro sentido. Yo me hacía valer con alegría, y con estusiasmo, y con la danza, y la cultura. Fui la primer México-Americana para dirigir la banda en el 1952, 1953, representar la escuela en Girl's State en Austin, Texas, en muchas cosas fui la primer Mexicana. Me pusieron de physical education leader en el eighth grade, que fui la única Mexicana. En el 1948 fui la primer Mexicana en educación física. Teníamos una profesora que se

---

4. They'd hit us on the head, but good, or they'd paddle us with what they called the board of education for speaking Spanish. I didn't understand what they were telling me, not one iota. That's why I'm so committed to the bilingual program, heart and soul, because I suffered horribly. I wasn't the only one, there were thousands of people who suffered in Arizona, Colorado, New Mexico, Texas, California; they stereotyped us horribly.

5. They degraded us horribly but we asserted ourselves.

6. I went to Morehead School, the old school that was on Arizona Street where the UTEP School of Nursing is right now. I graduated in 1948. I loved music. I remember they used to play music from *Peter and the Wolf* for us.

llamaba Jane Rush. Era muy estricta, pero yo la quería mucho.[7] I thought she was very fair with me. She gave me a chance; she gave me an opportunity; and I felt good as a leader. I felt tremendously great among all the lily-white people. I felt gorgeous and beautiful, brilliant and very rich, filthy rich. And I said, "Well, hay que hacerme valer." So I started being a model for my Raza in the 1950s there. I was kind of proud of myself because my mother and my father were very proud of me. I would come home . . . I wouldn't even tell them that I was running for this. I would come home and tell them, "I got this and I got that." I was president of the PE leaders, of the National Rifle Association, of the Courtesy Club, the Panamerican Club. In everything I was president. I had a very outgoing personality. My own kids call me the social climber of the fifties. I don't know what it was, but I just had to prove myself. I wanted to graduate from high school so badly.

My family thought school was all right. They wanted me to have high school. But I wanted to be the first one from the family to graduate from college. I was the first one to graduate from college and my sister Hazel graduated after me. We were the only ones that graduated. My brother went up to about the junior year; but has the best job of all. He is second in command with Blue Cross/Blue Shield in San Antonio.

During high school, I wanted to go to college. Thank God, I met the most beautiful man in the world, Sergio Guerrero. We were friends since grammar school and we started going around together our junior year in high school. I was the one that asked him for the first date. It was during "Twirp's Week," that I asked him for the first date. At first he didn't think I was serious, but I was. I said, "Sergio, vamos al baile. Yo te llevo al Baile de Febrero porque las chamacas, las niñas, las señoritas tienen que preguntarle a los muchachos." The boys did not let us call them "twirps." The girls had to do as the boys for the date, carry their books, pay for everything. Our senior year, Sergio and I were very

---

7. But I asserted myself because I had to compete with such intelligent people like the Jews and Americans who went to El Paso High School. The Mexicans, well, we had to assert ourselves in other ways. I asserted myself through my happiness and enthusiasm and in dance, and with my culture. I was the first Mexican American to lead the band in 1952, 1953, represent the school at Girls' State in Austin, Texas. I was a physical education leader in the eighth grade, and I was the only Mexicana. In 1948 I was the first Mexicana in physical education. We had a teacher named Jane Rush. She was very strict, but I liked her very much.

lovey-dovey. I told Sergio, "I always wanted to be a teacher." He said, "That's fine. We'll both go to school; we'll study, and we'll both be teachers."

In my freshman year, I went to Texas Women's University in Denton, Texas. It was the Texas Tech College for Women then. Me dieron beca de danza; I got a very small dance scholarship but at least it was an opening for me. That year, my husband, who was my boyfriend at the time (Sergio), supported me tremendously—financially, morally, and emotionally because I wanted to come back. There was no Mexican food in Denton; there was no Mexican music except for XELO. I would listen to the corridos y las canciones mexicanas and I would cry, six hundred miles away from home. My father wasn't there; my mother wasn't there . . . it was horrible! It was an eye opener for me. I saw all types of prejudices; I mean, horrible racism. But that's good though, sometimes. You have to learn that . . . you're not going to be born for people to like you. I wanted people to like me just because of myself, and that's not the way it is. Some people don't like you because you're black, or you're white, or you're brown, or you're Oriental, or whatever, and we can't help it. If the Lord made us that way, we can't turn ourselves into lily-whites. I can change my name to Rose Guerry from Rosa Guerrero and dye my hair, but that's not going to prove anything. I'm just kidding myself and I'm cheating myself.

In Denton, I was very active in the dance group. We toured Louisiana, Mississippi, East Texas, and it was an awakening experience. But for the rest of school (sophomore, junior, and senior years), I attended UTEP; it was Texas Western College then. I got married in 1954 and continued college at Texas Western until I graduated in 1957.

Then I got pregnant in my senior year and I had to practice-teach at Austin High School. I would nurse my baby, and go back to school, and even referee basketball and play basketball while I was pregnant and after while I was nursing the baby. It was very hard. I don't want to remember some of those bad experiences. But they were good in that they taught me a lot. I think that when you sacrifice and suffer a little bit, you appreciate life more. When I was practice teaching, my husband used to work night shifts, and go to school in the morning, and then take care of Bombi. He slept one or two hours in the twenty-four hours. Talk about a sacrifice! I would never have gotten my degree without my husband Sergio.

Sergio is a tremendously faithful human being; a beautiful, respectable man. I'm just very lucky to have met him and married him because we still, to this day, we have a lot of respect for each other and I just could not do without him. All the things that I've done, as a woman en la cultura, en la danza, en el folklore, it's because he's encouraged me. He knows that I've had to work very hard for everything and he encourages me.

I have three kids in my family: Ana, my beautiful daughter, is twenty-five; my baby is twenty-three (he's the youth director at St. Raphael's church); and then my eldest boy is going to be twenty-seven. They all live with me. This is a Mexican home, my children, my husband, and my animals.

I love teaching and to this day, I still find it very satisfying. I think the children are the ones who inspired me; their smiles, their hugs, even their little faces that are sad, that want some counseling and some love. I am trying to develop their potential as teachers, and as future teachers. They could be five, six, seven years old, but they could be teaching others. I'm trying to develop leadership abilities in them. And I hope that someday they will disseminate all over El Paso, or wherever they go, the art of dance, music, and folklore.

Oh, if I was sixteen years old again, I would just live my life with so much—first of all, I would take care of my legs like I've never taken care of them. I never took care of them; I didn't warm up right; I didn't wear leggings; I danced on cement. I would take care of myself. I would take care of my legs. I would eat well and I would drink milk, which I never did. My mother says que a mi nunca, nunca me gustó la leche. So my arthritis is the consequence.

I have just continued; I have never stopped working, never. I have been married nearly twenty-nine years. We got married; we continued school; and we haven't stopped teaching. The only time I stopped working was to have my children. And right after I had my dieta, my forty days of resting and my examination, I went back to work. And I've never stopped. I'm always doing something and I'm always building something. I have so many dreams; I have so many goals. That's me, I have many dreams. And every day is a new horizon and every day is a new dream.

References

Peter Copeland, 1983. "Border 'Ambiente.' " *Special Report: The Border. El Paso Herald Post*, Summer.

García, Mario T., 1980. *Desert Immigrants: Mexicans of El Paso, 1880−1920.* New Haven: Yale University Press.

Ligon, Betty, 1983. "Rosa's Fantasy Lives: Folklorico in Barrio." *Accent on Arts and Entertainment.* Supplement to *El Paso Herald Post*, December 23.

Martínez, Oscar J., 1980. *The Chicanos of El Paso: An Assessment of Progress.* El Paso: Texas Western Press.

Conclusion

Susan Tiano and
Vicki L. Ruiz

Each of these chapters provides a glimpse of Chicanas and Mexicanas bearing little resemblance to the caricatures so prominent in popular and academic folklore. The delicate *madre* who basks in the security of home and hearth, the uninformed conservative who retards Mexico's progress by supporting reactionary politicians, the docile wage-worker who impedes the coming-to-consciousness of the Mexican working class are not the women we are likely to encounter in the markets, homes, and factories of Nuevo Loredo or El Centro. That Chicanos in the U.S. Southwest have one of the highest poverty rates of all American ethnic groups is not, as the culture of poverty thesis would have it, chiefly because Chicanas prevent their families' upward mobility by teaching their children fatalistic values or by dispensing their husbands' hard-earned income to shiftless relatives or to the Catholic Church. Similarly, that male underemployment and joblessness in border towns is reaching unprecedented levels is not, as some politicians assure their constituents, because women are taking all the better jobs. Such stereotypes may help maintain the status quo by deflecting blame from the structural causes of poverty and unemployment onto the female victims of these political and economic dynamics. Yet they present a distorted image of women's public and private lives.

The Mexican frontier and the American Southwest are in many ways peripheral to the political and cultural centers of their respective nations. In some ways, border residents' marginality has hampered their ability to make their voices heard in Mexico City or Washington, D.C., and has contributed to a sense of dissociation from historical and cultural roots. At the same time this marginality has afforded border populations unique opportunities for cultural and social innovation. Customary beliefs and practices that constrain creative action at the center lose their power when diluted by distance and are more easily rendered invalid by their inappropriateness to frontier life. Moreover, the challenge of confronting an inhospitable physical environment, an unpredictable economic landscape, and an often unresponsive political system militate against passive acquiescence. That border residents have transcended these obstacles to forge an adaptive yet dynamic culture is testimony to their individual initiative and collective solidarity.

These chapters underscore women's vital role as architects of this sociocultural framework. This freer context is enabling many Mexicanas and Chicanas to venture beyond the domestic sphere and to reformulate accepted notions of female roles. Women are not, however, assuming their public roles at the expense of their domestic responsibilities. Instead, by learning to balance the competing demands of their productive and reproductive roles, they are composing new definitions of femininity that bridge the gap between public and private. As they move between the two spheres, they apply expertise and resources gleaned from one arena to enrich the other. The income and personal contacts generated through extradomestic work can enhance their families' economic well-being and social status. Conversely, the nurturing and integrative skills enhanced through reproductive tasks can increase women's effectiveness as managers, organizers, and negotiators at the workplace or in the political arena.

Still, the ideology defining women primarily as wives and mothers persists, contributing to their vulnerability in the public sphere. Many are confined to poorly paid, deadend jobs as domestic servants in other women's households or as unskilled laborers in U.S.-based factories. Rather than resigning themselves to the exploitation inherent in these roles, however, many Mexicanas parlay them to their own advantage. Women often use these positions to learn English and other skills which enable them and their families to maneuver more easily in U.S. border cities. Women's gender-based marginality has probably helped them pass more freely between the Mexican and Anglo worlds, mingling assets from each to produce the synthetic borderlands life style.

For all its faults, the Border Industrialization Program has helped northern Mexican cities weather the fiscal crises that have plagued

Mexico in recent years. The BIP owes its success in stimulating maquiladora investment to the quality of its predominantly female labor
force, whose productivity is unsurpassed by women in other export
processing zones. Were this not the case, many multinational firms
would likely have located their assembly operations in Southeast Asian
nations whose wage rates are lower and worker safeguards more minimal than those in Mexico. Mexicanas have also stimulated the border
economy through their roles as domestic servants. Describing women's
support of public transportation and other urban services, Ruiz reveals
a subtle but important contribution women regularly make to Southwestern cities. Moreover, by spending wages earned on the U.S. side of
the border in northern Mexican cities, domestics and other women
workers inject needed foreign exchange into a struggling economy.

As Staudt, Pena, Young, and Ruiz all demonstrate, female factory and
domestic workers are not submissive victims of exploitation and abuse
by multinational firms or middle-class housewives. Domestics have
shown themselves capable of organizing to protect their collective
interests and have maintained their self-respect in the face of demean-
ing treatment by their employers. Similarly, assembly workers have
individually resisted company efforts to intensify exploitation through
nonremunerated production speed-ups, and they have organized successful strikes aimed at improving working conditions. The Juárez-
based women's center illustrates their capacity to organize and sustain
over time an institution dedicated to raising women's political consciousness. Through this facility, women have helped one another
understand the structural roots of their oppression as women and as
workers, stressing the need for alliances that transcend barriers of class,
ethnicity, and nativity. Graduates of the center's classes have sparked
collective action at the workplace and in the community. In a similar
way, the Company of Mary's long-standing tradition of educating lower-
class girls illustrates its commitment to helping poor women overcome
the double disadvantage imposed by class and gender inequality.

These essays also provide insight into the ways Chicanos have maintained their ethnic identity and collective cohesion despite the steady
Anglicization of the Southwest. As Williams's discussion makes clear,
women organize the fiestas and ritual gatherings that fortify social
bonds and galvanize collective identity. Similarly, Ruiz's and Goldsmith's
accounts reveal how women, in their roles as teachers, performers, and
spiritual leaders, have engendered a sense of ethnic pride among Chicanos of all ages. The dedicated efforts of women like Mother Serrano

and her colleagues in the Company of Mary have empowered Chicano men and women to become leaders and role models for others in their communities.

Whether as assembly workers, artists, teachers, labor organizers, or community activists, Mexicanas have revealed considerable creativity in performing their public roles. The Company of Mary was perhaps unusual in its social and spiritual commitment; yet it exemplifies how women have surmounted the challenges of an alien environment to enrich the border region. Though members of an all-female community organized to serve a primarily female constituency, the nuns had to operate within the confining strictures of a patriarchal institution. When their religious affiliation exposed them to repression at the hands of the anticlerical Mexican government, they reestablished themselves in a desolate Arizona town. This adaptive strategy brought a new set of hurdles: their new homeland was in the throes of the Great Depression, bringing poverty and unemployment to vast numbers and stimulating restrictive immigration quotas that limited their own and their students' ability to reside in the United States. Furthermore, the sisters' lack of facility with English made it difficult to fulfill their mission as educators. Nevertheless, they met these challenges with resiliant determination, maintaining their organizational integrity and economic viability while reformulating their goals to match their new circumstances. These nuns' experience, though distinctive in its particulars, is continually relived by other border region women. Each Mexicana who crosses the border to emerge in an alien land, each Spanish speaker who faces the isolation of communicating in a foreign tongue, each Chicana who inculcates in others a sense of respect for their rich Mexican heritage repeats the challenges and achievements of the sisters who created a cultural oasis in the Arizona desert.

Every Mexicana reaffirms the beliefs, values, and practices of her cultural heritage as she fulfills the responsibilities of her domestic roles. Women bear major responsibility for socializing their children into the nuances of their collective culture and for orchestrating the ritual activities that make culture a living force in people's lives. Yet as William's essay indicates, Mexicanas and Chicanas are not conservative guardians of a static culture to be preserved and transmitted without modification to subsequent generations. Cultures are dynamic systems elaborated and transformed with changing circumstances. When several cultures coalesce, as they have in the border region, and when the socioeconomic fabric is rapidly changing, as it has been throughout the twentieth century, the opportunities for cultural innovation are especially pronounced. These essays suggest that *el ambiente fronterizo*, with its merging of traditional and modern, Anglo and Mexican, owes much to women's creative energies. Rosa Guerrero's enduring impact is perhaps exceptional; few have developed their talents to a comparable extent, or have been so committed to helping others excel artistically. Guerrero's account should alert us, however, to the existence of countless women whose stories have not been told and whose cultural contributions remain, for now, largely unacknowledged.

Despite their increasing participation in extradomestic work and community service, Mexicanas and Chicanas somehow manage to fulfill the duties mandated by their private roles. These essays provide no evidence that women's entrance into the labor force is jeopardizing the Mexicano/Chicano family. Ruiz, Solórzano-Torres, and Tiano concur that women typically enter factory, domestic, or other types of service work out of economic need, and their wages are critical to their families' subsistence. Yet whether women work *por necesidad* or *por gusto*, there appears little indication that they shirk their homemaking and child-rearing responsibilities. As Tiano's research suggests, many northern Mexican women drop out of the work force to devote themselves to full-time parenting while their children are young. Tiano also challenges the notion that women's wage work weakens the family by exacerbating male joblessness. To the contrary, many women enter wage work to support families headed by underemployed or unemployed men (see also Fernández-Kelly, 1983). In the face of inflation, the removal of price controls, and other concomitants of Mexico's economic crisis, a growing number of households are unable to subsist on a single breadwinner's income and require women's economic contributions. Ironically, women's wage work may be the main factor buttressing the family against the disorganizing effect of economic destitution.

The need for working-class wives and daughters to take jobs to help support their families is not a new phenomenon. As Rosa Guerrero relates in her oral history, it was her mother who supported her family while Rosa was a child, because Rosa's father was unable to secure employment. The high rates of male joblessness during the Depression made it necessary for many women like Rosa's mother to participate in the labor force. Rosa herself began to earn a wage when she was eleven so that she could contribute to her family's upkeep. Rosa's experience, like that of the domestic and *maquila* workers discussed in these essays, belies the notion that women need not work for wages because they and their households are adequately supported by husbands or fathers. Some researchers (Saffioti, 1975; Beechey, 1978; Vaughan, 1977) have suggested that this ideology serves the economic system by justifying low female wages and by making it easier to mobilize women into and out of the work force to meet the economy's fluctuating labor needs. Its applicability, however, is limited to upper-middle and upper-class households which constitute a small proportion of the Mexicano and Chicano populations. Historically and currently, most women have had to earn a wage at some point in their lives.

These essays also reveal how women fortify their families by maintaining extended kinship networks. Studies of lower-class families in the United States, Mexico, and elsewhere (Stack, 1974; Rapp, 1982; Bolles, 1981) have demonstrated that these networks cushion the blow of unemployment, physical disability, or other crises that might otherwise lead to economic destitution for the unfortunate relative, creating in turn an obligation to reciprocate when circumstances improve and other members are in need. Such obligations may, as the culture of poverty thesis charges, limit an individual's upward mobility by draining personal resources; yet the negative effects of this "leveling" are counterbalanced by the security of sustaining an economically viable kinship system. Kinship linkages provide contacts and information that help individuals gain employment in tight labor markets and influence in closely knit communities; they also facilitate the exchange of personal services, and integrate individuals into support systems important for emotional health and personal autonomy. At the nodes of these kin networks are women who organize the affairs and ceremonies that revitalize social bonds; send the letters and notices that keep members apprised of each others' circumstances; cook the food, grow the flowers, sew the clothing, and decorate the homes for the celebrations that reinforce kinship solidarity. Mexicano/Chicano networks have survived the entropic influence of urbanization, migration, and the bureaucratization of family functions, Williams' essay suggests, thanks to the ongoing efforts of women.

In sum, by bringing to light women's contributions to family and community life along he United States–Mexico border, the essays in this volume help Chicanas and Mexicanas gain the recognition they deserve but rarely receive. Too, they provide insight into the ways border region women are adapting to the social and economic changes that are transforming their world. Perhaps these essays' most valuable service is to alert researchers to a plethora of issues waiting to be explored.

Throughout this discussion we have stressed the similarities be-tween women on the two sides of their shared geopolitical border. We believe this approach is justified by the common cultural, historical, and socioeconomic circumstances of the Mexican frontier and the U.S. Southwest, and by the fluid movement of people, ideas, and resources across what often seems to be an artificial boundary. Yet as numerous women living in continual fear of INS apprehension would attest, the political border—and the legislation and activities aimed at "securing" it—are daily confronted realities. This issue underscores the pressing need for more information about women's role in the migration pro-cess. The factors motivating women to cross the border, the conditions they encounter at their destination, and the impact of female immigra-tion on the Mexican and United States economies are not yet well understood. Solorzano-Torres's analysis opens up many questions about the connection between the maquiladora program and interna-tional immigration, as well as women's role in sustaining the networks that structure the migratory flow.

Despite their commonalities, however, border region women are not a homogenous group. Social class, ethnicity, locale, and nativity all affect their opportunities and experiences. Furthermore, their produc-tive and reproductive activities vary as they move through the life cycle and their household composition changes. Researchers are just begin-ning to examine how these variables interact with gender to influence the lives of women on the United States – Mexico border. In reconstruct-ing and comparing histories of different constituencies in the region, or in ferreting out their similarities and differences through comaprative case studies or cross-sectional analyses, they will augment our under-standing of women's distinctive and shared circumstances.

There is little reason to assume that the forces propelling Mexicanas and Chicanas into the labor force will diminish during the coming decades. The economic and social consequences of their wage labor for women themselves, for their families, and for their communities form an important research focus. The factors influencing women's occupa-tional qualifications, the economy's demand for women's labor, and the terms of their employment are also fruitful avenues for further study. Remaining to be verified and theoretically elaborated is the hypothesis that women's reproductive roles—and the ideologies defining women primarily in these terms—are major factors relegating women to poorly paid domestic service or insecure factory jobs. Conversely, the effects of women's productive activities on their reproductive roles are not yet well understood. Would their wholesale entrance into the labor

force alleviate the high fertility that retards Mexico's economic development and dooms increasing numbers to lifelong poverty? Could secure,
adequately paid employment enable women to combat the extreme
machismo that subjects many to verbal and physical abuse? Will
women continue to be burdened by the "double day," or will their
menfolk come to bear a larger share of domestic duties? Answers to
such questions can inform efforts to ameliorate wage labor's exploitive
effect while strengthening its liberating potential.

Women's roles in creating, preserving, and transmitting border culture are other areas requiring further research. Are Mexican American
mothers in the border region more likely to teach their children Spanish
than those living in other areas of the United States? Do border families
demonstrate a greater persistence of extended family networks than
Chicanos/Mexicanos in other regions? How has Americanization affected women on both sides of the United States–Mexico border? To
what extent have women's cultural responsibilities and contributions
changed over time? These are but a smattering of possible questions for
humanists, social scientists, and educators to tackle.

The creativity and determination with which Chicanas and Mexicanas have confronted the often-overlapping challenges of *machismo*,
ethnic discrimination, and economic hardship demonstrates that they
are not hapless victims of oppressive social relations. Women's efforts
could be aided, however, by well-conceived policies aimed at eliminating existing barriers to their effective role performance. The provision of
federally funded child care facilities and the enforcement of fair labor
standards would help women combat exploitation at the workplace; the
creation of shelters for battered or abandoned women would help
empower them to resist oppression in the domestic sphere. As they
unite across the lines of class, ethnicity, and nativity which once divided
them, women are pressing for these and other reforms important for
their personal and collective well-being. The growing solidarity of border region women will make them an increasingly effective political
force as their societies enter the twenty-first century.

Women on the United States–Mexico border are no longer shadow
figures lingering in the landscape of scholarly literature. The composite
picture emerging from recent research is tinged with economic hardship and discrimination, yet it is also illuminated by the courage,
warmth, creativity, and strength characterizing *las mujeres en la frontera*. We are only beginning to explore and appreciate the complexity of
their experiences and their contributions to all facets of border life.

References

Beechey, Veronica, 1978. "Women and Production: A Critical Analysis of Some Sociological Theories of Women's Work." In Annette Kuhn and AnnMarie Wolpe (eds), *Feminism and Materialism*. London: Routledge and Kegan Paul, pp. 155–197.

Bolles, Lynn, 1981. "Household Economic Strategies in Kingston, Jamaica." In Naomi Black and Ann Baker Cottrell (eds), *Women and World Change*. Beverly Hills: Sage Publications, pp. 83–96.

Fernández-Kelly, María Patricia, 1983. *For We Are Sold, I and My People: Women and Industry in Mexico's Frontier*. Albany: SUNY Press.

Rapp, Rayna, 1982. "Family and Class in Contemporary America: Notes toward an Understanding of Ideology." In Barrie Thorne and Marilyn Yalom (eds) *Rethinking the Family*. New York: Longman, pp. 168–187.

Saffioti, Heleieth, 1975. "Female Labor and Capitalism in the United States and Brazil." In Ruby Rohrlich-Leavitt (ed) *Women Cross-Culturally: Change and Challenge*. The Hague: Mouton.

Stack, Carol, 1974. *All Our Kin*. New York: Harper and Row.

Vaughn, Mary, 1979. "Women, Class, and Education in Mexico, 1880–1928," in William Bollinger, et al. (eds) *Women in Latin America: An Anthology from Latin American Perspectives*. Riverside, CA.: Latin American Perspectives, pp. 63–80.

Index